WISDOM IN THE PRACTICE
OF PSYCHOTHERAPY

WISDOM IN THE PRACTICE OF PSYCHOTHERAPY

T. BYRAM KARASU, M.D.

BasicBooks
A Division of HarperCollins*Publishers*

Library of Congress Cataloging-in-Publication Data
Karasu, Toksoz B.
    Wisdom in the practice of psychotherapy / T. Byram Karasu.
      p.   cm.
    Includes bibliographical references and index.
    ISBN 0–465–09192–X
    1. Psychotherapy. 2. Psychotherapy—Methods.
3. Psychotherapist and patient. I. Title.
    [DNLM: 1. Psychotherapy-methods.   WM 420 K178w]
RC480.K283   1992
616.89'14—dc20
DNLM/DLC
for Library of Congress   91–57907
                                              CIP

To my patients, who are my teachers

Contents

Contents

Contents

Contents

PART VIII. ON TECHNIQUE AND ITS BOUNDARIES

PART IX. ON CURATIVE AGENTS AND THEIR DECEPTIONS

Contents

Acknowledgments

This book would not have been possible without the contributions of a number of very special individuals, to whom I would like to express my appreciation and indebtedness.

My wife and colleague, Sylvia R. Karasu, M.D., has provided invaluable comments on the content of the book. Louise Notarangelo, Philomena Lee, Rita Segarra, Shirley Kreitman, and Laurie Hillman have agonized over my handwriting, typed and retyped, and corrected the manuscript with ability and dedication. Ms. Betty Meltzer, with extraordinary skill and commitment, translated the rough drafts of my contemplations into the full text of a book. Nola Lynch meticulously copyedited the manuscript; and under the competent guidance of Melanie Kirschner and Stephen Francoeur, David Haproff began and Michael Wilde ably completed the shepherding of the manuscript through the production stages. And throughout the entire process, Jo Ann Miller, Senior Editor at Basic Books, maintained her usual comforting and capable leadership.

I am most grateful to all of them.

Preface

Let me begin with the title of this book: *Wisdom in the Practice of Psychotherapy.* The word *wisdom* has been defined as a combination of (1) knowledge—accumulated philosophic or scientific learning, (2) insight—the ability to apprehend or penetrate inner qualities and relationships, and (3) judgment—good sense *(Webster's* 1989). Knowledge forms the foundation of wisdom through education, which offers a reservoir of diverse thought and information from which to draw upon and build. Insight derives from that base, but goes beyond the scholarship per se. It comprises a second step toward wisdom by making useful connections between often unrelated and otherwise unrecognized fragments of data that lie buried beneath the surface. These in turn form new ideas and patterns that can combine and transcend what is already known. Last, the exercise of sound judgment is the consequence of, or reward for, informed inquiry and discernment of events. Judgment comes through the careful testing of premises and weighing of evidence.

It is thus no surprise that wisdom does not come quickly or easily. Indeed, the three ingredients of wisdom share this requisite: they must be tempered and refined by training, experience, and maturity. Wisdom is the opposite of dogma and, by its very nature, admonishes the repetition or reification of unchallenged ideas. Moreover, it is never a fixed state; rather, it is a gradual, open, and painstaking *process.*

Like many before me, I have tried to capture the meaning of *wisdom* in a series of aphorisms gleaned from many years of teaching and practice in the field of psychotherapy. Nearly fifty axioms are designed to amplify and sharpen the therapeutic process for the reader. I liken them to Gregory Bateson's (1979) "simple necessary truths (that every schoolboy knows)," although I do not wish to cast them in too elementary or too lofty a light. Should there be any doubt about the connotation of the term, this preamble asserts my wish to offer these teachings *not* as immutable verities, but with the sobriety and restraint that they deserve.

With the word *practice* I am concerned with what psychotherapists *do* when they treat patients (which may be inextricably connected to who they are). How psychotherapy is applied and how its goals are accomplished raises one of the most vexing issues of the field—to what extent psychotherapy can be considered a science—defined by such criteria as systematic organization, operationalism, empirical validation, replicability, and measurability—and to what extent it merits a more creative and humanistic status as an art or craft. Put differently, it remains unclear how far its techniques can be directly taught and learned; and as a pedagogical problem, how best to blend didactic with experiential learning.

The axioms presented here are an attempt to locate the interface of theory and experience. The discussions based on the axioms combine theoretical material on each topic with clinical vignettes that are selected analyses of the therapist and patient in the very act of their joint clinical work. Excerpts of verbatim dialogue are offered to highlight the course of psychotherapy as a narrative communicational process; simultaneously, explanations of the therapist's responses have been inserted at crucial points to provide a parallel line of thinking. This commentary articulates the practitioner's rationale for the particular stand he takes—rightly or wrongly—at a particular moment. Thus the reader has access to the clinician's inner voice during actual practice.

The third main term of the title is *psychotherapy*. Victor Raimy's (1950) sardonic definition of psychotherapy as "an undefined technique applied to unspecific problems with unpredictable outcomes, for which vigorous training is required" (p. 93), is, I believe, accurate only to the extent that Raimy recognized the rigors of educating the psychotherapist. With so many different schools and strategies, the concept of psychotherapy is varied, if not elusive. But we are gradually learning more about both its specific technical and its nonspecific relational aspects. Operational treatment manuals have made explicit the therapist's tools and techniques, which act as a blueprint for others in the field; these are parallel to the growing search for what all psychotherapies have in common that transcends individual differences or partisan allegiances.

My orientation in this book represents the merging of the two trends: elucidating specific techniques as well as presenting an orientation of rapprochement in regard to theory and strategy. The book distills several existing complex views of the human psyche, its ills and their cures, and identifies basic principles of treatment that are relevant for real-life therapeutic endeavors. The work is grounded in the overriding theoretical concepts of four major psychologies: drive theory, ego psychology, object relations theory, and self psychology (Pine 1990), in juxtaposition with language and communication theory as well as existential philosophy; the emphasis is on synthesizing these schools, on thinking simultaneously in multiple frameworks, and on shifting from one to another perspective. Likewise, versatile concepts, including therapeutic alliance, transference, encounter, insight, and empathy, are used because they are applicable to a wide range of patients within many types of psychotherapeutic practice. These concepts fall along a continuum of "expressive" (uncovering and confronting) to "supportive" (strengthening and sustaining) approaches within the basic context of dynamically oriented psychotherapy.

In keeping with the above, the clinical principles presented here rarely represent a single school or point of view; I believe that there is never one "right" strategy (such as a single correct interpretation) that must take precedence over all others. As an expression of this open orientation, the book is arranged not in conventional chapters but in thematic sections. I might venture further to say that I have tried to combine clinically commonplace activities (such as providing a safe environment, forming an alliance with the patient, removing resistances) with therapeutically exceptional events: unexpected (the exit line), paradoxical (the perils of positive transference), and dramatically deceptive (sudden insights) phenomena. Each section follows philosophical lines of inquiry into a variety of unresolved therapeutic concerns that have made their random but repeated appearance over the years of my clinical practice. Pressing questions are posed at the start of each section, the replies to which each clinician must continue to search for. Each maxim is simply a steppingstone.

Finally, this book is primarily directed toward the clinician who is already familiar with the basic premises and practices of psychotherapy. This does not mean that the novice or the highly experienced therapist has been exempted from its potential readership, nor that I believe there to be a best recipient. It is my wish that the writings reach a broad interdisciplinary audience representing many levels of learning and development—in short, the volume is designed for that wide and diverse group of yesterday's "schoolboys" (and schoolgirls), the psychotherapists of today and tomorrow. I hope that it will benefit all psychotherapists—and ultimately their patients—by offering general understanding as well as the experiential wisdom that is needed for effective practice.

The case illustrations in this book are based upon composites of actual persons and experiences of treatment. Any departure from "real" events is in part intended, in part unintended: details are deliberately disguised to protect the privacy of the patients; and the distortions of human perception and memory are unavoidable.

PART I

ON PSYCHOLOGICAL
THEORIES AND THEIR
LIMITATIONS

Since this book is primarily about clinical practice, specific theories of psychic function, personality, or psychopathology are considered only secondarily, despite the fact that clinicians typically must be trained in, and identify with, a particular school or schools of thought. In fact, this preoccupation with a preferred theoretical orientation has diverted practitioners' attention from experiential working principles that all clinicians can share.

Thus, my concern here is with the uses and abuses of theory as they interface with actual applications. By this I mean the benefits and limitations of theories in general, not the assets and deficiencies of one or another particular set of conceptualizations. Despite competition within and the polarization of the psychotherapeutic field, I believe that the specific content of a psychological theory, proven or not, can be less relevant to overall practice than the *purpose* (as a consensual belief system among professionals) the theory serves.

Naturally, the first issue addressed is the function that theories provide practicing clinicians, such as offering a body of beliefs to which they can hold professional allegiance and/or make a personal commitment. Many in the field assume that theories are meant for the therapist alone. But just as important to the therapeutic endeavor may be the role that the theoretical orientation plays for the patient. At the same time, although I recognize the positive uses of theories for both therapist and patient, I am also interested in the possible overuse or misuse of conceptual schemas for the healer as well as the person being healed.

This section therefore poses the following questions: What roles do theories play in clinical practice? Does a good clinician fare best with no theoretical boundaries? with a single school or system that preempts all others? with many, equally persuasive theories? How relevant is the clinician's ideology, not just for the clinician but for the patient?

CHAPTER 1

Theories of psychotherapy should anchor, not drown, the therapist

GREAT THINKERS have differed in their views of the role of theory in relation to practice. Albert Einstein (1969), for one, exalted the theoretical. He believed that "a theory could be tested by experience, but there is no way from experience to the setting up of a theory" (p. 89). Objective events might be sufficient for a scientist in the research or clinical laboratory, but the theorist could never derive formulations from them alone. The theorist needs the critical ingredient of creative imagination, which refers to the capacity to go beyond the "facts," no matter how many are collected. By contrast, Sigmund Freud (1916–17), whose elaborate conceptual formulations of the psychic apparatus may have been of equal invention and impact as Einstein's equations, did not agree. Instead he believed that the theory of mind was "an afterthought to the relatively direct inferences of the consulting room." More and more therapists are doubtlessly realizing that much of what they learn in regard to psychotherapy ideology, though intellectually intriguing and personally compelling, has limited utility in their daily practice. It may even be counterproductive, if the patient is forced to fit falsely into the practitioner's preordained premises.

This discrepancy between the philosophic plane of theory and the pragmatic plane of practice has been validated by comparative research studies of various psychotherapies. These suggest that the therapist's espoused theoretical orientation regarding the nature of the healing process and concept of the ideal therapeutic relationship may not be synchronous with his or her actual applications. In one study that directly examined four reputedly different therapeutic approaches— Freudian, Kleinian, Jungian, and Gestalt—to the same patient, descriptive ratings by objective observers failed to differentiate the respective schools of thought (Naftulin, Donnelly, and Wolkon 1975). This finding may have come as a surprise not only to the investigators but to the therapists themselves. Subsequently, a review of literature based on several research investigations of this subject concluded: "Effective therapists, irrespective of TO [theoretical orientation], behave similarly . . . for example, they appear confident, express concern, communicate clearly, are empathic, etc." (Sundland 1977, 215). It was further discovered that any significant differences in clinicians' technical function had more to do with their general level of experience than with their specific avowed theoretical allegiances.

If the relation of theory to practice is flawed, what then are the benefits—and risks—of learning and accepting a particular psychological theory? Every theory represents "an ideal or hypothetical set of facts, principles, or circumstances" (*Webster's* 1989). Theories are usually scientifically acceptable, or at least plausible, although they also can include completely unproven assumptions. Psychological theories are, more specifically, conceptualizations about the human mind and behavior, which may be especially speculative insofar as they relate to hidden intrapsychic events. Donald Spence (1982), who has been expressly concerned with the scientific and clinical status of the central assumptions of psychoanalysis, uses the word *metaphor* in assessing the theory's truth value (p. 296). He contrasts Freud's archaeological model of the mind as consisting of reconstructions of the past (that is, having "historical" truth) to an aesthetic alternative based on new constructions in the present that in effect create the past (that is, having "narrative" truth). In so doing he highlights the tentative or ambiguous nature of the clinician's interpretive formulations because their historical content cannot be separated from their context in current memory. Thus one's metapsychological premises, like interpretations themselves, are provisional although they are sometimes treated as fact.

Theories are nonetheless frameworks for the organization of data and explanation of events, which serve both to guide one's thinking to begin with and to continually shape it thereafter. Thus theories become anchors by constraining what is believed and what is thereby not believed. Depending upon the fluidity of their boundaries, theories may also offer possibilities for new ideas or for the incorporation of old ideas. For example, it may be easier to add to one's belief system the notion of a collective unconscious (a Jungian concept) if one already believes in the unconscious (a Freudian concept), than to reconcile a behavioral tenet (such as the symptom *is* the neurosis) with a dynamic one (such as the symptom is merely a manifestation of underlying conflict).

Unlike his predecessors, Jerome Frank (1991) has not addressed himself to the validity of specific psychological theories or clinical constructs per se, nor to their metaphoric value as temporary conceptualizations or templates that attempt to map reality. Rather, he proposes that the potency of a theory inheres in the belief system's consensuality for the healers. Based on an examination of the cross-cultural function of persuasion and healing, he considers a major theoretical aspect of psychotherapy to be serving to ground the therapist. Psychotherapy accomplishes this by providing a set of guiding principles—a belief system to which the clinician adheres—along with a group of adherents of similar orientation to whom the clinician can turn for professional confirmation and support. A significant implication is that the therapist had best not stand alone in theoretical orientation because he or she gains credibility and confidence through consensual validation.

Equally important, however, is that the conceptual foundation also represents a shared world view between therapist and patient. In the absence of this consensual set of beliefs the prospects for the patient's compliance as well as eventual change are diminished. This thesis further suggests that like all other theories, which simply set the stage for scientific exploration and typically precede factual validation, psychotherapeutic belief systems are to some extent professional myths. They are compelling and persuasive insofar as they are socially supported, although they have not necessarily been proven.

In fact, theories have a tendency to proliferate to fill the gaps in knowledge. Emotional appeal generally presides until scientific proof can prevail in its place. Spence (1990) has noted that as metaphors become cut off from their referents, they also tend to be reified and the objects of magical thinking. Instead of remaining provisional, the metaphor itself is transformed into the immutable essence. He suggests:

> If the metaphor cannot be falsified by direct contact with its reference, then the way is clear for the metaphor to be taken literally. Instead of one possible account of the stuff of the mind—a model or hypothesis—the theory in fashion becomes the final description. The temptation to accept it as final becomes particu-

larly hard to resist when the metaphor promises more than it delivers, that is, when it is couched in language that pretends to refer when it is merely operating heuristically, or when it is embedded in a fictional story so compelling that the reader has suspended all disbelief. (P. 7)

This brings me from the metaphoric and consensual value of theories—for the therapist and patient separately as well as together—to the tendency of theories to be misused. This is compounded by the further observation that theoretical constructs are susceptible to both sociocultural and private or internal influences. These can include the prevailing zeitgeist, the personal history of the theorist, and the reigning narrative metaphor. The last refers to the use of language or figures of speech that may go beyond the data but which gain appeal and strength from a long tradition of cherished themes. The metaphor is, in Spence's terms, what keeps the theory "afloat." According to this thesis, theories can thus obstruct progress by interfering with observation and by trapping the believer into testing irrelevant or inaccurate information.

In orthodox psychotherapy the so-called Oedipus complex may be an example of such a time-honored but sometimes overendowed term. Ever since Freud (1905) extrapolated the famous Greek legend to the guiding principles of psychiatry by claiming that "the Oedipus complex is the nuclear complex of the neuroses . . . which . . . through its after-effects decisively influences the sexuality of the adult" (p. 226), it has attained a level of credence and popularity probably unequaled in the annals of psychological thought.

Theories are at high risk of becoming self-fulfilling prophecies. The proposed theory, which is usually consistent with the personalities of its followers, can subjectively alter the perception and collection of clinical data; the alteration forms a feedback loop that returns to the original conceptual formulations. Thus the organizing theory of the observer (what Thomas Kuhn [1962] referred to as that person's "paradigm") inevitably influences his or her view of the ensuing events. Gerald Adler (1986) illustrates the application of this idea in his exposition on two contrasting orientations toward the psychotherapy of narcissistic personality disorders. In particular he reveals how the respective approaches of Otto Kernberg and Heinz Kohut serve to support and validate their own theoretical tenets. In brief, Kernberg's predominant technique of confronting as a defense the patient's grandiose self (as it presumably protects against hatred and envy of the therapist), means that the theoretician-clinician is often the recipient of the very oral aggression that he or she conceptually views as the core of the disorder. In comparison, Kohut's major strategy of allowing the transference to unfold and to become himself the empathic selfobject that was presumably missing in the patient's past (so that he can gradually explore the meaning of the patient's disappointment in the parent/therapist), supports *his* more benign theoretical contention that such aggression is at most secondary to narcissistic psychopathology.

Adler concludes, "Theory implies a clinical approach that leads to data collection, which tends to confirm the theory and encourage further clinical work, which supports the theory even more" (p. 434). Similarly, Adler believes that the personality of the clinician–theoretician will play a determining role in influencing which aspects of patients will be most likely to be observed and responded to and which will be more easily overlooked (presumably on the basis of the clinician's own unresolved difficulties). In the example of Kernberg and Kohut one would expect a difference in the relative degree of aggression and confrontation versus empathy and support each is more likely to apply—and receive—in the clinical situation, as he wittingly or unwittingly tests out his own preferred formulations.

In the final analysis—whether the theory is reverie or reality, proven or unproven—if the therapist relies too heavily on the persuasive power of a particular theory, it will overwhelm his or her thinking as well as constrict approaches to the patient. By so reducing or rigidifying the sphere of working assumptions, he or she is inevitably limited both as therapist and as human being. The patient in turn is also reduced. Edgar Levenson (1983) suggests that in the perpetuation of such an attitude, "The danger is that the theory becomes an ideological indoctrination *sui generis* and the patient becomes a disciple" (pp. 89–90).

At the same time, however, therapists must strongly believe in themselves and what they practice, and they must find a method that is most congenial to their personal needs and style. The more passionate a therapist is about his or her theories and personal healing powers, the more likely he or she is to have an impact on patients. One of the enduring ingredients of effective psychotherapy is transmitting one's beliefs, which do not have to be correct—just convincing. Indeed, the therapist's conviction is the basis for "doctrinal compliance" (Ehrenwald 1966) as a major ingredient of all forms of therapy.

Research studies of the efficacy of psychotherapy now confirm that attachment to a specific school or theoretical orientation may be necessary for the overall confidence and professional identity of the clinician. It has been proven, not merely recommended, that therapists need to be involved and committed to a particular point of view. A recent meta-analysis of outcome studies has scientifically concluded that "although all therapies are equally effective, one must choose only one to learn and practice" (Smith, Glass, and Miller 1980, 185).

The uses and abuses of theories of psychotherapy are therefore often tangled, and at times tread a thin line between their purposes and perils. Theory offers the therapist the foundation for personal conviction as well as professional allegiance—to prevent confused therapists with marginal identities. Theory serves a mutual and parallel purpose for the patient: a therapist and therapy to believe and trust in, at least temporarily. Despite the fact that each form of therapy may attempt to go beyond sheer suggestion or persuasion (the so-called placebo effect), on some level such suggestibility is still an essential ingredient of all psychotherapy interventions. The major risks, or abuses, of theoretical allegiance are those of personal indoctrination (blind faith as an individual) and partisan polarization (myopia as a member of a particular group). In either event, the therapist, alone or among ardent allies, becomes so convinced of the singular correctness of the theory that he or she cannot see beyond it.

But what does the clinician do with these two paradoxical prospects—strongly believing in one's theories, yet not so abiding by them that they erroneously restrict one's therapeutic view? The ability simultaneously to hold and reconcile these opposite perspectives is a quality the effective therapist needs to develop. It encompasses the capacity to accept a basic theoretical orientation while leaving room for alternative possibilities. It also means an understanding of theories in all of their mythic proportions, that is, as legends that endure because they contain collective inspirational value. Whereas such ideologies derive their potency from being rooted and remembered in human social and personal history as they continue to carry to their recipients the ring of truth, they need to be simultaneously seen, with equal fervor, as a form of fiction. The therapist's theory can thus serve as an anchor, yet not so envelop his or her thinking and practice as to drown therapist and patient in dogma.

PART II

ON THE PATIENTHOOD ROLE
AND ITS IMPLICATIONS

This section addresses my concerns about definitions of psycho-pathology and patienthood, where diagnosis resides in the current psychotherapeutic scheme of things, and in what direction I believe it can more profitably be headed. There are at least two major aspects to this issue: (1) how the therapist professionally defines or views the person who seeks help, and (2) how the individual may view himself or herself, in or out of treatment. What does the recipient want that standard diagnoses or symptomatology cannot necessarily reveal?

Embedded in the discussions of these axioms is also a consideration of psychotherapy as a special verbal treatment modality which may not fit the traditional medical model any more than the typical history suffices as a clinical interview. Psychotherapy as an intervention of the mind is concerned not simply with the individual's specific set of symptoms, but also with the personal meanings behind them. Integrally related to this is the idea that the person's problems in all their complexity may not be best defined by standardized diagnostic signs or syndromes, which are by their very nature reductionistic; they cannot describe the individual subjective depth and diversity that reside beneath the general objective diagnosis.

The initial interviews that are traditional for diagnosis have yet another inherent deficiency: they are insufficient for locating what is now believed to be a significant evaluative factor that extends beyond the patient's individual psyche—the type of interpersonal transference that is formed between patient and therapist. Thus, a highly personalized and interactive approach to patienthood is needed. At the same time, clinical efforts to recognize what is unique about each person, his or her particular problems and coping capacities, should not be antithetical to a simultaneous appreciation of what is universal. All human beings, including those in the therapeutic partnership, are engaged in the same existential struggles.

Alas, in speaking of psychological treatment I often still use the unfortunate word *patient*. I would like to redefine the concept to broaden its connotations, or, failing that, at least to neutralize the term. My hope is that the word be spared the stigmatic or social status associations that define the therapist–patient relationship in terms of inequitable power positions, and that can thereby undermine the potential for a mutual sense of shared humanity. (I am not convinced, I might add, that substituting *client* for *patient* will resolve this issue.)

This section therefore poses the following questions: How do traditional views and standard diagnoses affect both patient and therapist? Is there an orientation that may take a different look at the individual and that can more nearly bridge the gap between recipient and practitioner? What do we mean by the generic term *patient* in psychotherapy, and does anyone who happens to land at the therapist's threshold automatically fit that category? Beyond this, is there a difference between being merely a patient and being a "good" patient? Whether the clinician concludes that the person is or is not suitable for psychotherapy, what does the recipient wish to get from treatment?

CHAPTER 2

A patient is a sufferer who cannot cope and who believes in the therapist

CONTEMPORARY DEFINITIONS of the word *patient* refer to a person under medical care or other treatment. The popular alternative term *client*, which has its origins in legal, social welfare, and business transactions, is defined as anyone under the patronage or protection of another (*Random House* 1975; *Webster's* 1989). The drawback of *patient* is—that the word may undermine the person through the "sick" label. According to Carl Rogers (1965), who has been instrumental in applying the term *client* to the nonmedical domain of counseling, calling the counselee a client presumably represents a more egalitarian attitude on the part of the caretaker by emphasizing a negotiated partnership or contractual relationship. Yet this term's litigious, bureaucratic, or commercial connotations may have their own negative impact. Both rubrics are thus less than perfect. In this behalf I also dismiss as potentially pejorative the term *subject*, sometimes borrowed from the scientific research laboratory, whose innuendos of experimental manipulation and control are no less problematic.

None of the available labels does sufficient justice to the person who appears at the therapist's threshold, but I must make a selection. For me the term *patient* conveys the notion not only of helping but of healing. Without intending to denigrate the hurting person, I am therefore returning to an archaic definition of the term *patient* as simply "a sufferer" (*Random House* 1975).

Terminology notwithstanding, within the broad context of patienthood not every individual who has manifest symptoms (such as anxiety, depression, obsessive-compulsive behavior, or phobia), or discernible problems (such as marital dissension or job stress), or is diagnosed as having a recognizable or defined disorder (such as schizophrenia or bipolar mood disorder), automatically earns this designation. A patient is someone who not only has certain problems or symptoms but is also distressed by them. The chronic alcoholic, the compulsive gambler, the depressed individual, or the overt transsexual—who are untroubled by their drinking, gambling, depression, or cross-dressing, respectively—are as yet exempt as candidates for psychotherapy if they do not feel distressed or "demoralized," to use Frank's (1974) generic term. By *demoralization* he refers to a state of mind of an individual who feels unable to cope with a life situation that he or she is expected, by himself or herself or others, to be able to handle. This condition naturally varies from person to person, but it can encompass loss of confidence or self-esteem, guilt or shame, or isolation or alienation (especially when help is not forthcoming from those to whom the person ordinarily looks for support or understanding). Worse yet, it may mean a loss of trust or faith in the values or abilities of those particular significant others who have otherwise offered a sense of security, real or fantasied, in the past.

Whereas most demoralized persons may be thrown into a state of disorder and confusion or lose the will to cope, a certain degree of denial can also be operating. The denial consists of conscious or, more often, unconscious attempts to disavow the existence of unpleasant reality. Because denial must, by its very nature, ignore data presenting to the perceptory system of the psyche, such a defense as a primary protective mechanism usually dominates in those with an undeveloped infantile psyche or in persons whose ego is weak. As long as these problematic behaviors or feelings are fully fended off, the person is emotionally unable to admit to himself or herself or to others the need for help. The breaking through of such denial is therefore adaptive to the extent that it opens the way toward help seeking. The recognition that one has a problem, although painful, discloses one's inherent capacity to gain access to and reflect upon experiences and emotions, good or bad. However fragile one may be, feeling one's hurt is the first step toward health.

Even acknowledging one's problems and symptoms is insufficient for patient status if the individual is somehow able to deal with the distress for the time being. If the chronic alcoholic manages nonetheless to keep a job and marriage intact, if the compulsive gambler can make acceptable reparations for financial and psychological debts, if the depressed person doesn't decompensate into deeper despair or suicide attempts, and if the transsexual is socially supported rather than forced further into the closet, each may not yet qualify as a patient. More generally, this means that such persons become patients because they are not able to adjust or adapt sufficiently to the problematic situations at the source of their distress; despite defensive or adaptive maneuvers, they are still troubled by the faulty or ungratifying strategies by which they deal with one or another aspect of life's demands. Thus, two major criteria of potential patienthood must be intrapsychically met: (1) being aware of one's pain and (2) not being able to deal with it.

Yet the prospective patient may still feel demoralized but also despair of any remedy. Here, patienthood on an interpersonal level begins where patienthood on an intrapsychic level leaves off. The patient is both anxious to be rid of his or her suffering and believes that he or she can be helped by some outside source. Although many specific qualities of patients influence whether one or another ultimately improves in treatment, motivation to get better as well as belief in the therapist's ability to heal are essential criteria on the road to relief. If the person psychologically prefers his or her own illness and discomfort over the risks of attaining help, he or she will not become a patient; if the person is so fearful of change that he or she resists the very idea of it, the person will not make a promising candidate.

Much has been written about patient motivation. A major contribution to the patient's motives for health is the rational and conscious component of the patient's psyche that wishes to be free of symptoms through realistic cooperation with the therapist. Beyond this are psychological factors within treatment, such as wanting to please the therapist in order to receive his or her approval (or love), or needing to do what is considered appropriate or correct. Working against these motivating forces are the resistance to treatment generated by the unhealthy part of the patient that still needs the pathology and neurotic defenses, by those destructive motives unconsciously designed to displease the therapist through sabotaging therapeutic efforts, or by the needs for other benefits that may accrue from being ill—such secondary gains as getting special attention, being nurtured in one's vulnerability, or not having to meet the demands of reality.

The final criterion of patienthood relates to the general qualities of suggestibility, trust, and hope in relation to psychotherapeutic healing, which is based on receptivity to interpersonal influence. The person undergoing treatment must firmly believe in the powers of another, whether it is the shaman or the medical expert. This in turn is related both to the patient's hope of help and to any confirmation of the therapist's role as helper or healer. Such belief is very often supported by the cultural role and status assigned to such persons. In this regard, Kenneth Calestro (1972) has noted the similarities of faith healing and psychotherapy across the ages. As a primary observation, the patient's susceptibility to suggestion has always been enhanced by the healer's authority and socially sanctioned esteem within a particular environment.

For example, a noted research analysis of social structure and the dynamic process attempted to shed some light on this issue. The sociologist Talcott Parsons (1951) identified certain variables of the doctor–patient relationship necessary for successful treatment, one of the most critical being the "social distance" between practitioner and patient. In a related study of human organization, Temple Burling, Edith Lentz, and Robert Wilson (1956) similarly concluded, "We are coming to understand that faith in the doctor is a necessary element in cure, [and] that he will not be able to exercise therapeutic leverage if we, as patients, regard him in too prosaic a light" (p. 71). These authors suggested that the therapist's power to claim the patient's confidence and the therapist's effectiveness would be impaired by growing familiarity.

Religious shamans (the psychotherapists of their day) were typically of high intellect and demonstrated unusual emotional control. Thus certain personal qualities of the healer, in juxtaposition with the patient's expectation of help, have historically served to maximize the powers of suggestion. As Calestro (1972) put it, therapeutic suggestion is in part based upon "a recognition that the therapeutic agent holds a special position in the community, deriving from certain esoteric powers and knowledge about the universe which he has acquired. This position is not simply a matter of social status, but is a recognition of the unique relationship that the therapeutic agent enjoys with regard to . . . natural [or supernatural] forces" (p. 93). Addressing this particular factor, Jan Ehrenwald (1966) has further examined a phenomenon that he believes to be crucial to therapeutic outcome—the "therapist's myth." This has been defined as the therapist's personal belief or confidence in his or her own ability to be of help (that is, "therapeutic presence") in conjunction with an expectation of help on the part of the patient in response to it. Both the therapist's self-perception and the patient's confirmation of these endowments in light of his or her own needs, are significant. Beyond sheer suggestibility or persuasion per se, of course, is the person's willingness to work with the healer within the context of an interpersonal relationship, to put faith and trust in someone else. In short, two interrelated criteria of patienthood on an interpersonal level must be met: (1) desiring to change or be cured, recognizing that one cannot do it alone and (2) believing in another's capacity to help.

In sum, if the person is aware of his or her pain, is not able to cope with it, wishes to change the situation, and believes in the ability of another to help, that individual has the fourfold makings of a "patient." These criteria form the general requirements of treatment and are non-specific. They must be present before the clinician can even think about beginning work. And these intrapsychic and interpersonal factors are necessary regardless of the particular techniques of treatment.

CHAPTER 3

Diagnosis in psychotherapy means understanding human conditions that are both unique and universal

ALL CLINICAL PRACTICE begins with a person, a potential patient, who is essentially unknown. How the therapist proceeds to regard that person is often circumscribed by the preemptive purpose of making a diagnosis. This axiom is less concerned with the accuracy of diagnoses than with two overall orientations or attitudes toward the evaluation process that go beyond specific diagnostic formulations. It refers to a dual search for the *unique* (selective) and *universal* (shared). The former orientation looks for what makes the patient singularly special, at his or her worst and best; it seeks those individual qualities that define and distinguish the person from all others. The latter orientation takes a seemingly quantum leap in the other direction to locate what he or she has in common with others, not necessarily within the framework of psychopathology, but on the larger level of what fundamentally binds or connects him or her to all humanity with similar struggles. The clinical pendulum may continually swing somewhere between these two spectrums before it finally falls into place. In either event, how one views the person on preliminary presentation and how the dynamic assessment is made become a microcosm of these two stances toward the patient qua patient.

Since the initial interview naturally has important implications for the course of treatment as well as prognosis, there is usually a great deal of pressure to make a precise formulation as early as possible. The clinician may also have a personal stake in keeping to the initial construction as self-fulfilling proof of his or her diagnostic prowess, thereby prematurely closing off other possibilities. For practical purposes of assessment, the anxious clinician (who may believe he or she is being scrupulous) can easily become preoccupied with nosological matters of mental status tests, differential diagnostic categories, and the like. Such instrumentation and the designations derived from them are not without utility in orienting the therapist; they can provide succinct and even standardized guidelines that comfortably encapsulate a patient's problems.

But the focus and function of tests and categories is by nature highly circumscribed and simplistic. We are all familiar with the efficient physician's temptation to identify the patient by his or her "disease," in effect viewing the presenting person simply as the objective sum of pathological signs and symptoms, or, equally undermining, the mere repository of subjective complaints. Not only are these indications insufficient, but they are interpersonally perilous. Initial symptoms can easily belie what is really troubling the patient, insofar as diagnosis cannot be determined by overt appearance, or by initial subjective report, nor on a one-shot basis; rather, it is most often an unfinished procedure that takes repeated clinical impressions to reveal. Because patients with psychological problems are especially prone to want to hide their troubles from others as well as themselves, their overt symptoms become at best the tip of the psychopathological iceberg.

On an interpersonal level, the distance between the psychotherapist and patient is increased when the clinician falls back upon the familiar typical medical anamnesis as a major source or style of taking the case history and gathering information. This process often serves to separate clinician from patient, not only in terms of professional status accorded to the expert (which may in part be appropriate), but by unnecessarily placing them on opposite sides of the psychopathology spectrum. Creating a conceptual trench between illness and health, the approach erroneously makes each the presumed representative of a theoretical pole—the patient as "sick" and the therapist as "normal" (or "healthy"). Such unequal positions of power or dependency may then remain implicit throughout treatment. These can reflect the insecure clinician's need to reinforce the psychological space between himself or herself and the patient, needlessly exaggerating the victim status and rescuer role.

Nonetheless, to adopt this type of delimited diagnostic orientation toward the prospective patient is very tempting, especially to the novice who is eager for closure or the expert who may be overconfident of his or her capacity to pinpoint pathology. Accentuating neurotic or psychotic symptomatology, for example, takes the psychotherapist away from a broader and deeper look at the individual which is necessarily more flexible and demanding. Moreover, because such a stance is skewed toward preconceived categories or prototypic standards of behavior, it can be dehumanizing to the extent that it fails to regard the complex and subtle nuances of the whole person, whose psychodynamics are intricate and infinitesimal on one level, broad and boundless on another.

The problems, distresses, and disturbances that lend themselves to a more mutual psychotherapeutic endeavor and that help to establish common ground between the person who comes to treatment and the person who does the treating are the human struggles that both (we all) share. The therapist's open orientation toward the troubled person recognizes every individual's limitations as well as assets—difficulties and adaptations in interpersonal relations in love or at work, guilt and inhibitions, doubts about self-worth and concerns about being creative. These are viewed in light of the inherent need to express one's capacities and possibilities; the desire for independence and self-realization; the need for dependency and intimacy; and the acceptance of age-appropriate losses while nonetheless yearning for immortality and infinity. In short, it recognizes every human being's ontologic hunger as well as fragility and mortality.

This broader definition of patienthood in terms of a self-actualization spectrum sees every disorder or disturbance as an expression of self-growth versus self-diminution—the differential between what one is (or perceives oneself to be) and what one can conceivably become. At the same time, it implies an emphasis on positive and healthy aspects of the self to counterbalance the opposing predilection for pathology. It therefore opts for a more humanistic conceptualization of psychological difficulties, in Abraham Maslow's (1970) terms, serving to place on one continuum "all the standard diagnostic categories, all the stuntings, cripplings, and inhibitions . . . and also the existential disorders . . . that cannot be called 'illness' " (p. 124).

These are the very issues that the therapist can be struggling with, though presumably with less apparent disruption to his or her personal life and professional function. The recognition of this unifying fact—that the clinician works with an individual who is neither unknown nor unacceptable to himself or herself—is the leveler of psychotherapy. Such a stance can even make the therapist's task easier, if the therapist is not threatened by this kind of human identification with the patient.

The therapist need not be protected by an image of the recipient as different, whereby diagnosis can become a defensive maneuver applied as a form of emotional distancing. The unfrightened therapist's acknowledgment of shared humanity both binds the therapist to the patient as a philosophic position that appreciates their joint struggles and strivings, and more technically, influences the ongoing psychotherapeutic task as a cooperative venture and empathic process.

Thus, in conducting psychotherapy, to focus on neurotic or psychotic symptomatology—such as anxiety, panic, delusions, sleep and weight disorders, bulimic behavior, or impotence (even if overt behavioral manifestations are a prominent part of the presenting problem)—is not only diagnostically reductionistic, but on an interpersonal level can easily bring the sessions to an end or impasse. The patient's understandable feelings of being diminished may result in expressions of anger, exasperation, or aggression, and the therapist in turn may begin to experience frustration or alienation. Any of these will likely disrupt whatever semblance of therapeutic alliance has been, or can be, established.

What I am leading to is an overall orientation toward the patient that holds that no matter how striking the symptoms (for example, a preoccupation with or attempt at suicide) and no matter how aversive or socially unacceptable their behavioral expression (as in child abuse, incest, or adultery), the therapist's ongoing diagnostic question to himself or herself needs to be, Who is *this human being*, from whom these particular signs and symptoms happen to emanate? The function of such an internal query is twofold: (1) emphasis on the word *this* helps to direct the clinician to the individual's special problems and strengths in all their unique character, healthy and unhealthy, while (2) concentration on *human being* sensitizes the therapist to the person's shared struggles in all their universal character, good and bad. In clinical assessment and ongoing treatment, both of these alternate but complementary views need to be continually borne in mind in order to gain the fullest appreciation, evaluatively and therapeutically, of the presenting patient.

CHAPTER 4

---

*Behind the question, What do I
want? is the larger question,
Who am I?—or even, Am I?*

THIS MAXIM HAS LESS to do with the therapist's myopic or expansive view of the patient than with the ways in which the patient's problems may be masked, not only from the therapist but from the patient himself or herself. It pertains to clues regarding what the patient may often unknowingly want or need—despite superficial appearances, inconsistent complaints, or protestations to the contrary. This fourth maxim relates to the conduct of such patients within the treatment process, suggesting how the therapist had best address these unwitting wishes. As a clinical application of the development of object relations and self, maxim 4 takes the unconscious and unfocused yearnings of the patient from an endless search in the world at large to a more conscious and focused pursuit within the finite world of psychotherapy.

Today's patient frequently comes to treatment complaining of chronic but inexplicable dissatisfaction in his or her life. The major problem is not specific or easily identified, but rather a global discontent that occurs regardless of, or in concert with, varying overt symptomatology. Such a patient may neither be able to verbalize nor understand his or her unremitting struggle—trying to consolidate, organize, stabilize, or maintain, to *feel*, a sense of self. As Rogers (1965) observed: "In a very true sense the client never knows what the problem is until it is well on its way to resolution. Another way of stating this phenomenon is that the problem appears to be the same in all cases; it is the problem of assimilating denied experience into a reorganized self" (p. 104). The person seems to be on a relentless quest for something as yet undefined, which persists despite what one presumably has in terms of material comforts, success, or good fortune. A pretty picture may even be painted by the patient, at least initially, that soon belies the extent of deep-seated disturbance. This can be manifested by an early presentation of one's problems, in James Masterson's (1976) terms, "wrapped in romantic camouflage" (p. 9), or less superficially, defensively, and erroneously placed outside oneself—for example, projected onto one's partner.

A critical clue for the clinician is usually the sense of diagnostic contradiction. The therapist's own response parallels an overriding patient characteristic of externally deceptive or inconsistent clinical findings. Thus the practitioner can typically be greeted with marked discrepancies, either between the patient's outward appearance and underlying disturbance, or among his or her different areas of function. For example, upon fuller examination it may be that the individual does quite well in some arenas but very poorly in others. In these instances, at bottom can often lurk—to greater or lesser degrees—an early developmental defect in the sense of self. The wounded or faulty self may need to constantly assure itself that it is alive, not being really certain that it exists at all. The patient may adopt various forms of false self, or "pseudovitality" (Kohut 1977) (for example, eroticized life-style, preoccupation with youth, power, or fame), behind which lie a profound sense of worthlessness and the compensatory yearning for stimulation to counteract feelings of inner emptiness.

Viewed historically, the prototypes of the Freudian hysteric of the 1900s to 1930s, the high anxiety neurotic of the 1940s to 1970s, and even the mild to moderate depressive of the 1980s and early 1990s do not express the depth and diversity of disorders of self at the brink of the twenty-first century. As Erik Erikson (1963) anticipated, "The patient of today suffers most under the problem of what he should believe in—or indeed, might—be or become; while the patient of early psychoanalysis suffered most under inhibitions which prevented him from being what and who he thought he knew he was" (p. 279). Thus yesterday's psychopathology meant knowing who one was and what one wanted but being too repressed to seek and express those hidden desires and wishes. Today's psychopathology, on the other hand, in a time when the opportunity for recognition and accomplishment combines with an erosion of values and a loss of identity, means conceivably having it all—but not knowing what one wants, indeed who one is or *that one is* in the first place. This new breed of patient may also attest to Kohut's (1977) call for two psychologies, each evolved out of a different historical period: the earlier one is the "guilty man," whose modus operandi has been to try to seek gratification for his libidinal desires and drives; the more contemporary one is the "tragic man," whose modus operandi is to fulfill his nuclear self as he continually strives for cohesion of that fragmented or missing self.

More specifically, as Margaret Mahler, Fred Pine, and Anni Bergman's (1975) research on the psychological birth of the human infant concludes:

> Smooth and consistently progressive personality development, even under ordinary favorable circumstances, is difficult, if not impossible. This, we found, was due precisely to the fact that separation and individuation derive from and are dependent upon the symbiotic origin of the human condition, upon that very symbiosis with another human being, the mother. This creates an everlasting longing for the actual or coesthetically fantasized, wish-fulfilled, and absolutely protected state of primal identifica-tion . . . for which deep in the original primal unconscious, in the so-called primary repressed realm every human being strives. (P. 227)

What the patient "wants" when he or she has everything is to re-create this state of primal identification that characterizes the long-lost self; the desire is all encompassing if the person has never had those blissful moments. Although the yearning for that idyllic infancy occurs in every human being, an obsessive preoccupation with it occurs only when it has to be created anew. The fantasy of what one did *not* have preempts all one has.

The infant's wanting and being are indistinguishable. Especially in the preverbal stages the infant's inner sensations, which are predominantly proprioceptive-enteroceptive, become the core of the feeling of self. At the same time, external sensations are predominantly sensoriperceptive, which are instrumental in differentiating the self from the world. The most significant object in the child's universe is the mother, who helps the child integrate these proprioceptive and sensoriperceptive dimen-sions by providing the matrix for psychosocial and biological depen-dency and security. She allows the structural differentiation and innate individualization to take place. She is the symbolic organizer, in Mahler,

Pine, and Bergman's (1975) terms, the "midwife" of individuation and psychological birth. It is through the gradual internalization of this constant, positive, reliable image of the mother that the child develops emotional object constancy and a stable identity. The differentiation between a child's wants and his or her sense of self occurs gradually, as the child gives up primitive wishes for symbiosis and begins to establish a stable object relationship.

Of course, human development is not linear. Silvia Bell (1970) has even demonstrated experimentally that infants who have had harmonious relationships with their mothers develop "person permanence" prior to "object permanence," whereas the sequence is reversed for disharmonious maternal relationships. In spite of the child's immutable inborn endowment or constant "good-enough mother" (Winnicott 1965), there are ongoing events that may influence this development of a sense of stability; they especially occur at the crossroads of development (Erikson 1959). Particularly traumatic are the unfavorable events that impinge on the child's personality when the child is developmentally most vulnerable or that act upon the child's specific sensitivities. The earlier the occurrence of trauma, the more unfavorable the outcome, disposing the child to a greater proclivity toward later severe personality disorder. If the lack of good-enough mothering occurs in the symbiotic phase of development (the first six months of infancy), the child may never be able to "hatch from the common membrane" and may want to stay in the "delusional twilight state of the mother-infant common orbit" (Mahler and Furer 1960).

The more the deprivation at this phase of infancy, the greater the yearning, to a point that at times the child may renounce or distort autonomous functions (mobility, speech, and the like) to preserve the delusion of an unconditionally omnipotent symbiotic relationship with the mother. As a result, not only does the child not differentiate self from mother (that he or she is a separate being who can have independent wants), the child does not even crystallize his or her inner sensations to feel a self, that is, to recognize the self as an entity—in short, to gain a sense of *me*.

Case Illustration

An attractive, forty-seven-year-old businesswoman had married her "high school sweetheart" and was the mother of two "lovely" daughters. At the time of the patient's birth, her mother had been in a "depression" that lasted for two years. The patient had been in treatment with different therapists sporadically during the previous twelve years. She invariably complained about some elusive dissatisfaction in her life with which she was privately haunted, but that belied her otherwise comfortable circumstances and flimsily held illusion that all was well. She was told by her past physicians that she was suffering from "chronic depression."

PATIENT: What do I want? What is it that I want? I have everything I could need. I have had a storybook marriage: I have a good husband, healthy kids, thank God, none of them on drugs or anything like that. We have enough money. I enjoy my job, and I love participating in my church. My friends say it must be the "empty nest syndrome." I go along with the gag, but I felt this way even when I was very young, in fact, as far back as I can remember. . . . Every therapist suggested something different: first they checked my thyroid and took other tests; they were all normal. They gave me megavitamins, then antidepressants. Those almost gave me a stroke after the fourth month because by mistake I ate some cheese or something. It wasn't helping at all, anyway. They also sent me for exercise, jogging. One therapist suggested I take up some hobby, so I learned to knit and took painting classes. In group therapy, other patients suggested that I get a lover, that romance might be missing from my life, even though my sexual relationship with my husband is good. Believe it or not, I even found someone for a few weeks—then I was back to where I had been, if not worse. I read every self-improvement book. They say one needs friendship, intimacy. I do have some good friends, but I am not sure how intimate I am supposed to be with them. On the one hand, I seem to have everything I could want, but do I want that? If not, then what do I *want?*

THERAPIST: During the last twelve years of treatment you seem to have gotten no answer to your question. Is it possible that it's because that question "What do I want?" might not be the question?

PATIENT: What question do you think I should want answered?

THERAPIST: Maybe in all of those "I wants" the emphasis has not been on the right word.

PATIENT: You mean instead of what I *want* the emphasis should be on what *I* want?

THERAPIST: Hmm.

PATIENT: I still see that quizzical look of yours. So I know there's something more. . . . But I can't say what *I* want because I don't know what *I* want. I guess I don't really feel like there is any "me." So then maybe there's another question I should be asking. I mean, if there's no "me," then what am I? or better yet, Who am I? Tell me, who am I? because maybe you know.

This patient's rather superficial sense that she had "everything" temporarily masked what she did not have, deficiencies that resulted in deeper defects in the areas of both love and work. Sporadic episodes of desperate clinging, incessant imploring of the therapist for answers, and vacuous flurrying of activity in behalf of others instead of herself, alternated with an assortment of abortive involvements and emotional distancing that reflected her defense against intimacy in treatment as well as in her outside life. Despite repeated proclamations to the contrary, especially in the earlier sessions, her object attachments and love life with her husband were really experienced as empty and ungratifying; she felt alone and "unconnected." Similarly, her inability to individuate affected her inconsistent capacity to be employed as an independent and self-sufficient woman. The sense of failure in both arenas was viewed as a manifestation of a basic defect in the development of self.

In patients who have never evolved beyond the symbiotic union with mother to feel a self, not only a rational answer to What do I want? but even an awareness of Who am I? does not develop because a sense of "I am" has never been established. As Mahler, Pine, and Bergman (1975) define it, "We use the term *identity* to refer to the earliest awareness of a sense of being, of entity. . . . It is not a sense of *who* I am but *that* I am; as such, it is the earliest step in the process of the unfolding of individuality" (p. 8). In the case cited here, the "I am" was missing—the foundation upon which the "who I am" and "what I want" are built.

CHAPTER 5

Patients come to treatment in search of a substitute object, if not a substitute self

SEVERAL MAJOR THEORISTS since Freud, including Melanie Klein, W. Ronald Fairbairn, Harry Guntrip, Donald Winnicott, John Bowlby, and Wilfred Bion, have not conceptualized drives as being gratified instinctually through direct discharge; instead they have seen drives as object seeking. More specifically, mother–child attachment is not secondary to libidinal gratification, but rather is the infant's primary and fundamental desire. Even Klein, whose theory is perhaps the most orthodox in stating that perceptions of real objects are merely the scaffolding for projections of the child's innate object images, admits to the ameliorative value of real mothering beyond sheer fantasy. In essence, all of these theorists emphasize libido as the need for the breast in infancy, and thereafter, for special human contact—as hallucinatory wish, if not reality. Taken further, whether or not the mother is physically present, the child who experiences secure attachment can ultimately negotiate the difficult path of separation and individuation in the development of the self.

Following this line of thinking, it is likely that all patients, regardless of diagnosis—whether the less severe symptom neuroses and neurotic character disorders or the more pathological narcissistic, selfobject, and borderline disturbances—suffer problems in the establishment of self to varying degrees; that is, there may be some sense of inner cohesiveness and internal stability on one end, or fragmentation, even eradication, on the other.

At issue here is how that spectrum of self-disturbance naturally reveals itself in psychotherapy as a microcosm of the less than optimal relationship between parent and child. More specifically, this continuum suggests two underlying expressions of unfulfilled yearnings for mother, as manifested in the patient's relationship with the therapist: the search for a substitute object, and in more extreme instances, the search for a substitute self.

In the treatment itself, some patients who appear to be successful, desirable, and capable, but who constantly complain that they cannot find a spouse, lover, or friend, can turn therapy into a long quest for these real objects in their current life. This type of sojourn may include endless discussions of where to meet people or how to evaluate others in forming new relationships. And the therapist may be enlisted to provide information and guidance about how to meet people and how to form new relationships. At times the therapist may share the patient's search in sympathy and identification. Susceptible therapists even attempt to explore the patient's contribution to the fruitless pursuit of relationships at the risk of losing their empathic bond.

It should be remembered that patients usually speak to others as well about their unsuccessful efforts and have already received all sorts of advice, no doubt including comments about the part they play in their problem. What patients do not often get from others is the understanding that their problems in object relations go beyond the current situation. The problems represent at a minimum a yearning and searching for past relationships (the prototype of which is the maternal figure of childhood). Before patients can experience a new relationship, they need to find a substitute for the lost object. Patients will address the therapist as that past object; as such, the therapist becomes the primary focus of patients' thoughts, feelings, and narration, and a very intense and irrational transference is formed.

In these cases, the therapist can only help to locate the nature of this yearned for relationship, and then allow the same desire and disappointment that the patient is experiencing with other people to be repeated within the therapeutic relationship. The therapist's role is not to become that substitute object, simply one who will interpret the search in vivo. When the patient's unfulfilled wish is understood and put in proper perspective, then the patient may begin to accept others as themselves, not as substitute objects who are always falling short of what the patient seeks. Others eventually can become new objects in their own right and potential partners for relatively satisfactory relationships.

Other patients, however, in the guise of seeking a relationship, are not even looking for a lost substitute object from their past: they never had "good-enough" mothering (Winnicott 1965) in their childhood to begin with, so there was nothing in their past on which to base a search for a substitute now. For these patients the search is more complicated. Not only did the early loving relationship not exist, but its absence— marked by unresponsive "empathic failures" (Kohut 1977)—interfered with the development of the self. Such a patient will talk about himself or herself without interacting with or relating to the therapist. The patient seems to be speaking to anyone, and no one is special. The therapist is an almost interchangeable object.

In this situation, the therapist allows himself to be temporarily used as that substitute self, a stand-in for the self the patient has never had. However, the therapist does not interpret the patient's using him or her as a substitute self until the patient's sense of self has become relatively stable. An early sign of such stability is that the patient begins to speak to the particular therapist, that the patient starts to see the therapist as an object (that is, a person)—even if it is a substitute object.

Case Illustration

A thirty-nine-year-old divorced, childless, and successful professional woman had been in love with a man who left her after one and one-half years. The patient was depressed and felt rejected, experiencing the loss and the pain, and thinking that there was no reason to live. She was contemplating killing herself.

PATIENT: I never loved that way, if this is what love is. I mean, ironically, I did not even see him [her lover] that much, as if I didn't need to have him all the time. The fact that he existed for me was good enough. Of course, I always looked forward to seeing him. I wouldn't miss any opportunity, but I always felt him within me.

THERAPIST: It is a major loss. [The therapist's statement encourages the patient to feel the extent of the loss, what her lover meant to her, what kind of object he was for her.]

PATIENT: I don't think even my mother's death was such a loss. I remember having cried a lot. Please don't misunderstand. I loved her, but I felt I could survive. I remember during the funeral I couldn't completely focus on her. My mind kept wandering to other matters. I was just twenty-eight, not that I no longer needed a mother. Life was going to go on. I was married. Now I feel like the world is coming to an end. I've fallen in love with other men in my life and when the relationship ended, I would feel pain and suffer for a while, but then find someone else. This time I don't even want to. I can't. I don't feel I could love anyone else. I don't feel that I can love, period. It seems that not only did I lose him, but I also lost something else, the ability to love, a part of me—

THERAPIST: —which compounds your loss.

The therapist wants to shift the content from the loss of the relationship to loss of self; he uses the word *compounds* to bridge the two. Intentional shifts of topic or focus by the therapist, done by bridging, will generally increase the patient's collaboration. In fact, after a successful transition the patient may even drop the former subject altogether and follow the latter one, with no further effort by the therapist.

PATIENT: I am not sure which is worse. The loss is not just compounded—it is beyond anything that I have ever felt. I never thought of killing myself over a love affair. It was different when I wanted to wash a man out of my hair; I always did. This I cannot shake. It's as if it is stuck in my bones.

THERAPIST: Your relationship with him was quite different from all other relationships you had with men. [The therapist is following the same path. Now, instead of focusing on the loss of the lover, he is focusing on the larger issue, the "different" nature of this relationship.]

PATIENT: Quite different. As I was saying, I didn't really care. I mean I cared, but not this way. Maybe I didn't love them as much, or you think I did not love them really?

THERAPIST: Maybe John is the first person you really loved?

The therapist not only finishes the thought process of the patient, but desexualizes it and generalizes from the man to the person. The apparent generalization is actually intended to break the impasse of the specific loss of the love of one particular man to the more encompassing experience of loss of love or never having been loved; later on, this may even lead to the deeper sense of never having been.

PATIENT: In adult life, for sure. He is not even that special, mind you, not very handsome or smart or intellectual. Somehow, in fact, if you look at him objectively you wonder why, for heaven's sake, I am so preoccupied with him. He's so ordinary, but he really loved me. Even that is not so unusual. I have had many men fall in love with me since I was thirteen. I guess he let me love him, really love him. I was completely myself with him, the way I really am. He allowed me to be me. He loved that "me," and that "me" loved him.

THERAPIST: He made it possible for you to experience the ability to really love. [The therapist wants to solidify a baseline of understanding by repeating the patient's previous insight, and he also would like to slow the patient down.]

PATIENT: I never thought I had that capacity. I didn't even know it existed at all. I was just going along my own way, thinking that I loved people. I had no idea even of what I was lacking.

THERAPIST: Not only have you loved him this real way, you also discovered a dimension of yourself that you did not know existed. [The therapist is reinforcing these observations by rewording the patient's statements. He both agrees with the patient and begins to narrow the field of inquiry from interpersonal behavior to internal discovery—from loving another to loving the self.]

PATIENT: How does one know what one does not have? I guess it's like the blind or deaf person: How does he know what he is missing?

THERAPIST: You discovered that you have other eyes and ears. [Semantic congruity promotes cooperation, so the therapist is using the same metaphor as he zeros in on the self of the patient.]

PATIENT: Not even other, just having eyes and ears I never thought I had. I can see and hear, not again, but for the first time.

THERAPIST: And you love that seeing and hearing self of yours that you never had before. [The therapist, having gained some ground on the issue of discovery of self, has again approached the next frontier—loving that self.]

PATIENT: Yes. I walked around smiling. People looked at me amused. I had a secret. It was wonderful. I found *me!*

THERAPIST: And John's leaving you not only caused you to lose someone you really loved, but you also lost that newly found part of you.

Loving the self, in turn, sets the stage for the next topic, the corollary issue of *not* loving the self, the patient's current situation. The therapist is also concerned with the pace of self-revelations. He wonders what the patient may be avoiding by such eager self-exposure, or if this is a sign of fragmentation. The therapist thus wants to lessen the pace, hypothesizing that perhaps the patient is trying too hard to deny the pain of the actual loss.

PATIENT: I guess that's why I want to kill myself when I think of killing him. When I hate him, I hate myself, too. He deprived me of himself and of myself. I feel I could never love anyone else anymore. That "me"—the new me—died. I don't have to kill it. It's not as if I lost my arm or a part of my body. It's more than just an arm. I feel empty, like "me" just moved out of my body. I have no sense of me anymore. I don't like anything else in life. I resent every other existing thing— people, my friends, you. *(Remains silent for about two minutes.)*

The therapist breaks the silence slowly here, not only allowing more time for the patient to experience the loneliness just expressed, but hoping that she may talk about it again. The therapist also gives himself extra time when he needs it.

THERAPIST: None of us is able to make you feel like you, the way that you were with John.

Here the therapist wonders what path to pursue. Should he move back and talk about her loss of John? Or speak about her "self" as a loss? Or drop both subjects and follow the new material the patient just presented, that she "resents other existing things"? The therapist further asks himself whether he should start with "all existing things" and dilute the resentment, or risk focusing on himself as a target of that resentment.

Although this patient presented herself as suffering from depression because of a specific loss, she understood early in the treatment that she was always yearning for love that she had never received in her childhood. All her love affairs were failed searches to find that missed union. Therefore, virtually every relationship had been disappointing, insofar as most men did not want to be a substitute object; they grew tired of her narcissistic demands. In fact, these relationships never lasted long even with nurturing men, because the search for a substitute object was a thin cover for her search for herself in someone else (that is, for a substitute self).

In this instance, the therapist will not only clarify the patient's desires and losses but provide that transitional self as a buttress or temporary bridge. The therapist will be a selfobject (Kohut 1971) to this patient, until she develops a relative sense of herself. He does this first by letting her feel comfortable and accepted in his presence (to experience a feeling of realness comparable to what she experienced with her boyfriend). In essence, the therapist will offer himself as an empathic, benign object so that she can begin to make contact with him. Once some successful transformation of the selfobject into the psychological structure is achieved, she will be ready to reveal herself further to the therapist. Then they may productively explore her difficulties in outside relationships as well. The therapist recognizes the patient's request for him to replace John in order to help her to find herself. In this crucial interim, while the patient is in search of her real subjective self, the therapist will serve as a stand-in.

PART III

ON THERAPEUTIC SETTINGS AND THEIR MYTHOLOGIES

A therapeutic connection or relationship does not automatically happen between all patients and all therapists. The general atmosphere, which has both physical and psychological components, provides a form of sanctuary that is separate from everyday living—at first as a new place and activity and thereafter symbolically. The atmosphere supplies the conditions of safety, which must accompany or precede the development of trust. It is assumed that the patient feels vulnerable by definition and cannot proceed without some semblance of a sense of security, however temporary. But safety alone does not suffice; without optimism for the future, therapy cannot begin. Here the interpersonal ingredients of psychotherapy emerge as a continual balancing act, as the therapist attempts to realistically combine legitimate concern about the patient's problems with some modicum of hope for the future, in a way that is neither too solemn nor too idealistic. The goals must not be beyond either member's reach.

Setting the therapeutic stage is also embedded in another aspect of the patient's (and therapist's) preparation for a psychotherapeutic encounter: the need to have a shared concept of the nature of illness and its treatment. Cross-cultural studies suggest that such a mutual belief system need not be scientifically proven; it must merely be a "shared myth" which is usually culturally inherited or sociologically supported by the surrounding environment. Beyond this mutual mythology, however, are individual aims or intentions that are based on the realities of each person's needs and psychological capacities.

Finally, in conjunction with the initial ingredients for an aura of receptivity is the nitty-gritty of having to enter the patient's psychic world. Reaching a conflicted and defended individual means that the therapist must unfreeze long-held attitudes and behaviors. This requires altering the recipient's arousal system, either by heightening it or by lowering it. Only then can the therapist hope to penetrate the inner recesses of the individual. But altering the patient's arousal is only the beginning of the therapeutic path to change.

The following questions are therefore posed: Are there general principles for setting the stage for receptivity, which apply above and beyond making contact with an individual patient? Does a sense of safety suffice? Is expectation enough? What roles do suggestibility and arousal play? What qualities are required in the therapist and patient, or better yet in the two together, not to change or cure the person, but simply to get started?

CHAPTER 6

---

*The therapist must establish a
psychologically safe environment,
wherein anything can be said and
any feeling experienced*

WE ARE ALL SUSCEPTIBLE to our surroundings, in therapy as in
life. (The patient may be more susceptible within treatment than in the
outside world.) Although some individuals are relatively insensitive or
oversensitive to their immediate environment, how one responds is
usually more a matter of the symbolic meaning of the presented situation than a function of physical or logistical factors alone. Alerted to
this, the psychotherapist is able to make use of rather than play down
a sometimes underestimated contextual factor, the therapy setting.

To begin with, the interaction between therapist and patient is conducted within a particular environment that is not incidental; it is an
integral part of the total therapeutic experience. The setting can be
considered a core feature of all psychotherapies, past and present. The
clinical setting or atmosphere (including location, furnishings, decor, and
equipment) not only incorporates tangible conditions that help to create
the proper ambience to facilitate therapeutic communication, but has
symbolic value and metaphoric meaning.

Frank (1979) refers to the "healing setting," which serves the primary
role of sanctifying the procedure by certain traditional rites that are
designed to reinforce the therapeutic relationship. Its main function is to
heighten the patient's regard for the therapist via the presence of vali-
dating symbols of health and cure. Reminiscent of the shaman who must

perform a special ceremony dressed in his particular priestly apparel in order to raise the recipient's belief that he can heal the sick, divine the hidden, and control events, or the gypsy fortuneteller whose crystal ball becomes more than a mere accoutrement of her prophetic powers to gaze into the future, in modern Western medicine the physician's influence is nonetheless facilitated, at least initially, by the nature of the environmental ingredients and the particular aura they create.

Modern legitimizing representations of the credentials of the therapist as a professional learned person (for example, framed diplomas on the wall, books, the office desk) serve covertly to communicate his or her qualifications and special capacity to conduct psychotherapy. At the same time, special representational objects, whether a statue of Buddha or a photograph of Freud, are indicative of allegiance to esteemed masters of one's particular belief system.

Whatever its actual or symbolic valence, the setting of dynamic treatment shares with other forms of therapy a professional area that is intentionally removed from everyday life and sharply distinguished from it. This ideally provides a special space, a sanctuary or personal refuge, set apart from the realities of daily life and psychologically divorced from it—rather like a religious temple. It is in these private protective surroundings that the patient can be offered both physical and emotional safety.

The verbally monitored interpersonal ambience affects one's intrapsychic state of mind. In dynamic psychotherapy this therapeutic context bears little resemblance to other interpersonal situations insofar as the patient is encouraged to say whatever he or she wants to say about anyone (including the therapist) as well as to experience the entire gamut of feelings without the normal risk of reprisal. The result is not strictly the same as the classical Freudian technique of free association— which may constitute a unique example of having the patient report whatever comes to mind, however nonsensical, trite, or taboo—but in both free association and other therapeutic approaches the patient is made to feel safe in the light of unleashed shame, guilt, or fear.

An overall sense of protection, support, or acceptance, no matter what is divulged, must characterize the noncritical and caring therapist's orientation to the patient in any psychotherapy. This interpersonal atmosphere of unconditional approval permits generally uncensored speech on the part of the patient because the patient is not inhibited by everyday attitudes or values.

More specifically, the patient's "bad" (inappropriate, undesirable, or socially unacceptable) ideas, wishes, and feelings are allowed—in fact expected—to be expressed in words without the loss of the therapist's interest, respect, or concern. As a form of unconditional regard, the therapist's orientation conveys the message that the recipient will be protected from the therapist's personal reactions, especially those that reflect rejection or disdain; likewise, the patient will be shielded from endangering himself or herself with unacceptable thoughts and feelings.

Spontaneous and otherwise censored ideas or emotions, which would ordinarily remain untapped, may take the negative form of hate and its variations: anger; jealousy or envy; wishing harm or death to others; incestuous or aggressive feelings; unpopular, deviant, or perverse fantasies; or the like. The therapist neither condones nor condemns the feelings while eliciting their full verbal expression. Nonetheless, the patient, who naturally wants the positive respect and esteem (love) of the therapist, inevitably has difficulty in exposing weaknesses such as feelings of self-hate, inadequacy, or unimportance. This special permission to experience one's psychic life under the interpersonal shelter of a psychologically safe environment gives psychotherapy its unique quality, allowing the patient to gradually shed the accumulated layers of defensive armor.

In conjunction with a nonjudgmental posture, the therapist does not retaliate or reciprocate, maintaining instead a benign but dispassionate attitude. Although the therapist does not express his or her own feelings, so that the patient will not be burdened with them, paradoxically the therapist induces affective experiences that the patient cannot experience elsewhere. In this kind of unprecedented accepting atmosphere, the patient is given the opportunity to be free in the presence of someone else—perhaps for the first time. Ideally such a benevolent atmosphere is inconspicuously available so that neither the patient nor the therapist has to be consciously occupied with it. In Michael Balint's (1968) words, "The therapeutic environment should be there . . . but . . . the subject should be in no way obliged to take notice, to acknowledge, or to be concerned about it" (p. 180).

Henry Stack Sullivan (1954) thought along similar lines about the psychotherapeutic environment; he considered it a refuge for releasing the obstacles that stand in the way of the patient's being true to himself or herself. Thereafter everything will take care of itself. In Sullivan's words, "in well over twenty-five years—aside from my forgotten mistakes in the first few of them—I have never found myself called upon to 'cure' anybody"; the patient is self-generative, in effect self-curative, once the therapist has done "the necessary brush clearing" (p. 238). Recognizing that the patient is the suffering one who opens himself or herself to the therapist with all the potential vulnerabilities of such a trust, the therapist in turn neither ignores nor satisfies the inevitable needs of the patient. Especially in the early stages of treatment, the therapist avoids interpreting needs as defenses or as derivative expressions of infantile drives or desires; rather he or she permits the patient the untarnished freedom of revelation or confession.

Leston Havens (1986, 1989), who is concerned with the nature of the therapist's language in supplying this sense of safety, delineates three types of empathic statements that the therapist can draw upon: (1) imitative statements, which are a kind of simple cognitive mind-reading, whereby the therapist speaks out loud with the patient's inner voice (for example, "Is there any hope for me?"); (2) simple empathic statements, which are short emotional utterances or exclamations that affectively share the patient's experience (such as, "How awful!"), or (3) complex empathic statements, which reflect the patient's dilemma by in effect giving equal weight to both sides of a conflict; these are bridging statements that serve to reiterate the patient's own ambivalence ("It is a wonder that you have been able to accomplish your goal, considering how much you would rather not do it"). Of course, even the fine art of empathic language does not constitute the whole of providing a psychologically safe environment.

Setting the physical and symbolic stage is also, practically speaking, a matter of "finding a working distance," verbally as well as nonverbally (Havens 1986). The therapist and patient seek the state of being alone together while respecting each other's space. Noninvasive closeness has its developmental origins in the child's early experience of sharing the emotional environment with mother. In therapy, that childhood situation of being alone with the maternal object without being invaded—in fact or in fantasy—is recapitulated in the living space of the therapist's office and the psychological space that it signifies. The establishment of a viable working distance is thought to be especially pertinent in addressing today's common interpersonal problems of isolation and intimacy, domination and self-sufficiency.

When the therapist provides such security, treatment proceeds with no special need for the clinician to *do* something. He or she will certainly be doing (giving) something that is implicitly offered in such an environment and that is not very different from what a child needs, according to Kohut (1971), "empathically modulated food giving, not food." It is not the substance of the "food" itself, but how one is fed that is important.

CHAPTER 7

The therapist establishes the optimum therapeutic environment through a balance of neutrality and empathy

THE QUESTION MUST NATURALLY BE RAISED, What consti-
tutes the best therapist position to help the patient to feel safe enough
to reveal secret and otherwise long-buried or offensive thoughts and
desires? Two pervasive terms have been taken to encompass this crucial
interpersonal stance: *neutrality* and *empathy*. Yet much controversy has
broken out over the meaning and application of the original Freudian
neutral or value-free stance. Ideally, technical neutrality may be considered synonymous with psychological safety insofar as the therapist
attempts to remain impartial, not taking sides in any psychological
conflict; in Anna Freud's (1966) terms, the therapist thus retains a non-
preferential position of "equidistance" from the patient's "three harsh
masters" (id, ego, and superego) (Freud 1923). Clinically impartiality can
include the safety that inheres in not being intruded upon. That is, the
therapist does not press for a particular goal; does not demonstrate
strong feelings for or against the patient, whether paternal, seductive, or
the like; and in general, does not become overinvolved (or under-
involved) for personal countertransferential reasons.

Unfortunately, *neutrality* can also connote a dispassionate manner
that comes across not as impartial equidistance but as impersonal distance. Historically, the predominant "blank screen" orientation toward
the patient first led Sandor Ferenczi (1920) and then others (such as

Rogers and Kohut) to question whether this type of dispassionate or detached therapist was not simply neutral but emotionally withholding. He saw this stance not as unilaterally accepting but as insufficiently caring, unwittingly fulfilling the patient's neurotic expectations that significant others would be bad or rejecting. In this view, maintaining neutrality inevitably meant depriving the patient of natural emotional warmth and affection and was therefore reminiscent of poor or absent mothering. Paradoxically, such a presumably neutral environment could easily become more threatening than safe for the patient.

In his research on the impact of the therapist's neutrality Joseph Weiss (1990) has come up with some illuminating findings with implications for the therapeutic atmosphere and the therapist–patient relationship. He has presented empirical evidence that therapeutic neutrality was, as expected, significantly related to an increase in the patient's verbal expression of warded-off forbidden material. However, this came about not because repressed impulses had become intensified by frustration (as the "dynamic hypothesis" would suggest), but because the therapeutic setting made expression seem safe (their "control hypothesis"). In the author's words, "Because patients will feel safer, they are likely to become emboldened—free to express themselves more directly" (p. 107).

The research also found that while patients made unconscious demands on therapists as a way of assuring themselves that they could safely confront the thoughts, feelings, and memories that were blocked by repression, they were *un*disturbed by the lack of gratification received. Instead, when the patient tried to get the therapist to satisfy certain infantile wishes and the therapist did not do so, the patient became more relaxed rather than more anxious. The author suggests that this response may be explained by the thesis that most patients want to "master, rather than gratify" unconscious urges, keeping at bay the infantile ideas and desires that caused their conflicts. What most patients apparently needed was the assurance that the therapist would *not* be drawn into their infantile or irrational demands; they want to be reassured that the therapist would not be seduced by their sexual wishes or destroyed by their aggressive wishes.

In these ways the traditional therapist neutrality can foster a feeling of safety in some patients. The clinical evidence presented by Weiss indicated, for example, that only when one patient learned that she was not actually hurting the therapist did she feel safe enough to express omnipotent fantasies and wishes. Similarly, only when another patient felt completely assured that the same-sex therapist would not be aroused by him could he express his homosexual feelings and fears. Fred Pine (1990) has more recently suggested that what may be facilitating and mutative about this particular stance—which is most characteristic of adherents of drive theory—is the absence of condemnation that it affords the patient, as well as the reassurance that no matter how treacherous the thoughts and feelings expressed, the therapist survives.

Others who have addressed the issue of what constitutes a protective psychological environment or therapist attitude increasingly claim (like Ferenczi) that a position of neutrality needs to be shifted to one of more expressed interest, warmth, and understanding. Emphasis on the role of an empathic therapeutic atmosphere in recent years falls midway between the earlier principle of Freud's freely suspended attention, in which the analytic nonjudgmental stance was a way of dispassionately listening to the patient, and its previously unorthodox psychodynamic antithesis, "support," which was actively nurturing and directly responsive. But the new emphasis on an empathic environment calls for some satisfaction (however partial) of the patient's needs.

This type of orientation often accompanies theoretical views regarding the differential psychodynamics of the patient. For example, although the neutral therapist stance may be appropriate and safe for neurotic patients who are warding off unconscious libidinal and aggressive feelings, an empathic model may better serve patients with faulty self-development and unfulfilled narcissistic needs. Kohut's (1977) attention to the importance of empathy in the construction of the self and the need to find an empathic object in the figure of the therapist came out of the expanded populations of today's therapeutic practice, which includes patients with borderline and narcissistic personality disorders.

Kohut believes that the infant's psychological survival requires a specific psychological environment—the presence of responsive empathic selfobjects plus a specific structure formation within that environment, called "transmuting internalization," through which the nuclear self becomes crystallized. Ultimately, the autonomous self replaces those who served as selfobjects and develops within the context of secure caretaking that forms the nucleus of self-confidence and inner security. With the individual in psychotherapy, empathic understanding on the part of the therapist both helps the patient to gain access to archaic narcissistic needs and functions as partial gratification of those needs. The patient, in expressing, becoming aware of, and accepting preoedipal needs, can convert them into normal self-esteem and the formation of ideals. No longer simply a tool to increase the therapist's knowledge, empathy is viewed as having mutative value for the patient.

As the clinician communicates an understanding of the patient's problems and psychic pain, this empathic resonance not only enters the inner world of the patient to meet unmet needs, but may facilitate insight. Clinical observation (Havens 1986) increasingly suggests that even the most accurate and well-timed interpretation will not be effective in the absence of an accepting, empathic atmosphere. It is also proposed that the reality of a benevolent object in the here-and-now also provides insight by differentiating the fantasied (frustrating) figure of the past from the real (gratifying) one of the present. In sum, the therapist's neutral, empathic, or supportive stance itself may be less important than the extent to which the type of stance represents conditions of safety for the particular patient (Weiss 1990), that is, "without risking internal dangers such as guilt or shame or external dangers such as loss of love" (p. 109).

CHAPTER 8

The therapist and the patient need to share a view—or myth—of illness and its cure

WHAT IS THE LEAST that therapist and patient must have in common in order to initiate psychotherapy together? As a generic aspect of treatment, every therapeutic enterprise, from the magico-religious healing practices of the shaman in primitive treatment to the scientific methods of Western psychiatry, has invariably involved a conceptual doctrine that provides the justification for the procedures used. It is the sociological and psychological matrix upon which the therapist understands and explains the nature of the presenting problem and conveys it to the patient. What appears to vary historically, cross-culturally, and even among schools and theorists, is the particular thera-peutic model that is presupposed. The choice of model is nevertheless linked to a dominant world view of the time, as well as to the assump-tive beliefs or standards of both patient and therapist. Frank (1961) defines a person's "assumptive world" as a "complex, interacting set of values, expectations, and images of oneself and others, which guide and in turn are guided by a person's perceptions and behavior and which are closely related to his emotional states and his feelings of well-being" (p. 27).

Each dominant theoretical model provides both patient and practi-tioner with a reasonably acceptable explanation of the cause of the patient's distress and a set of techniques for altering it, a proposed method of relief. To be effective, both parties' assumptions must be compatible with the world view shared by the two. In fact, treatment procedures created, developed, or chosen in one society or in the context of a particular belief system may not be transposable to another, as has become evident in failed attempts at cross-cultural psychotherapy (Wittkower and Warnes 1974; Neki 1973).

The implication for patient compliance is that "the more closely the conceptual framework of the therapy fits that of the patient, the more readily he can accept it." (Frank 1974, 370). The impact of the conceptual system upon cure is demonstrated in the clinical observation that the closer the value system of the therapist concords with that of the patient, the more potentially effective the treatment will be (Hogan 1979). To the extent that such schemes are also synchronous with sociocultural norms, one of the ways they may be therapeutic is by reducing the patient's feelings of estrangement or alienation, not only from the therapist but from the outside world. This serves to explain why the popularity of different therapies at different times often relates to the extent to which they fit the dominant belief systems of society at large.

Throughout the twentieth century, fundamental orientations have influenced shared therapeutic concepts about illness and its treatment. Freud's psychoanalysis and other dynamic psychotherapies came out of, and in answer to, an "age of sexual repression," which viewed the psychopathology of its day in terms of underlying, unconscious sexual conflicts and unresolved oedipal strivings which needed to be wrested from childhood memory. Subsequently, with the mid-twentieth century's rapid rise of technology and the impending replacement of humans by the machine, arose an "age of anxiety," which a group of newly developed behavioral therapies attempted to address by systematically desensitizing the patient to environmentally derived anxieties and directly reconditioning him or her to relaxation responses. Finally, in the last part of the 1900s, with the wholesale subordination of humans to overwhelming outside forces and with the depersonalization and dehumanization that resulted, the individual was unwittingly ushered into an "age of alienation" in which one felt diminished and alone, if not entirely out of touch with one's feelings. A host of experiential therapies sprang up to fill this particular void. As Calestro (1972) put it, "It may be that whether one evokes devils, hierarchies, or id, the process and net result are the same—so long as the particular technique is relevant to the assumptive world shared by patient and therapist and derives from an influential source to whom the patient is susceptible" (p. 100).

It is of great significance, however, that such belief systems need not have proven truth value. Rather, they may refer to a "shared myth" that by its very nature does not require a factual basis or historical validity. Such a view suggests that as long as both parties accept the basic terms of the prescription for change—believe in it, so to speak—therapeutic influence is possible. Ehrenwald (1966) has used the term "doctrinal compliance" to describe the notion of accepting a therapist's myth *as if it were fact* and behaving in a way to verify it. The remarkable observation that patients in Freudian analysis produce oedipal dreams of sexuality and rivalry, and those in Jungian analysis dreams of primordial archetypes, legendary spirits, and demons, has been offered as a succinct expression of this phenomenon (Calestro 1972). In short, mutual belief in a doctrine of healing is central to the activation of the therapeutic process. But, as with insight, it is the *function* of the shared myth, its compelling or persuasive nature rather than its specific content, that is of integral importance.

Frank and others have chosen the perhaps provocative term *myth* to highlight the point that although Western therapies, unlike primitive healing practices, do not typically invoke supernatural or magical forces, they have in common with the myths of ancient times a set of beliefs or assumptions that are neither shaken by therapeutic failures nor subject to scientific disproof. That is, myths often carry with them a sense of infallibility insofar as they rest on the power of suggestibility, not objective validity (Ehrenwald 1966). In addition, the "therapist myth" has several related therapeutic functions: it supports the therapist's self-confidence insofar as it complies with the therapist's group identification or academic affiliation; it also indirectly increases the patient's confidence in the therapist. More important, the myth supplies a "conceptual scheme" (Frank 1974) for making sense of the patient's symptoms, which itself is reassuring.

In fact, it has long been recognized that giving something a name is the first step in gaining control over it. Referred to as the "principle of Rumpelstiltskin"—based on the fairy tale about a young queen who had to guess that particular name in order to save her infant child—it is suggested that the sheer act of naming the problem has a therapeutic effect (Torrey 1974). It has been further hypothesized in this regard that the problem, once identified, thus becomes the "enemy" (Reider 1954), something tangible that both patient and therapist can begin to attack together. The therapeutic myth, however culturally imposed or inherited, thus serves both as a label and explanation for the patient and as a symbolic carrier of the therapist's creed.

The following are three different scenarios between therapist and patient at the start of treatment with regard to their shared (or unshared) myths.

1. *Shared myth and the knowledgeable patient.* By the time a mental health professional enters a psychoanalytic institute, it is reasonable to assume that he or she has some idea of what to expect in the analysis. Generally, the person is already well versed, in theory at least, about notions of etiology and method of cure, and, more specifically, about the dynamic nature and the psychosocial/intrapsychic source of problems. Beyond this, the initiated patient more or less understands and accepts the thesis that problems are somehow related (albeit unconsciously) to childhood experiences, and that certain unresolved conflicts will be verbalized and analyzed within the context of a special "transferential" relation with the analyst. He or she is relatively prepared for the fact that this is a "talking cure" with the clinician in the primary role of listener. Although the therapist may go over the basic tenets or procedures at the beginning of treatment, there is no need for basic indoctrination. The practitioner and patient share a similar point of view about the nature of illness and its cure.

2. *Shared myth and the novice patient.* When a patient comes to the therapist with little previous knowledge or experience and few preconceived ideas about the treatment, the therapist's task is more complicated. There will be a need for some preparatory education, an induction phase which demands patience and tolerance of the therapist. For example, an uninitiated patient may wait to be asked questions (perhaps based on previous medical experience) and may expect structure and guidance; after reciting his or her symptoms, the patient may quickly run out of material. One such patient, after a cursory, fifteen-minute recitation on his presenting problem and the circumstances surrounding it, promptly asked, "Now that you know all about me, what shall I do?" Even at the beginning of treatment, such specific questions do not have to be replied to concretely; it is more important to understand the patient's underlying request: "Help me to proceed." The therapist may have to ask many questions to get the patient to elaborate in detail on the material presented. The therapist may also have to teach the patient how to articulate carefully the nature of their shared myth.

3. *Unshared myth.* When a patient (inexperienced or experienced) comes to a consultation room with preconceived ideas about what caused his or her problems and what cure he or she expects, and when these are not shared by the therapist, there is an immediate problem. Therapy may end very quickly. If the patient's position is within the range of clinical

reason, a proper termination or referral is in order. For example, if the patient identifies his relationship with his wife as the crux of his depression and there is sufficient evidence for this, individual treatment may be presented as an alternative to or as a simultaneous approach with marital therapy. However, lack of consensus in regard to the nature of the complaint (for example, if the patient can view the problem only as residing outside himself) may only bring the sessions to an impasse, unless the patient is persuaded to accept, at least partially, the therapist's point of view. This shift requires a revamping of the patient's orientation to be consistent with that of the therapist. But such doctrinal compliance—the net result of the therapist's myth and the consequent existential shift by the patient in its direction—is perforce tenuous and needs to be replaced soon thereafter by genuine concordance between practitioner and patient.

The shared myth, however, does not indefinitely suffice in any of the three instances; it must be accompanied or supplanted by real shared intentions or specific goals that have to be mutually wrought or contracted between the parties involved. In fact, the two requirements— shared myth and shared intention—have different derivations as well as different functions. The need to incorporate both elements into treatment leads to the next maxim.

CHAPTER 9

A shared myth between therapist and patient may be culturally inherited, but their shared intention must be mutually cultivated

SHARED INTENTIONS OR GOALS are less contingent than shared myths upon the overall cultural context and can be much more specific and personal. One classic issue in psychotherapy is to agree on whether the patient should be helped to make alterations in his or her social or family situation, or rather, should be helped to adjust to the status quo (Szasz 1978). In a world of changing sexual mores, for example, does the therapist still consider heterosexuality an ultimate goal or should the patient be encouraged to continue and adjust to his or her homosexual life (Garfield 1974)? May the unhappy mother leave her husband and children, or should the family unit be preserved at any cost?

Whereas most therapeutic myths are implicit because they are culturally embedded and do not have to be negotiated, the shared intention—which may or may not be implicit—must be carefully cultivated and, at times, actively negotiated. Doubtless the issue of shared intentions between therapist and patient is highly complex and subtle, for it often represents covert or unconscious expectations that must be made explicit before mutual goals can be pursued.

For example, the patient may come in with a certain request, a conscious or unconscious intention about what is to be accomplished in treatment. At times such an intention will be shared by the therapist. For example, a mental health professional may apply for analysis to foster personal maturity and modification of personality. Or, following the loss of a spouse, a person may seek to ease the pain, to speed up recovery from depression. These are naturally shared intentions.

At other times, the patient may come to treatment with certain expectations that the therapist cannot share. The troubled patient may have already decided that his treatment goal is to separate from a spouse, or to find one. Other intentions can be subtle and hard to articulate. A patient who comes to treatment with the basic complaint that no one appreciates her and who is searching for an appreciative therapist, may be disappointed with a therapist who, rather than attempting to fulfill the patient's expectations by complying with them (that is, by gratifying them), wants to explore the patient's contribution to her situation. The discordance in these intentions is not to be resolved through interpersonal negotiation. Rather, the therapist's role is to listen, comprehend, and even at times temporarily comply with the patient's request, thereby establishing a reasonably stable relationship before beginning to introduce an alternative intention. The workable shared intention in this case might be for the above patient to become "appreciable."

For the patient who says "I don't feel appreciated," the shared intention may be fostered by the therapist who first "appreciates" the patient's dilemma by sharing her pain. Especially if the therapist comes to appreciate the patient even in some small ways, he then can safely ask the question, "Do you also, at times, wonder what it is about you that generates such a reaction from so many different people?" Such statements may be in question form, if they do not demand an immediate answer. Slow and careful repetition of the same theme, if accepted each time, will prepare the base for a shared intention or goal that facilitates the establishment of a working purpose or plan.

Case Illustration

A thirty-six-year-old attractive, single woman, who grew up with a narcissistic and dependent father and a masochistic mother, was now an assistant professor in a small college. She identified her major problem as not having a man whom she could love and marry. She was beginning to worry that it would soon be too late to have children. She was unhappy and bitter. She complained that men were selfish and unreliable and that the few good ones were married, while the rest were either homosexual or too disturbed to bother with. About eight years before, she underwent psychotherapy for six months on a once-a-week basis after she broke up with a man and was depressed. She thought it was not all that useful. In her fourth session she raised a concern that would lead her and the therapist toward a shared intention.

PATIENT: I am not sure what I need, a psychotherapist or a coach or a matchmaker. Well, you are a man, so you must have men friends and you must know where men go to meet women.

THERAPIST: You would like me to play the role of therapist, coach, and matchmaker, all rolled up into one.

At this point the therapist simply registers the general nature of the patient's attitude toward the therapist (her transferential disposition) for future reference, knowing that patients usually come to treatment with varying degrees of unspoken expectations that will not be met. He observes that this patient is explicitly setting the stage for early frustration. The therapist also intentionally dismisses the partial put-down in her statement because an ambivalent attitude toward treatment is a common characteristic; moreover, the signs of negative transference preempt any conscious mutual negotiations because they invariably will be rejected.

PATIENT: That would be nice. Frieda [the previous therapist] suggested that I put an ad in a magazine, which I did. I met a bunch of creeps; I felt humiliated. This is what things have come to. I'm an attractive professional woman. Lots of men used to fall in love with me. Now I have to advertise. Frieda met her husband at a singles weekend in the Catskills, so I tried that, too. There were at least twice as many women as men. I met this forty-six-year-old dentist. It turns out that he had four kids, had been separated from his wife for seven years, and was still not divorced. I have no patience for this. I think my problem is a real problem, not a psychological one, but Arlene [a friend] insisted that I come to see you. You apparently helped her a lot. But, I don't know what you can do for me.

THERAPIST: The concrete suggestions of Frieda did not do much good anyway.

Here the therapist wants to close the door firmly on any matchmaker role by emphasizing its past failure. He is alerted to the tendency for the patient to draw the therapist into a "role responsiveness" (Sandler 1976), which is defined as "a compromise-formation between the therapist's own tendencies and his reflexive acceptance of the role which the patient is forcing on him" (p. 46). It is the converse of doctrinal compliance. By being aware of this phenomenon, the therapist can open the way to a more useful shared intention.

There is an even more compelling reason for not making suggestions or giving advice to patients. As in Ferenczi's ([1919] 1926) active technique, such a posture puts the therapist into the role of parent/teacher, which may present problems if they are construed as strong superego figures. As Herbert Strean (1985) points out, "Then clients can legitimately contend that they must obey orders in order that they may be loved, which is often one of the cardinal factors in the etiology of their neuroses. Consequently, one of the hazards of the active technique is that it can induce unnecessary compliance in many clients. It can also provide in other clients a wish to spite and take revenge against the therapist who reminds them of their punitive parents. These are clients who wish to defeat the therapist anyway, and suggestions and advice from the therapist can exacerbate this negative therapeutic reaction" (p. 64). However, Ferenczi may not have sufficiently focused on the fact that the use of active techniques can often evolve from countertransference problems of the therapist, who may be lured into meeting the patient's requests.

PATIENT: Yes, everyone has some idea, especially the married women. God knows how they got their husbands. But I'm telling you, if these girls were single today, they could never find a man.

THERAPIST: Including Frieda? [The therapist wants to elicit the patient's feelings and reactions to the previous therapist, in order to learn more about her transferential disposition and receptivity to a shared intention.]

PATIENT: Especially Frieda. She'd be utterly lost.

THERAPIST: Is that the reason you didn't go back to her?

The therapist not only wants to find out why she did not go back to her previous therapist, but to learn about that relationship—if for no other reason than not to repeat it. Examination of the patient's relationship with the prior therapist would teach the therapist a great deal about the patient's transferential disposition. It is quite likely that the same scenario will be repeated unless the therapist has been forewarned; otherwise, despite any effort to establish a shared intention, he may fall into the same script written by the patient and accept an assigned role that perpetuates her neurosis.

PATIENT: Well, she is a sort of friendly therapist, an older sister type. But she wasn't smart enough for me and I used to criticize her. Many times she got really offended. She thought I was too demanding. Now, what am I supposed to do, take care of my therapist? It is bad enough that all the men I meet are babies; they all want to be taken care of. Well, what do they bring to a relationship?

THERAPIST: You want a therapist who at least will not be a burden to you. [The therapist tries to establish a shared intention, however small.]

PATIENT: Well, I hope so. Frieda used to say, "Look, men are babies. If you don't meet their needs they brood, they mutter, they sulk, they blame. That is their way of crying. That's it. You just have to accept that fact. They are all looking for a mother." Well, I'm not interested in mothering these grown-up selfish people. She said that if you want to get married you have to follow certain gender strategies. Not only marriage, but even romance, includes some degree of calculation. If this is what it takes to get married, I am not interested.

THERAPIST: Everyone seems to want to be mothered by you. . . . So, where do you get your needs met? [The therapist recognizes the patient's burden within his first sentence, and he sympathizes with the patient with his second sentence, recognizing that she has no one. The therapist is seeking to take the shared intention a step further by acknowledging the patient's plight.]

PATIENT: Nowhere. If I got it, maybe I would be willing to give it, too. But it seems like it's all a one-way street. I'm sick and tired of being at the giving end all the time.

THERAPIST: Everyone wants to be taken care of by you, but you wonder who will take care of you.

Although this comment may sound redundant, it is intended to solidify their alliance insofar as it is already agreed that this is a safe subject. The idea is also to repeat the same dynamically significant subject again and again, each time with different thrust, until the patient has exhausted the current material and begins to have past associations connected with it. Instead of saying, "Tell me about your childhood," which is too intellectual, the therapist focuses on the affectively loaded subject itself in order to elicit a more natural flow of material from the past.

PATIENT: No one takes care of me. No one ever did. My mother was always busy with my father. I more or less grew up without a mother. As if that is not enough, I had to take care of my younger sisters.

52

THERAPIST: [The therapist begins to feel the weight on his shoulders.] Oh, how burdensome! [This is an explicit expression of empathy. The therapist uses it as an opportunity to focus on affect and explore the patient's accessibility to empathic bonding as a emotional base to generate their shared intention.]

PATIENT: Maybe my reaction is coming out too strong. Maybe I am responding to the wrong people, but that is how I feel. [If the therapist is empathic and the patient is responsive, there will be a gift of significant material.]

THERAPIST: Coming out too strong, to the wrong people? [The therapist narrows the affect and the target.]

PATIENT: The men—I'm rejecting their neediness, but maybe it's normal neediness. I don't know.

THERAPIST: You mean your rejecting of their normal neediness comes out too strong?

Using a guideline of "affect first, content afterward," the therapist emphasizes the intensity of her emotion first, rather than its target. Also, the therapist in his tentative (questioning) presentation of this understanding attributes it to the patient. With this style of interpretation, the clinician can begin to close the door on her request that he be her coach. (She was disappointed with the first therapist in spite of what seems to have been her good coaching.)

PATIENT: Yeah, I think so. The last guy that I was going out with was a nice man, but he always wanted to eat in and then criticized my cooking. Either the vegetables were overcooked or the meal wasn't hot enough. He didn't notice that the meal had been on the table for ten minutes while he was grooming himself. Somehow I was always wrong and he was right. Didn't I see that he was shaving and should have kept the meal in the oven until he was ready? I should have known when we first met. He looked at me that night and said, "You know, everything is fine with us, except that you are too tall."

THERAPIST: Instead of, "I am too short!" [Even though the therapist did not know how the patient was going to finish this train of thought, he did not want to miss the opportunity to be in alliance with the patient, picking up on the topic of how her last boyfriend had tried to make her wrong, no matter how blatantly the facts were on her side.]

PATIENT: I am not even that tall—just five-eight. I began to wear flat shoes and walk hunched over. I didn't mind doing that, but on the top

53

of all this was his dependency, which I could not tolerate. Everyone thought that was the least of the problems. My friends thought I was wrong in not tolerating his dependency. It is true I am not as intolerant of my girlfriends, even though they deserve more of my intolerance.

THERAPIST: You said earlier that not only did you come out too strong, but also to the wrong people, meaning to *men?* [Now the subject is narrowed to intolerance of men's neediness. The therapist no longer sees the need to ally with her against men, and begins to present a potentially ego-alien part of her.]

PATIENT: Why am I so harsh with men? Do you think it's because I have such a dependent father?

THERAPIST: Who also took most of your mother's attention? [The therapist, instead of concretely responding to the patient's question, accepts it and, sharing her feelings, permits her to penetrate further into her past.]

During the next ten minutes the patient talks about her father's selfishness, neediness, never spending any time with her, his abusive relationship with her mother.

PATIENT: I don't want that kind of man, that kind of marriage. Is there any other kind? I cannot believe it, maybe I shouldn't get married—just adopt a child?

THERAPIST: You said earlier that maybe you are coming on too strong to the wrong people. There is some negative feeling toward the men you meet; do you think that they stand in for your father?

PATIENT: Well, obviously. But I can't seem to stop behaving that way to other men.

THERAPIST: And they don't much appreciate it.

The therapist again finishes the patient's sentence in order not to lose the connection—her behavior is not being appreciated. The emphasis at this time is not on her failure to be appreciated but on her *behavior,* insofar as it may be under the patient's control even though she says she cannot help what she does. The therapist emphasizes the behavioral aspect, because feeling unappreciated may be equated with *being* no good. In addition, it is a more hopeful posture, as the therapist tries to maintain an optimistic outlook, recognizing that pessimism would inevitably undermine any shared intention.

PATIENT: No, they don't. Of course, they have no idea where I am coming from.

THERAPIST: I guess for that they have to get to know you very well. Even we have only just begun to understand. [The therapist is again hopeful that if people get to know her better, they will appreciate her. He also introduces the word *we* to reinforce their shared concern and shared intention of getting to know her.]

PATIENT: *We* have a long way to go. . . .

CHAPTER 10

By heightening or lowering arousal, the therapist enters the patient's world

Entering the patient's psychic world may require reaching beyond the relative decorum of the individual's intellect to the turbulence of his or her emotions; conversely it may call for quieting excessive anxiety or agitation. To accomplish either of these, the therapist often has to recognize that each person usually attempts to maintain a certain level of affective equilibrium in everyday life. Routine interactions are conducted at a particular level of emotional arousal, with only moderate fluctuations. This is a comfort zone that each individual strives to achieve, whereby all external as well as internal stimuli are relatively balanced and contained. Ordinary interactions do not typically alter this desirable homeostatic level of excitation. However, unexpected, unusual, or especially meaningful external events—positive or negative (such as getting an award or having an accident) or internal events (daydreams or nightmares) may naturally change this established affective level. Anxiety in particular is thought to be the emotional expression of a state of aversive arousal due to uncertainty (Hoehn-Saric 1978).

An alteration in emotional state, however uncomfortable or unsettling, brings about the disequilibrium that is necessary before information can be received. Applying Kurt Lewin's (1958) theories of social change to that of cognitive modification, it has been suggested that for an attitude to be altered, it first has to be "unfrozen," then shifted, and, finally, refrozen into a new position. A marked change in arousal is thus the foundation for the attainment of insight and a new knowledge of self. In fact, all learning occurs best if received in an emotionally engaged state of mind. Information about one's self especially remains a sterile intellectualization if it is not embedded in affective receptivity, a state that requires a change in the individual's arousal level—it must be either raised or lowered.

Viewed as a way of penetrating the patient's intrapsychic universe, emotional arousal has a long history in therapeutic practices. As early as 25 B.C., Aulus Cornelius Celsus (1935–38) suggested, "Beneficial to [mental] illness . . . in general, is anything which thoroughly agitates the spirit." Some form of strong stimulation was probably the primary tool in the psychotherapeutic cures of primitive man. Often séances were conducted in the presence of a select group of individuals (the psychotherapists of their day), and intense affect was induced through smoking, drinking, drugs, and rhythmic music. Such emotionally charged situations facilitated regression and eased the confession of sins. This type of affective purging process was the prototype for the earliest known structured psychotherapeutic attempt to deal with human problems.

The oldest Freudian version of this is, of course, the now classic cathartic method, whereby abreaction occurred with the emergence of repressed memories uncovered through the technique of free association. Behavioral therapists also have their arousal counterparts in reproducing anxiety-evoking stimuli either in imagination or in vivo. Flooding and implosion procedures, for example, re-create high intensity exposure to feared objects or situations; patients are expected to experience their anxiety as fully as possible and, exhausted with fear and relief, no longer respond as they used to. Similarly, aversion therapy, by presenting an unpleasant and sometimes painful stimulus, at least temporarily disrupts emotional equilibrium as a precursor of change through reconditioning.

Yet other extensive therapeutic use of emotional arousal and release occurs in the new "experiential" approaches. Such approaches as Reichian therapy, Lowenian bioenergetics, and Rolfian structural integration aim to express the affect trapped in the body posture, not by analyzing defensive character armor, as Reich originally did, but by physically manipulating the muscles that underlie it. Psychodrama plays out the expression of feelings through dramatic improvisations, while uninterrupted marathon sessions seek emotional access through the by-products of physical exhaustion. Comparably, the primal scream and Morita methods use prolonged isolation and sensory deprivation to lower resistance and break down cognitive defenses—the former expressed in a screaming, sobbing, seizurelike episode to recapture the pain of one's primal past, the latter by activating anxiety and distress as a preparatory step toward the creation of a state of spiritual readiness for rediscovering the beauty of life. A basic rationale for such diverse methods of affective arousal is that they aim to facilitate therapeutic change by "producing excessive cortical excitation, emotional exhaustion, and states of reduced resistance or hypersuggestibility" (Kiev 1966, 174).

Controlled research studies now confirm emotional arousal as one of the major effective ingredients of successful psychotherapy. So universal is its application across a broad spectrum of treatments that it is now considered to be a basic generic feature. Rudolf Hoehn-Saric's (1978) work indicates that following strong abreaction there occurs a period of exhaustion which produces heightened acceptance; that is, "The patient appears bewildered, dependent and eager to find a comforting solution from the therapist" (p. 103). Three different experiments demonstrated that heightened arousal made patients more receptive to suggestion and therefore more willing to change attitudes than they were under low arousal conditions. Interestingly, arousal combined with cognitive confusion yielded even better results than arousal in patients with undisturbed cognitive functions. Evidence also suggests that while highly dissonant messages tend to be rejected, some cognitive disruption and need for clarification can be created through conflicting messages. The author concluded that heightened arousal under conditions of at least some degree of cognitive disorganization helps to unfreeze attitudes as a prelude to change.

What makes psychotherapy unique is its intentional application of the alteration in arousal level to prepare for change. Dynamic therapists often use understimulation (rather than overstimulation) by limiting the sensory input during the therapy session. The receptive role of the therapist, the relative simplicity and isolation of the office environment, and the use of the couch can also have an altering effect on the arousal system, enhancing the patient's ability to reprocess experiences; quiet physiological states, like deep relaxation or meditation, have demonstrable effects on brain wave activity. Perhaps paradoxically, by reducing the affective response to external stimulation, the techniques can help a person experience emotionally laden inner events.

Attitude change can thus be facilitated by different kinds and levels of arousal, each causing a disturbance of ordinary consciousness sufficient to warrant a shift in perspective. Hoehn-Saric (1978) has therefore concluded that external means of unfreezing attitudes and enhancing uncertainty can be induced by overstimulation, understimulation, or the introduction of unsettling messages, by "any method which enhances uncertainty about the existing attitude [and] causes sufficient discomfort in the patient to motivate him to change." In short, all create a "temporary disorganization . . . and subsequent restructuring within a functional frame" (p. 104). In effect, most often an overload phenomenon occurs, in which the organism is unable to rationally process all incoming information. Although in the initial phase of treatment inducing strong arousal has the advantage of increasing the patient's receptivity to the therapist's influence, a change in arousal may be used whenever the patient is resisting the influence of the therapist. Havens (1986), in his book on making contact with the patient, refers to the use of empathy as "establishing an affective baseline" (p. 49). The therapist not only needs to form an empathic alliance from the beginning, but must view each interpretation as a new danger that arouses anxiety in the patient and potentially opens or closes further communication pathways.

More specifically, in setting and sustaining the stage for dynamic psychotherapy the therapist attempts to change the patient's frozen emotional state in order to gain access to his or her ordinarily inaccessible world, while trying to maintain a receptive attitude and establishing trust. Verbal confrontation and interpretation are the specific arousal strategies that the therapist may primarily use. Silence may also be introduced as a form of underarousal that induces regression, while dissonant messages over which the patient is conflicted—ones the patient is unable to accept but cannot completely ignore—create cognitive confusion and the need for clarification. This is especially the case for patients who have already formed a relationship of benign dependency upon the therapist and thus have an emotional commitment to accept the therapist's interpretation. In such instances the affective aspects of the patient's ongoing dilemma have been posed as a psychological conflict regarding acceptance versus resistance to each interpretive effort. If the patient rejects dissonant interpretations by the clinician, he or she lands in the anxiety-producing position of either having to discredit the therapist, and thus becoming freer emotionally, or risking eventual rejection for being uncooperative and potentially untreatable.

The patient comes to treatment with relatively rigid patterns of feeling, thinking, and behaving. These patterns are maintained whether they are adaptive or not, whether they are causing pain or not; indeed, the patient may be inclined to repeat unconsciously the patterns that are most conflictual and unresolved. In the initial therapeutic encounter, as expected, the patient brings these same modes of relating to the sessions. The clinician who allows such accustomed attitudes to continue will have limited access to the patient. Instead the therapist is responsible for the "maintenance of a state of tension" (Strupp and Binder 1984). For the patient a state of chronic discomfort is created that must be strategically converted into a kind of temporary acute disorganization at the beginning of and intermitently throughout treatment. That the patient has made an appointment, shown up at the therapist's office, and naturally is somewhat anxious (not knowing exactly what will occur), all contribute to his or her potential for becoming more or less unfrozen.

Especially during the initial phase, the therapist may in fact have to decrease the patient's fear and anxiety in order to heighten his or her positive affect toward the therapist, providing permission to express deep feelings. During the initial session, the patient tends to state the circumstances of his or her problem as they are remembered. The patient may also tentatively open up to express his or her fears and pains. Much of this material is prepared in anticipation of the session—preparation keeps anxiety at bay. But as the patient gets too comfortable, he or she may slowly freeze up and return to old patterns of relating. The therapist may inadvertently speed the freezing process by getting anxious about either the material presented or the pace of its presentation.

Case Illustration

A forty-seven-year-old, physically healthy man was referred after having had a complete medical workup, which failed to show any physiological reason for his impotence, which had lasted over a year. The patient had already gone to a sex therapist, who conducted marital therapy and used the Masters and Johnson technique for a period of three months, without success. The sex/marital therapist reported that the man and his wife were a loving couple, interested in each other and in their teenage daughter. There were no hostilities to be found; the husband denied any extramarital affairs or even masturbation. He was very cooperative and she very understanding—but to no avail. In fact, the man could swear that the only problem this couple had was his impotence, and that he needed individual treatment.

The current therapist initially tried to explore what had happened, if anything, a year earlier. He found out that one and one half years earlier the patient began to work for a new boss, who was somewhat sarcastic and put him down in front of others. He wondered about the resultant stress and its impact on the patient's sex life, but this line of thinking was not very productive and apparently had been explored unsuccessfully by the previous therapist. In the third session the new therapist asked him whether there was any information that the patient had not shared with the sex therapist, his internist, or his wife.

PATIENT: Well, there's one thing I did not talk about to my wife or to the sex therapist. I don't know how relevant it is, but I did speak to my internist about it; he is also a good friend of mine. He reassured me that it was a normal thing. (*Hesitates and looks searchingly at the therapist*)

THERAPIST: [Since the therapist does not want the patient to get too anxious and possibly hold back important information, he intervenes directly. He deliberately does not prolong the silence.] You wonder whether you should talk about it here or not?

PATIENT: (*Hesitates*) Yes . . . it is sort of embarrassing, but I understand it is quite normal, kind of an Oedipus complex. My daughter is growing up, going out with boys, boys a little older. I know she is having sex; I can tell. Maybe I am a little preoccupied with her. Joe [the internist] says it's very natural; he went through the same phase with his two daughters.

THERAPIST: So Joe has tried to reassure you; but in spite of his reassurances you don't seem to be fully comforted. [The therapist uses the first name of the internist to generate a sense of familiarity, to ease the eliciting of material.]

PATIENT: No, I guess I'm not very reassured.

THERAPIST: [The therapist still does not want to discomfort the patient unduly, but he suspects that there is more information to be revealed.] You said you are a little too preoccupied with her. Did you tell all aspects of your preoccupations to Joe? [The therapist is not sure whether to ask directly if there is more to it, or to assume that the patient did not tell everything to his internist. So the therapist allows for both possibilities.]

PATIENT: Well, it's hard to talk about the details of family life, even to one's friends. I don't even believe in doing that. I believe in the privacy and dignity of an individual. People go around gossiping about their intimate matters, exposing their innermost selves. I am a very conservative person. Those sex therapy sessions, I must say, were the most humiliating things I have ever gone through in my life. But I had to do it. I'll do anything to resolve this because I want our marriage to be a good one. It is not normal not to have sexual desires at this age. I am sure that there must be some disease in there, like a prediabetic condition or some neurological disease not yet detectable.

THERAPIST: [The therapist decides to hold in abeyance the patient's undetectable disease theory until he knows more. He chooses instead to return to the earlier statements about privacy and fear of exposure.] You said you did not believe in talking about your innermost private matters to others. Do you feel the same way here? [The therapist is still trying to gauge the patient's discomfort, *not* heightening the arousal level for fear of closing off communication.]

PATIENT: A little bit, because one does not know how people will take it. But I suppose you're used to this kind of thing. *(Long pause)* [This time the therapist waits in silence, believing that the heightened arousal may be facilitative.] Well, it is just a dream. I dream about her. I have no sexual desire for her during the day; she is just my little girl. We are a very traditional family. I have no sexual interest in anyone else, let alone my own daughter. Joe said he had sexual dreams about his daughters. Does *every* father have such dreams? *(Becomes increasingly anxious)*

THERAPIST: Well, I guess, as Joe says, there is something called the Oedipus complex; it's quite universal. Some may not even remember their dreams. [The therapist is feeling a little off guard: Should he deal with the patient's anxiety first? Should he focus on the issue of incest? Is there a real danger he must deal with? The therapist chooses intentionally not to answer the patient's direct question and allows additional silence to heighten arousal. Then, to reduce his *own* anxiety, he responds with partial (somewhat unconvincing) reassurance.]

PATIENT: *(Apparently not gratified, because he has not received a direct reply, and not reassured by a statement made more for the therapist's benefit than for the patient's)* Boy, what a perverted world! I'm not going to survey my friends about their dreams. . . . I still want to know from *you* how abnormal this may be. . . . You must have a daughter. [This comes as an attack on the therapist by implying that the therapist is as "perverse" as the patient. As Robert Langs (1973) has pointed out, offering the patient unconvincing reassurance can cause him to feel demeaned; in return he attempts to defeat the therapy and the therapist.]

THERAPIST: [Believing that by addressing the patient's insult per se, he will further increase resistance, the therapist returns to the subject of the patient's discomfort.] Even if Joe or I have a normalizing name for it, like Oedipus complex, that does not really comfort you.

PATIENT: Because I know it is perverse; it is disgusting—my own child, my own baby. Nothing can be normalizing this; nothing is normal about it. I've seen child abuse, sexual abuse on TV. I cannot believe how a father could abuse his own child.

THERAPIST: [Here the therapist empathizes with the patient, no longer needing to reassure himself.] I see how disgusting it is to you, to even dream about your daughter. This must generate a lot of guilt.

PATIENT: Terribly. I cannot look at her face during the day, as if she knows it. I am avoiding her. We used to roughhouse occasionally, but I am afraid to touch her. Even my wife thinks I am behaving strangely these days. It is all consuming. We have been trying to make love— the first time in our long marriage I cannot have an erection.

THERAPIST: *(After a long silence)* I guess you are taking every precaution.

PATIENT: I don't understand, what do you mean? [The patient is startled, a sign of cognitive disorganization or uncertainty.]

THERAPIST: *(After another long period of silence)* [The therapist rewords his previous statement.] I mean, your not having an erection because you may be guarding against it.

PATIENT: I still don't understand. [The patient is getting even more confused, albeit temporarily; the confusion is a precursor to a "cognitive shift."] You mean that I am losing my potency as a way of precaution, so that I will not have sex with my daughter, either?

PART IV

ON CLINICAL LISTENING AND ITS NUANCES

Psychotherapy is a primarily verbal interaction, which has as the basis of treatment the patient's words and their meaning. It is therefore incumbent upon the clinician, first and foremost, to be a good listener. In this part, the origins of therapeutic listening are traced from the Freudian principle of "evenly hovering attention" (also called evenly distributed, evenly suspended, or free-floating attention), and some of the major connotations of the concept are examined, as understood—and, at times, misunderstood—by Freudians or their detractors.

The first issue that arises concerns two major ingredients of the dynamic therapist's listening role: neutrality and empathy. Can these phenomena be construed as antithetical? And how does the clinician combine the two in actual practice, insofar as *neutrality* implies distance and *empathy* implies reaching toward the patient. More specifically, an *objective* orientation of being dispassionately detached—or, in Anna Freud's terms, "equidistant" from the three components of the psyche—is explored in relation to an *empathic* attitude for making contact or affectively connecting with the patient. Both elements are considered essential and potentially complementary in meeting the reciprocal needs of each party during treatment.

Various types of listening as well as different definitions of empathy are explored to bridge the gap between the two elements. The attentive therapist is one who carefully oscillates between different degrees of engagement and disengagement, communion and noncommitment, as part of the listening role.

The nonverbal attentive aspect of the therapist's behavior also raises a complex and sometimes confusing issue: the relationship between listening and silence. Silence has many meanings for the practitioner and for the patient. It is a therapeutic paradox that the therapist's technical use of silence is designed to *facilitate* the verbalization needed for dynamic exploration, whereas the patient's silence is usually meant to *resist* it. Other underlying meanings emerge, including the notion that the patient's silence may express a wish to be understood without having to speak.

This section thus raises the following questions: What are the components and functions of the therapist's listening role? In what ways may such attentiveness be understood, or misunderstood, especially in relation to silence as a therapeutic technique? What does silence mean to the therapist? to the patient? How might we expect the patient to react to the silent therapist and, perhaps more critical, how does the therapist deal with the silent patient?

CHAPTER 11

The therapist's suspended attention is not only objective but empathic

ATTENTION IS ONE OF THE BASIC ELEMENTS of communication; in psychotherapy its role is critical for the benefit of both practitioner and patient. Without it, there would be no meaningful interaction; with it, the therapist is able to listen properly to the patient, while the patient in turn is aware of being listened to. Although the patient may not especially take note at the time of the therapist's undivided attention, the loss of such attention, however brief, can become an issue of treatment.

Lapses of attentiveness or inconsistent periods of interest may reflect natural fluctuations in concentration, or perhaps, distracting personal stresses. Unfortunately, these times can convey to the patient a lack of care. Patients, whose self-esteem is quite fragile by definition, often cannot tolerate such a message from the therapist and may react with depression, anger, or flight. Others may overtly respond with masochistic acceptance or denial, which perhaps deceives the therapist into believing that the inattention has not been registered by the patient. No matter how the patient responds, the lapse is countertherapeutic to treatment because it implicitly does a disservice to both parties: the patient loses contact with the therapist, at least briefly, and the therapist loses his or her link with the patient.

Perhaps paradoxically, the direct or persistent focusing of interest on particular events or details can create a tense, if not inhibiting, atmosphere, especially when the topics themselves are traumatic or threatening. Focused attention is required nonetheless on those special occasions when the therapist needs to stay with a particular content to gather more information or to be clearer about what has already been revealed. In this regard Lester Luborsky (1984) has pointed out that the clinician's ways of listening may vary throughout the course of treatment. Three basic modes have been distinguished; they manifest themselves at different times and are used according to the needs of the therapist. The first occurs most frequently at the beginning of psychotherapy—when the therapist has little knowledge of the patient—or when a new subject comes up at any point in therapy: the therapist is most likely to be in a position of having to listen afresh, open and primarily unreflective. The second mode is applicable when the therapist has to arrive at some hypothesis to help the patient deal with a pressing issue; it is a somewhat more focused manner of listening. A third mode is brought to bear when the therapist must check the accuracy of his or her understanding thus far, to be able to affirm, discard, or revise what is tentatively known; it is perhaps the most focused form of listening.

The Objective Function of Listening (for the Therapist)

The much emphasized concept of the therapist's "evenly hovering" (or "evenly suspended") attention (Freud 1912b) is neither a heightened attention nor a lack of concentration, but rather represents a special way of listening that has been compared with the scientist's empirical attitude. It is a way of being therapeutically impartial by mentally divesting oneself of preferential thoughts about the patient's presentations. It is intended to prevent any excessive vigilance, or selective interest, on the part of the therapist which would interfere with his or her ability to maintain professional objectivity. The therapist is supposed to suspend judgment and give the same dispassionate recognition to every detail. As a specific technique it "simply consists (to the extent possible) in making no effort to concentrate the attention on anything in particular, and in maintaining in regard to all that one hears the same measure of calm quiet attentiveness" (Freud 1912b, 118). It is a way of keeping at bay the intrusion of any personal reflections or private preferences, expectations, or values.

This "suspended" therapeutic stance is often misunderstood, however, as an intellectual orientation or sterile laboratory method that in its nonsubjectivity necessarily distances the therapist from the patient. In particularly vulnerable or needy cases, the listener's technical neutrality may be misconstrued as a form of aloofness or lack of care. In fact, there has been much controversy over the idyllic and stereotyped concept of the therapist as value-free, as represented by the technique of evenly distributed attention to all that is (and is not) said. Hans Strupp (1974), for example, regards such a notion as a fallacy. Clinical experience attests that the purely objective function of this attentive stance for the gathering of clinical data does not suffice as the sole rationale for its use; yet the therapist's professional conduct as an unbiased scientist is still an ideal of both researcher and clinician.

The Empathic Function of Listening (for the Patient)

Perhaps paradoxically, the concept of evenly suspended attention is now better understood not only as a way of sustaining objective *detachment* and being emotionally removed in the manner of a scientist, but of also establishing an empathic *connection* to the patient. In Freud's (1912b) terms it held a special valence for the therapist—to "turn his own unconscious like a receptive organ towards . . . the patient" (p. 115). It is an expression of unconditional acceptance or regard, no matter what the patient says or what the therapist really thinks.

In fact, psychotherapy increasingly focuses on the therapist's empathy (in addition to warmth and genuineness) as a necessary (Kohut 1971), if not sufficient, condition for patient change (Rogers 1957). Two decades ago Carl Rogers and Charles Truax (1967) theoretically defined such "accurate empathy" as "the ability of the therapist accurately and sensitively to understand experiences and feelings *and their meaning to the client* during the moment-to-moment encounter of psychotherapy" (p. 104). Although this empathic listening was posed as a non-Freudian, client-centered approach, it is nonetheless reminiscent of Freud's principle of freely suspended attention insofar as the therapist's nonjudgmental stance is not meant to be cold or cerebral, but actually a way of empathically communing with the patient. Havens (1986), who broadly defines empathy as "a capacity to participate in or experience another's sensations, feelings, thoughts, or movements" (p. 16), bridges the earlier (that is, objective) and later (that is, empathic) functions of therapeutic attention by suggesting a distinction between "passive" and "active" empathy. The former emphasis is regarded as a "waiting, sentient attitude" (p. 17), whereas the latter is more searching and embracing of another's world, in Martin Buber's (1957) terms, a "bold swinging . . . into the life of the other" (p. 110). The first, I believe, best addresses the subject matter of what the patient says, the second the emotional tone or meaning of the message.

Thus, as a fundamental principle of psychotherapy practice, focused attention secures the "content presence" of the therapist, who is tuned in with specific material offered by the patient, while the predominant empathic listening mode of free-floating attention secures the "affect presence" of the therapist, an expression of genuine concern for the patient. Affect presence is essential to the maintenance of the therapeutic relationship. The therapist who provides focused attention and offers content presence may be a good objective technician who can set up a reasonably productive therapeutic condition without imposing his or her values or opinions through prejudicial or preferential attention. But the ideal therapist is present in both content and affect, altogether in synchrony with the patient.

The complexity of the clinician's listening role is compounded by historical changes in our understanding of its purposes and effects. The notion of therapeutic attention has evolved over time, from Freud's (1912b) sometimes misunderstood evenly suspended attention within an aura of neutrality and anonymity, to Rogers's (1957) and Kohut's (1971) emphasis on empathic listening as a way of conveying genuine regard for the patient. Consequently, the function of listening in psychotherapy has had major implications for both clinician and patient. No longer primarily a technical tool for objective observation in the quest for unbiased knowledge of the patient (that is, predominantly for the therapist's benefit), therapeutic attention is increasingly viewed as having mutative empathic value as a direct agent of healing (that is, for the patient's benefit). This shift in conceptualization highlights the complexity of the therapist's dual attentive role, as he or she carefully modulates objective content presence and empathic affect presence.

CHAPTER 12

The therapist who "completely understands" the patient has stopped listening

HOWEVER SIMPLE a person may seem, however obvious his or her psychological conflicts may appear to be, with exploration the person's complexity will become more apparent. Winnicott (1965) writes:

> In health there is a core of the personality that corresponds to the true self. I suggest that this core never communicates with the world of perceived objects and that the individual person knows that it must never be communicated with or be influenced by external reality. Although healthy persons communicate and enjoy communicating, the other fact is equally true, that each individual is an isolate, permanently non-communicating, permanently unknown, in fact, unfound. (P. 187)

Moreover, when stressful experiences lead to the organization of defenses in psychopathology, there has been a threat to the isolated core. At bottom, then, the patient's defensive structure is designed to hide that secret self, to protect against the dangers of being communicated with, known, or found.

The following is an example of how a relatively simple consultation unfolds as the therapist gets closer and closer to the core of the individual's conflict; alternatively, the endangered patient again and again must fend off being known. Here each new facet of the patient's traumatic or stressful experience that is exposed contains the seeds of other, as yet hidden and uncommunicated, aspects of self. To show how the secret self gradually unfolds, I will present the therapist's successive responses to the patient: the first one (in brackets) relates to the immediate issue at hand, with the clinician's effort focused upon what is being introduced at that moment; the second (in brackets and italics) indicates the therapist's attempt to understand the patient better with each exposure as well as his renewed puzzlement each time a new facet is revealed.

Case Illustration

A forty-eight-year-old physician commented about his "confusion" over what course of action to take after his wife attempted suicide. Then he announced that he wanted to leave her for another woman, a much younger and successful physician, whom he had been seeing for two and one half years. The patient felt terribly guilty about his wife's suicide attempt (she had cut her wrists in front of him).

PATIENT: I don't really passionately love her, but I care about her and feel responsible for her. We have two boys; both seem to understand my problem, but of course they want us to stay together, primarily for her sake. Both boys are grown up and out of the house, so I don't feel guilty for them. The older one is engaged to be married this July; the younger is eighteen years old and is smart and a great student. They are OK.

THERAPIST: The boys seem stable and their future looks fine without your marriage being maintained. [The therapist restates the patient's comments to see whether he is really conflict-free in regard to the subject revealed. Upon the therapist's unambiguous restatement, the patient may restate his own position with a more balanced view, especially if he is ambivalent about what he has just said.]

[*I think that the patient's dilemma as to what course of action to take is related to his relationship with his children in spite of, or because of, his denial.*]

PATIENT: Well, not exactly fine. I am sure they need to see a stable marriage. I wonder how this is going to affect their view of marriage, having children, et cetera. How are we going to maintain a relationship with grandchildren? There is bound to be some fragmentation.

THERAPIST: Some fragmentation, but they will survive. [The therapist introduces the term *survive*, reminiscent of the wife's suicide attempt.]

[*I think that kids may not be the cause of the confusion after all; let's go back to the survival issue.*]

PATIENT: Oh, they'll survive, better than survive, and I'll be there for them. I'm not leaving them, I'll always be their father, their children's grandfather. Then the question is, Shall I sacrifice my life just to make sure that she survives? You know, we all go around only once. As I was saying, I feel guilty about leaving her. I was brought up in a highly religious home. The idea of divorce was not even in our vocabulary.

THERAPIST: [Although important issues are being brought up, the therapist chooses to remain silent until he hears more.]

[*I wonder whether I should pursue the patient's worries about his wife's survival and guilt associated in leaving her, or expand on his betrayal of his religion, culture, and original home; I wonder about the best course of action to take.*]

PATIENT: I had a very rigid upbringing. My parents were married until my father died about two years ago. Did they have a good marriage? I have no idea, but they stayed together—that was the point. As they say, you don't desert your partner.

THERAPIST: As *they* say? [The therapist wants to see whether the patient will come up with the specific source for his strong guilt.]

[*I now think that what might be causing confusion is not the present issues, such as the children's well-being or whom he loves the most, and so on, but a powerful unconscious guilt coming from earlier years.*]

PATIENT: Well, my father used to say that. I grew up on a farm in North Carolina. I, my youngest brother, and my sister all had our daily chores; we were a team, as he used to say; we helped each other if one of us had too much to do. You certainly never quit your part of the chore. You would get a long lecture at dinnertime in front of the whole family if you ever failed in your task. The same thing was applied to schoolwork; he always made you feel guilty.

THERAPIST: Your father would have been disappointed in you if he knew that you are deserting the team now. [The therapist uses the same metaphor; it is not just the divorce but "desertion of the team" that is producing severe guilt.]

[*I am now almost sure that the father is the internalized superego, creating guilt for the patient's deserting his wife (who tries to desert him in turn).*]

PATIENT: Yes, I would have been called in to be lectured about the sanctity of marriage, the sins of giving into one's desires, that life is a series of responsibilities, the denial of your needs is the source of salvation, et cetera.

THERAPIST: Now that he is not here to tell you all that, you are saying it to yourself. [The therapist points out to the patient that he has internalized his father's value.]

[*I have found confirmation of my minitheory, and I think that is it.*]

PATIENT: Yes, but I can't really accept it. I never fully believed all the high falutin' sermons. Yes, one should be honest, decent, altruistic. But, God, I am not Jesus, the world does not work that way. I used to resent his holier-than-thou attitude. . . . As a kid, I at times hated him, praying that he would be dead. I never said this to anyone before: I am still ashamed of having thought that way. He was a good and very caring father, a little stuck-up but a well-meaning, religious man.

THERAPIST: Ashamed and guilty. [The therapist singles out the affectively loaded words in the patient's statements and pairs them (*guilt* and *shame*) as used by the patient in connection with his father. Such focusing might provide further related material.]

[*Are these—shame and guilt—deriving from the same source, the father—the superego? Let's see.*]

PATIENT: He wasn't that old, nor that ill when he died. It's silly, but at times I wonder whether my childhood prayers were finally being answered. I guess you can't shake your beliefs no matter how educated you are. Yeah, I guess I feel guilty about his death, not about the wish I had, but more that I did not believe his chest pains. He was known to the family as being a hypochondriac and his physicals were all OK, but I should have known better and insisted that he go for a stress test. A simple EKG isn't enough, but I just let it go. Did I still have some unconscious hostilities towards him, that I let him die? I don't know. When he died, I cried a little, but I did not really miss him. I felt sort of relieved, as if now I can do what I want, without his looking over my shoulder.

THERAPIST: Within six months of your father's death, you met Kathy [the girlfriend]. [The therapist merely introduces the time sequence of two events. He does not tie the package too neatly, but helps the patient to do it. When the patient wraps it not only will he own the package, but also he'll learn how to wrap other packages.]

[*How could it be that after his father's death he breaks the rule? Is it possible that the issue of his having a harsh superego was a false theory?*

Maybe he did not internalize his father's values as I once thought, and instead of an abstract superego he was just afraid of his father.]

PATIENT: It is the first time in my life that I actually slept with another woman. Although I was very conflicted initially, eventually it became rather natural; I loved her and I still do. She became more of a wife for me than my wife. It was just incredible that I could be that way. I was sexually freer, socially more comfortable, funny and entertaining, a different person, like being let out of jail.

THERAPIST: After the warden died! [The therapist is in metaphorical synchrony with the patient.]

[*I am now convinced that it is not the harsh superego generating all his presenting problems and confusion, either. The father actually exerted external control until he died. The patient's confusion may be related to having lost that external control.*]

PATIENT: It was as if my real self had been hiding somewhere; then after I met Kathy, I became a new person, a person that I always wanted to be. It was just an unbelievable transformation. Finally, I decided that this is what I really wanted and I was going to get divorced. That night I sat down and told my wife the truth. Well, you know the rest. How can I leave her? I deeply care for her, a special love, a sisterly love. I cannot hurt her. She has called the boys, telling our close friends what I am doing to her. In reality they all know how difficult she has been, an oppressive character. The boys call her Mother Superior.

THERAPIST: You have more than one warden. [The therapist tries to connect the two oppressive characters in the patient's life.]

[*So, it is not team desertion, but killing the wardens that creates guilt. Are we back to superego and aggressive drive theory?*]

PATIENT: I am not sure which one is worse. For both of them I had to play the perfect-person role. First an obedient son and then a dutiful husband. Until I met Kathy, I didn't realize what a relationship could be like. I just accepted it while grinding my teeth in my sleep.

THERAPIST: Did you have any death dreams for your wife? [From sleep to dreams is a little too quick, but a reasonable jump, especially in view of the fact that the patient was grinding his teeth.]

[*Of course, he wants her to die, too, the way that he once did his father; and her suicide attempt is just her explicit compliance with his wishes.*]

PATIENT: Not dreams, but plenty of guilt-producing fantasies of her dying in a car accident or getting cancer.

THERAPIST: Or suicide? [The therapist completes what the patient avoided among his fantasies and wants to come to the present subject.]

[*Let's solidify the specific guilt as it relates to her suicide attempt.*]

PATIENT: No, I don't think that. I never thought she would try to kill herself, especially over me.

THERAPIST: That she did not love you and care? [The therapist wants to make sure that the patient means what he said, especially the issue of caring.]

[*Is this to relieve his guilt and justify his fantasies about her dying?*]

PATIENT: Yes, but I saw her basically as just demanding, a drill sergeant without much feeling, rather cold and methodical, a Nazi. To make such a drastic gesture in order to keep me is strange for her.

THERAPIST: Then the guilt is related to being the cause of her potentially killing herself, like you felt you caused your father's death.

[The therapist interprets present guilt historically as related to the patient's wishes.]

[*The patient must have married his wife because she was very much like his father. Besides the obvious homosexual incestuous connection, he may have wanted to replicate the same controlled environment in his marriage and then complain about it. With all that came the same aggressive, murderous thoughts and wishes in the new relationship.*]

PATIENT: That would be worse than what I did to my father. This is actual murder, murder of the warden.

THERAPIST: Murder of wardens who seem to care for you? How awfully confusing the different feelings must be. [The therapist does not want the wardens to be separated; he also points out their multiple roles as they relate to the patient, the confusion this must evoke.]

[*So, the patient wants to kill the father again by his fatherlike wife's suicide, which is also reactivating earlier guilt. The whole thing is a passive oedipal victory and his guilt has little to do with the wife; she is just standing in for the father. Also I am somewhat confused and feel empathic for his dilemma. Therefore I go back to the beginning of the patient's initial presentation, his confusion.*]

Psychotherapy proceeds both in a linear way and in circling back repeatedly. This approach helps the patient and the therapist to be oriented to and connected with the unfolding story. Each time the therapist goes back to the beginning or comes to a point of the past session, the connective tissue of narration is strengthened.

PATIENT: I am rarely, if ever, confused at work; I am clear as a crystal. I guess as long as I got my marching orders from someone, I was always clear and I in return could give marching orders. I like the orderliness. I suppose emotional issues are not so easily put in order. I guess there is nothing you can do, so I have to deal with this matter myself. I don't know what you could do for me; it is something I alone have to make decisions about. I have made many decisions in the past.

THERAPIST: Are you disappointed that I have not given you a marching order? [The therapist noticed the first negative message "nothing you can do," and will not allow it to fester. The choice of wording—the semantic congruency of "marching order"—may help the patient accept the interpretation.]

[*The telltale signs of negative transference! This is not so surprising, but it immediately followed my empathic statement. Did I present myself too much as a better father image? Is the patient feeling bad about so quickly opening up and betraying his own father? Or have I not been able to relate as a caring individual to the patient?*]

Guntrip (1968) views the ego as consisting of extremely deep introjects and projective identifications (whether bad or good). He thus points out the patient's fear of losing his or her malevolent introjects to the extent of looking upon the therapist not simply as someone who can rescue him or her from bad parents, but also as someone who may destroy the parents or take them away. In therapy there is a difficult transitional period when the patient is afraid of losing these introjects because he or she is not yet sure that the therapist will truly replace them, can really be a better parent. This shift takes a long time, until both the child and the adult can believe in the new parental image. Long after the patient is reasonably convinced that the therapist can adequately replace his significant others, there is still an element of doubt. Under such circumstances of uncertainty, it is hypothesized that even as benign an activity as accepting the therapist's help may feel like a fundamental disloyalty to parents and arouse guilt.

Richard Chessick (1974) goes further and suggests, "The patient cannot be weaned from, and become independent of, internalized bad parental objects—and so cannot become healthy and mature—unless he can consolidate and introject a good relationship with the therapist as a real object" (p. 317). Therefore, it is believed that what takes priority over all other concerns of the patient is whether the therapist, as a real human being, is able genuinely to regard the patient as a person in his or her own right.

PATIENT: I presume it would be easier if someone said to me: "You have the right to live your life as you think best; you don't need to feel guilty—it is her problem. You are entitled to be in love; go ahead, marry her and just be happy."

THERAPIST: And I am not providing such comfort. [The therapist here had different options: to go ahead to discuss the patient's neediness and his lifelong dependency on others; or to follow the thread of his feeling resentful afterward toward those who give the marching orders, even though he needs them. The therapist chooses to deal with the transferential aspect of the patient's comments because of their emerging negativeness. But the therapist also uses a different wording this time, thinking that the patient does not want to hear the term "marching orders" again, perhaps finding it too deprecatory in his connection with the therapist.]

[*No, he is not finding me an uncaring person; he actually still thinks that I do care. That is the reason for his negativity, his transference—for him, caring means controlling.*]

PATIENT: I thought we would have one or two sessions at the most to figure out which woman I should be with. Instead, I see us digging into my relationship with my father, my guilt about his death, my wishes to kill both my father and my wife. I don't know where this is taking us, especially if all of this has to be resolved before I make a decision. At this rate, it'll take a few years. This whole thing can't wait until I resolve all my deep-seated psychological problems.

THERAPIST: On the one hand, you would like to have a quick answer to the problem, and on the other hand, you realize that in the last two weeks all the advice you got did not help much. [The therapist recognizes the truth of what the patient is saying, but he is not going to rationalize the situation, since there are no shortcuts. This point will only be rebuffed by the patient. The therapist thus decides just to reflect on the dilemma that the patient is in.]

[*He wants to kill me off too quickly, even though I hadn't in actuality established a controlling relationship. I certainly avoided it so far; so his confusion may be not knowing how to relate to me, or others. I wonder what Kathy is like.*]

PATIENT: The people I asked did not have all the facts, of course. But, nevertheless, I got all kinds of advice, mostly not useful.

THERAPIST: Now I may be the only one who has all the facts; and even so, I am not coming up with any useful advice. [The therapist, recognizing the patient's differentiation of him from others giving advice, remains focused on the negative feelings.]

[*He is telling me that I don't have all the information, so look for some, but get this negative transference under control first. He is trying to get me to give advice and then reject it, or feel controlled by me and resent it; if I don't give him the advice, he'll be disappointed that he did not get any, and that will leave him more confused because he cannot play out his typical scenario.*]

PATIENT: Well, you are either too smart, or you are also lost and don't know what advice to give.

THERAPIST: Either way, disappointed! [To lecture on the importance of being neutral in treatment would represent defensiveness on the part of the therapist. Instead, once the therapist catches the thread of negativity, he shouldn't let go (see maxim 27).]

[*How did Kathy relate to him, that he was so liberated? What was the mother like? There must be someone, some positive introject I can be identified with. I've got to avoid being identified with the father and wife; otherwise, this treatment will end very shortly.*]

PATIENT: Not really. Both internists think highly of you, that you helped many patients; they have enormous confidence in you. Well, also, I am not sure what I am expecting from you. You really can't give me advice, tell me what to do or not to do.

THERAPIST: Especially now that you are finally freed from your father, who all your life told you what to do and what not to do. [The therapist points out the patient's need to be independent, in order to emphasize one side of his ambivalence (a healthy one), and thinking that the patient will provide the other side.]

[*His conflict is not just oedipal but belongs to even earlier stages. He is still to some extent in a dependency/independence struggle: control or be controlled. He is thus confused, a confusion that is not limited to deciding which woman to be with. His fluency of self-presentation is just a superficial facade, not warranted by what he really feels. Rather than appear incoherent and really confused, he is presenting me a pseudoconfusion, and not necessarily just to confuse me.*]

PATIENT: At the same time, I seem to be seeking someone to do exactly that, and I then resent and fight that person—go figure that out.

THERAPIST: Not only have I not given you any advice, but I have deprived you of a justification to resent me. [The therapist, instead of comforting himself with the insightfulness of the patient, deepens further the search for negativism.]

[I think enough has been done to dilute the negative transference for the time being. I'd rather go after some yet undiscussed subjects, but for this I need more material: Is Kathy like his mother? Is he really not confused at work? What about all the other questions that I don't even know how to ask?]

PATIENT: (*Laughing*) Well, you are not all that home free—I still resent you. I don't know why, but we are going in a circle. This is fine and interesting, but I can't move to either side; I'm just sitting on the fence.

THERAPIST: Not a comfortable place to be! Let's continue next session. [The therapist stresses the difficult but also inevitable position of the patient.]

[Well, the patient may be on the fence while I feel reasonably in the saddle. But I'm not that comfortable either; there's still a little bit of hurting where the old saddle sores are.]

This case illustrates that there are various levels of understanding a patient and thus intervening accordingly, each time heading toward different consequences. The therapist can stay at the most superficial or conscious level (with the presenting problem), dealing with the women by viewing the pros and cons of each and attempting to decrease the patient's rigid superego and guilt feelings—thus implicitly encouraging the patient to leave his wife. Or he may interpret the patient's love for the new woman as an acting out against his father, thereby underplaying its importance and its authenticity—thus helping the patient to disengage from his lover. Some therapists may fall into an assigned role, give advice, and end up terminating the treatment quickly. There can be other options, mostly countertransferential ones, justified and fortified by the therapist's theoretical bias.

Because there are multiple meanings at any level, compounded by the existence of many changing layers, the therapist can never be sure which meanings are the most true, and what information supplies clues to understanding a patient. In fact, the search for ultimate understanding may be what preempts the unfolding of various partial understandings. The therapist can count on only one thing: there will always be more to know if he or she keeps looking.

CHAPTER 13

Therapists tend to underestimate the power of listening and overestimate the power of speaking

IN OUR DAILY LIVES we become well acquainted with the power of speech in interpersonal communication and emotional discharge. In the clinical setting, however, the power of speech is more than matched by the power of listening. The patient may not be quite prepared for the therapist's quiet, reflective stance and may not always appreciate it. This is especially the case when silence conspicuously contrasts with the therapist's concerted interest in the patient's verbalizations as he or she tries to reach inaccessible thoughts and wishes. Thus, at some time or another during the therapeutic encounter, every practitioner knows well the pleading expression of the patient, asking for a word.

Ralph Greenson (1965) has suggested that for some patients who have strong reactions to the discrepancy between their verbal output and the therapist's, this type of response can be a direct reflection of a transference reaction to the clinician, whether positive or negative. Here the clinician has become the tender, loving, milk-giving mother, or the reverse. When this occurs, verbal utterances of the therapist are experienced as food, interpretations as special nourishment, and any semblance of silence as rejection or desertion. Such patients usually have "oral" responses to the speaker; they insatiably need to take in every word. Greenson observed that in one such patient, "My speaking . . . meant that I was willing to feed her. If I would talk, then it meant I was truly concerned about her, would take care of her, feed, and not abandon her. . . . [Another patient also] insisted that I insert even a small comment into her silence and then she would be able to let out all her stored-up communications" (p. 249). With the occasional or less pressing request to speak, the therapist can reply, "You seem to want some response." The danger is that the therapist, like the patient, may begin to overestimate the power of talking.

When it is the patient who remains silent, the therapist can merely comment, "You wonder how to proceed." Or he or she may ask a simple content question. There are times when most patients would rather be left alone in the flow of their thoughts. In fact, they can get somewhat disoriented when even momentarily interrupted. The patient may naturally respond to the therapist's statement but then try to go back to the reverie, at times openly wondering, "Where was I?" Some patients actually resent these interventions by the therapist. A patient once said to me, "You know, as much as I want you to talk, when you do I feel as if I lose contact with you."

The permission the therapist gives the patient to speak without interruption establishes a special relationship between them; the patient in turn has assigned a reciprocal role to the therapist as listener. Thereafter any statement of the therapist will interrupt the designated process by deviating from the expected roles. This phenomenon is part of the transference, but it is different in the sense that the content of the material is not directed to the therapist (thus it will generally not require a transferential interpretation).

On many occasions, however, the therapist may well feel obliged to talk, overestimating the necessity for talking and underestimating the power of listening, in part due to pressure from the patient and in part due to the therapist's own need for activity and participation. In general, susceptibility to speaking occurs because saying something is equated with doing something. Due to the general suppression of physical activity in verbal psychotherapy, the therapist's expertise or personal ego tends to dictate the display of professional prowess with words, as an overt sign of being a good or smart clinician. The insecure clinician at least temporarily loses sight of the fact that silent intervals are neither random intermissions nor rest periods for the therapist. Indeed, there is a hidden component of silence in every verbalization, just as there is a hidden component of verbalization in every silence. Balancing these is part of natural tact as well as therapeutic judgment.

In short, what the therapist usually needs to do is simply to let the patient talk while he or she just listens, first with two ears and later on with a "third ear" (Reik 1949). This means that the therapist not only scrupulously observes conscious perceptions, but receives, records, and decodes what narrowly escapes from the net of conscious observation. In Reik's words, "The voice that speaks in him [the therapist] speaks low, but he who listens with a third ear hears also what is expressed almost noiselessly, what is said *pianissimo*" (p. 145).

In this kind of attentive listening, so much of the communication is conveyed that nothing more than occasional empathic sounds are needed (which reside somewhere between silence and words). The therapist is never completely silent or doing nothing—he or she is caring, understanding, concerned, interested, and accepting; the therapist is just quietly there, actively attending to the patient and to his or her own inner voice. This type of listening supercedes talking. If "words are also deeds," as Ludwig Wittgenstein (1951) has asserted, then we might venture to extend this axiom by suggesting that silences are also words.

CHAPTER 14

Do not strangle the patient's questions by answering them

RELATED TO THE IMPLICIT PLEAS on the part of the patient for the therapist to speak is the issue how to handle the patient's explicit questions of the therapist—*if* they should be answered in kind. The topic has been a matter of concern and controversy in psychodynamic circles. Some have recommended that the therapist directly answer the patient's questions, that he or she spontaneously meet the request for concrete information, opinion, or advice. They note that by virtue of the reciprocal nature of the therapeutic endeavor the patient deserves to have queries replied to. And on the face of it, one can hardly argue with such consideration for the patient.

Nonetheless, to respond humanely to the patient does not mean to answer decisively his or her particular questions. Rather, the clinician must be alert to the pattern and purpose of the patient's queries—and not be sidetracked by the compelling nature of their content. Sidney Tarachow (1963), for example, has examined the multiple motives behind a patient's series of questions about her patienthood status, such as, "When am I going to get well?" "What is the cause of my problem?" and "Am I your worst patient?" He suggested that this type of interrogation, which may take the form of a repeated verbal barrage, can have many psychological functions: an aggressive attempt to provoke the therapist or to make the therapist defensive; a disguised way of requesting reassurance; a test of the clinician's expertise or commitment, a rivalrous effort to be measured in relation to other patients; a maneuver for gaining control of the session according to the patient's will and against the therapist's agenda; an act of dependency, setting up a situation in which neediness is satisfied through answers; or, more simply and often overlooked, a desire for the fundamental gratification of hearing the therapist's voice. Expressed curiosity about the clinician's life or qualifications, general questions about therapy, requests for help with dilemmas, or even seemingly simple requests for specific information may reflect various kinds of solicitation for "something," not always a specific answer, from the clinician.

Therefore, to answer the most obvious requests immediately may strangle underlying inquiries, which are often much more relevant for the progress of psychotherapy. It may also be stultifying to respond to every query of the patient with the return query, "Why are you asking me that *now?*" This kind of reply, which has virtually become a rigid formula for some nonanswering therapists, is unnecessarily frustrating to the patient; it is also reductionistic in its assumption that hidden dynamic data can be reached only in this way.

On the other hand, obvious "realistic" questions, to which a prompt reply would facilitate the patient's exposition—for example, asking in the midst of a football narrative whether the therapist knows what a T-formation is—are best briefly responded to, so that patient and therapist do not have to spend time on details with which both are already familiar. However, long responses may divert the direction of dialogue, thereby casting doubt on the motives not only of the patient but also of the therapist. (Is the therapist's need to demonstrate know-how to the patient interfering with further exploration?)

Greenson (1965), for one, has suggested a straightforward approach. When a question is asked by the patient for the first time (as when the single patient wonders whether the therapist is married or the quasi-sophisticated patient asks if he or she is supposed to fall in love with the therapist), the clinician explains that his or her not answering has the therapeutic purpose to shed greater light on the patient's curiosity about the matter at hand. Thereafter the therapist may neither answer the question nor explain why; rather, he or she suggests that the patient think about his or her own thoughts or fantasies regarding the query as well as any anticipated answer by the therapist. If the clinician can resist complying with the patient's immediate request, there may result the larger gain of the patient's capacity to go beyond the desired answer. Alternatively, even if the frustrated patient becomes aggressive against the therapist for failing to reply directly, he or she may learn a different unanticipated lesson of therapy, that is, that the therapist can survive the patient's wrath. As Strean (1985) has suggested, "If requests are gratified by the therapist rather than understood by both client and clinician, the anxiety that evoked them is not confronted, the conflict that is being expressed is not mastered, the autonomy that the client fears is not considered, and the resistance that is being demonstrated is not re-solved" (p. 132).

Case Illustrations

A thirty-four-year-old woman, who had recently lost her four-year-old daughter, her only child, to leukemia, could not talk about her pain. Several sessions went by without the subject being broached.

PATIENT: Doctor, do you have children?
THERAPIST: You would like to know whether I've lost any?
PATIENT: Yes, otherwise I don't think you could understand how I feel; no one can; I cannot put my feelings into words. It is just a frightening black hole, an abyss.
THERAPIST: (Makes a pained empathic sound)
PATIENT: (Continues to describe her pain)

There is no need for the therapist to tell the patient how many children he has, whether they are girls or boys, their ages, and so on. Such information at worst may generate envy or unnecessarily burden the patient; at best the responses can clutter communication because the patient's request for specific information is usually unwarranted. Not answering directly also has another advantage: setting a pattern of communication wherein the patient learns to ask the real questions or broach underlying issues instead of masking them with interrogation of the therapist. Of course, not every question may lend itself to easy categorization. At times further inquiries are necessary, especially when the patient's concerns are carefully camouflaged, and the therapist's "answer" needs to take the form of more detailed clarifications.

A professional woman whose son was not academically up to her expectations managed nonetheless to get him into a reasonably good college; there he became rather successful. At the end of his first year the mother wanted to transfer him to a better college.

PATIENT: What do you think? Do you think I am doing the right thing?

The therapist would do best to avoid simple counterquestions (such as What do *you* think?), which tend to be unproductive, caricatured patterns of communication. Let's look at the therapist's possible responses.

1. Well, college *A* is a better one. [Under the disguise of the objective statement the therapist encourages the mother to pursue her wish, but leaves her dangling with unresolved feelings.]

2. What are the pros and cons of the transfer? [The therapist is opening up the subject for discussion, for the mother explicitly to identify the advantages and disadvantages of the transfer. At the same time the therapist is gaining time to learn more about the matter. But since he has not answered her question and he may not be off the hook, the question will no doubt come up again at the end of this exploration of the pros and cons, whereupon the patient will again ask what he thinks.]

3. Do you think that you may have some mixed feelings about transferring him? [The therapist focuses on the patient's real concern that is causing her ambivalence, moving from an external problem to the internal psychic conflict.]

The therapist made response 3, and the following dialogue ensued.

PATIENT: Yes, he's so well adjusted there, happy, he has friends; I wonder whether I am too prestige oriented and going to do some harm to him.

THERAPIST: I guess part of your indecision is related to the fact that you are not sure how much that transfer is for your agenda versus for his.

PATIENT: I know that he would rather stay where he is. He has friends there and he is popular, but is he not shortchanging himself? It is, I guess, my agenda. Wouldn't it be better if he graduated from Yale? But I'm always being accused of being a climber. I don't know. Maybe I am a superficial person who is more impressed with names and titles than with substance. I guess saying that my son goes to Yale, that kind of stuff . . . oh! how awful that sounds. I must be some selfish person.

THERAPIST: Then your earlier question, what do I think of the transfer, is more like the question, what do I think of *you?* whether you are a good mother or not.

PATIENT: Yes, I feel like I need you to tell me that I am OK; I need someone to tell me that it is OK, that I should not feel so guilty. You are not my father; I mean, why should I even care what you think—isn't it crazy? [Here the patient has sequentially shifted from her son to the therapist, and finally, to her overcritical father.]

The questions of both patients, "Doctor, do you have children?" and "Do you think I am doing the right thing?" are not directly answered, but they are nonetheless therapeutically responded to by the therapist.

CHAPTER 15

The therapist's silence is intended to facilitate treatment; the patient's silence unintentionally resists it

THE THIN LINE between listening and silence is one that the dynamic psychotherapist is often obliged to tread. Silence can have many meanings or functions for both therapist and patient. According to Mayer Zeligs's (1961) study of the psychology of silence, which highlights its manifold and often perplexing forms, it may mean

> agreement, disagreement, pleasure, displeasure, fear, anger, or tranquility. The silence could be a sign of contentment, mutual understanding, and compassion. Or it might indicate emptiness and complete lack of affect. Human silence can radiate warmth or cast a chill. At one moment it may be laudatory and accepting; in the next it can be cutting and contemptuous. Silence may express poise, smugness, snobbishness, taciturnity, or humility. Silence may mean yes or no. It may be giving or receiving, object-directed or narcissistic. Silence may be a sign of defeat or the mark of mastery. (P. 8)

Moreover, because of the economy of silence—which invariably occurs in a much briefer time interval than does the speech that precedes or follows it—it is endowed with the power of parsimony, reflected in such expressions as "pregnant silence." It may also be highly susceptible to an individual's projections, the need for filling in the soundless void. When a Romantic poet confessed his great yearnings to his beloved, for example, and she failed to reply, he in turn responded, "She is silent. And in that silence I am more than answered."

In psychotherapy, two broad categories of therapist silence can be distinguished, especially insofar as they are prospective sources of misunderstanding by the patient and/or therapist: (1) silence for the purpose of attentive listening and (2) silence as an intentional (or sometimes unintentional) means of producing frustration and anxiety. Both types are considered major elements of the therapist's technique. For the most part prolonged silences do not reflect countertransferential responses, although occasionally a perplexed, bored, or irritated therapist may reciprocate a patient's silence with his or her own; these retaliatory reactions are thought to occur when the therapist is feeling deeply discouraged about the progress of therapy (Fenichel 1945) or personally eradicated by the patient's absence of response (Greenson 1967).

The patient's silence also comes in various guises that reflect an assortment of possible uses to the individual and to the recipient. Nonetheless, it has been suggested that because a major function of speech is to discharge instinctual feelings, silence can readily represent an unconscious defense against those feelings. In addition, since all silence (whatever its individual functions) enhances the formation of thoughts and fantasies, it is more conflictual than speech. As in fantasy, greater aggressive and libidinal energy is believed to be discharged (Kris 1950).

A major implication for psychotherapy is that insofar as silence tends to hold in ideation and affect, it often acts as a cover for the very thoughts and emotions that are most unacceptable. Indeed, some patients can cope with the terror of their dangerous fantasies and feelings only by being rendered speechless. Thus silence is safer than speech.

Silence also can have individual meanings. Ferenczi (1916–17), who pointed out the relation of silence to the patient's dynamics, suggested that obsessional patients (for whom silence is an expression of oral eroticism) may unconsciously equate strength with the retention of words. Other personal meanings within treatment can include silence as revenge against the therapist (when the patient knows that the therapist wishes for him or her to speak), silence as teasing or as a power struggle (as when the patient selectively withholds speech, but lets the therapist know when he or she is doing so), silence as a defense against aggression (where the patient fears saying something that will incite the therapist), and silence as depression (whereby the patient is both physically and psychologically hypoactive, and silence becomes equated with death or loss of self). Examination of the psychodynamic literature in fact suggests that patients' silences, when they occur in the midst of ongoing discourse or exploration and are not preceded by the therapist's silence, are usually an expression of underlying aggressiveness, resistance, or negative transference; or, when they immediately mimic the silent clinician, are most often vengeful reactions of the threatened patient, accompanied by the belief or fantasy that the therapist has, albeit temporarily, gone away.

It can be said that the overall motives of the silent therapist and those of the silent patient in psychotherapy are not only different, but antithetical: the clinician's silence is technical (that is, nontransferential), whereas the patient's silence is personal (that is, transferential). More specifically, the clinician's silence is primarily designed to *facilitate* the therapeutic process, whereas the patient's silence is predominantly meant to *resist* it. Greenson (1967) cited the case of a breathless patient who arrived late, saying that she had had difficulty parking her car. The therapist felt that it was premature to confront the patient's lateness immediately. He anticipated that not only would any immediate interpretation be denied, but that such an encounter would divert the session from pressing content that the patient otherwise wished to communicate. Instead the therapist chose to remain silent. Soon the patient began to report a dream that she had had the night before—but much of whose content she had forgotten. The partially reconstructed dream, marked by the patient's silent intervals, became a source of frustration to both participants. But the therapist's silence, he believed, had permitted this event to occur as a confirmation of the patient's rising resistance. It follows that patient silence serves, in Greenson's (1961) terms, as both communication and resistance, or in Jacob Arlow's (1961) more alliterative terms, as discharge as well as defense. In either event, whether by patient or by therapist, silence (nonspeech) sends a potent message.

CHAPTER 16

Silence is not always golden; it can be misused by the therapist and misunderstood by the patient

DERIVED FROM an ancient Talmudic proverb (Brewer 1953), the concept that "speech is silvern, but silence is golden" reflects a long-standing belief in the high value of silence; words may come cheap, ring false, or be transitory, but the purity of silence endures. In psychotherapy, however, this adage does not always hold: the gold of silence can also tarnish as the clinician overrates its utility and the patient in turn misinterprets its intent. In short, the special role of the therapist's silence, an inherited part of the Freudian legacy, can easily be misused by the therapist or misunderstood by the patient.

How and when to use silence as a therapeutic tool is perhaps one of the subtlest skills in the conduct of psychotherapy. One is reminded of the concert pianist Artur Schnabel (1958), who commented upon the nuances of his own musical ability when he said: "The notes I handle no better than many pianists. But the pauses between the notes—ah, that is where the art resides."

There are many occasions in psychotherapy when the therapist chooses to remain silent; it is a select therapeutic prerogative. Indeed, the therapist's benevolent silence may grant permission to the inhibited patient to be likewise silent if he or she feels unable to speak. It may even work paradoxically, insofar as both silence and the breaking of silence are seen as equally acceptable. However, the therapist's not speaking for purposes of attentive listening (see axiom 11), versus not speaking for purposes of sustained silence (the intentional withholding of words), are very different. They can be almost antithetical: the former is ideally an empathic expression by the therapist that reflects patience with, interest in, and concern for the patient, whereas the latter can be an act of deliberate deprivation, although temporary. Withholding speech is therapeutically designed to frustrate the patient in order to induce further anxiety and regression. Greenson (1965) refers to silence as the therapist's way of letting the patient's resistance increase; it permits the patient to experience the internal forces that are barriers to change or cure and to become aware of their tenacity.

Depending upon its nature and length, the therapist's pause can either promote or impede the subsequent therapeutic process. If the silence is prolonged and the patient misunderstands why the therapist waits to speak, the patient may be erroneously receiving the "silent treatment" rather than the "talking cure." The patient may naturally impute negative meaning to such silences, especially when they occur inappropriately.

One inappropriate occasion for protracted silence is during the initial interview, the first contact between therapist and patient. Here, if the patient is not forthcoming about his or her problem and background, unnecessary silence on the therapist's part will not help him or her obtain the needed information. The therapist's choice to say nothing (not knowing how to draw the patient out) will invariably have an adverse effect, especially if the patient has no idea why he or she is being treated in that way. The therapist may have made a defensive decision not to speak out of indecisiveness, for fear of saying the wrong thing; this discomfort in turn can be sensed by the patient, who then may get frightened by the therapist's insecurity.

Case Illustration

A young college student who came to treatment for a "second opinion" on a school-related crisis said that he had had his first therapy experience six months earlier and had been "turned off" by the therapist. In fact, he had gone for only one session and never returned.

PATIENT: The therapist just sat there and hardly said a word. . . . He asked me what brought me there, and I told him what I've told you, you know, dropping out of school and all . . . I mean, I asked him if

I would have to come to treatment for a long time and he just said, "We'll have to find out more about you, then we'll see." And when I asked his fee, he seemed suspicious; he didn't answer right away. I told him that I couldn't really afford much. I was sure he would challenge me, but he didn't; we never really went into it. Frankly, I didn't know what he was waiting for. He kept quiet, so I kept quiet. But I began to go into a cold sweat. He didn't seem to care one way or the other. I suppose I thought he wouldn't want to treat me anyway, if I couldn't pay what he wanted. But I really don't know that for sure. All I know is my anxiety kept going up and as time was passing I was feeling progressively worse than when I came in. I started to think that I would just walk out, but somehow I was afraid to say anything or get up. My mouth was dry and I just kept thinking about leaving, but felt frozen to the spot. At the end, he took his notebook out, I suppose to write down his schedule, so I just blurted out that I didn't think I was coming back. For the first time, he behaved the way I would expect; he said, "I'm sorry to hear that." . . . But that was it. I couldn't wait to get out of there. . . . After I left I thought maybe he'd call me, but he never did. If that's therapy, it's not for me.

Not verbally interacting may also serve as a thin screen for the therapist's unconscious hostility toward the patient for being difficult, a silent retaliation. Silence at such times is mutually disadvantageous, for it increases the anxiety of the patient and of the frustrated or confused clinician. In his observations on the psychopathology of silence, Edward Glover (1955) points out that when the therapist's silence is pitted against the patient's, the therapy has degenerated into a pugilistic encounter that can be settled only by the competitive winning of points; in effect, therapy becomes a no-win contest. Even intervention or the interruption of this dual silent state with direct questions or comments, like "Tell me what is on your mind now," or "Is there more you'd like to say about that?" is not likely to improve the impasse. The therapist may already have completely lost the uninitiated patient.

At other times, however, if the message behind the therapist's silence is received as a benevolent one, then silence will be supportive, granting the patient the same permission and reassuring right—to remain silent or to speak—as the therapist has.

CHAPTER 17

Behind the patient's silence is a wish to be understood without verbalizing

THE PATIENT HAS MANY UNCONSCIOUS or implicit wishes in relation to the therapist. One of the more pervasive fantasies is that the therapist will defend the patient forevermore from the dangers of himself or herself and the world around him or her, without active participation on the part of the patient. By virtue of being nearby, the clinician as sorcerer and shield will protect the patient. In a similar vein are the underlying fantasies or wishes of the noncommunicative patient. The patient expects to be understood, as if by osmosis, in the absence of any natural effort to communicate. (This wish may also make the patient impervious to the therapist's extended silences.)

The clinician must make an educated judgment about whether the patient is comfortable with the silence (as if beatifically content in the quiet presence of another) or, more likely, whether the lack of communication is based on intense anxiety or resistance. The former (likened to the young child who is quietly content with mother nearby) is clinically contrasted to the latter, which has unconscious traces of the same fears of rejection and wish to be magically understood. The contented silence need not be interrupted or interpreted (it may even be counterproductive to do so), whereas the conflicted type is subject to intervention.

Therefore, what seems like a simple matter—when to interrupt the patient's speech or silence—does in fact require some consideration. Obvious circumstantial thinking or obsessive ruminative repetitions aside, rarely is the therapist's active intervention needed to interrupt or alter the flow of the patient's speech. These unusual circumstances are primarily related to the following: the patient's avoidance of certain topics, especially transferential ones; defensive emphases on the past or the present; excessively affective or intellectual presentations; or instances of acting out.

Silences of the patient are often difficult to read. Misreadings tend to alienate the patient and thus are potentially damaging to the relationship. There is merit to the well-known advice not to break the silence so that a certain level of anxiety is maintained in the patient; but that course can also be unproductive. The management of silence cannot be based solely on generating or decreasing anxiety.

The patient who appears to be in a pensive state is usually associating or processing some material that he or she is trying to remember. Obviously, the last thing a therapist should do is to interrupt such a potentially productive state of mind. If the therapist waits long enough, the patient spontaneously will begin to speak again. Or the patient will come out of the thoughtful state, stay silent, and begin to look again at the therapist. Since the therapist does not want to lose the material at hand, he or she may say something like: "Were you thinking about something?" or "For a few minutes you were somewhere else," or "You did not want to talk about what you were thinking?" Usually the patient either responds with a wealth of associations or says merely, "Oh, some irrelevant daily stuff." In the latter case, the therapist does not let go; nothing is irrelevant, especially if it occurs daily.

If the patient remains in silence for a long time, how long should an unanxious therapist wait? A simple rule is for the therapist to break the silence when he or she can no longer stay with the patient and begins to drift away. At such times, breaking silences must be done gently and with little intrusion. In order to recapture the already elusive material, the therapist must be careful not to introduce an emotionally laden subject.

When the patient actually comes out of the pensive state and becomes unproductively silent, the therapist may respond, "You did not want to talk about that." But when the therapist is commenting on silence in the middle of the pensive state (there is not yet a defensive elaboration evident), an encouraging statement or, even better, a short phrase suffices. The therapist may say, "In deep thought!" or "A little louder."

On the other hand, when the patient looks at the therapist or avoids the therapist's eyes but is not in a pensive state—the patient is, rather, anxious and lost—long silences are unlikely to be productive and usually condition the patient negatively to the sessions. Equally unproductive are affect-exploring interpretations of these silences (such as, "The silence seems to be making you anxious"). The therapist would be better off to acknowledge its presence: "Long silence!" Or the therapist may acknowledge the difficulties in the situation: "You wonder how to proceed?"

Instructing the patient to say whatever comes to mind rarely works. Such permission or encouragement remains implicit, unless a regressive atmosphere is established. So, if a simple acknowledgment does not break the unusually long silence, the therapist may need to open up an area. An opening should not be in the form of a question; a pattern can develop wherein the patient will repeatedly fall into silence, waiting to be questioned each time. Instead, the therapist may say: "The last thing you began to talk about was your relationship with your brother," or "Earlier you were beginning to remember what it was like to have your mother ill during your teenage years." If the patient understands such statements as a request for elaboration, he or she will start expanding on the subject. Of course, the subjects are chosen by the therapist as potentially conflicted issues for the patient, therefore productive arenas for discussion.

Not uncommonly, frequent silences are manifestations of resistance, which do not respond to any of the above techniques, only to interpretation.

Case Illustration

A sixty-eight-year-old lawyer sought help for his acute depression and anxiety immediately after having learned that his wife of more than forty years had lung cancer. During the first few sessions, he spoke extensively of his fears of losing her, as she had become his main support over the years. Although quite capable and successful at work, he remained emotionally highly dependent on her. No one, including his own mother, provided him such love and affection. He spoke repeatedly of his need for her and his lifelong hidden dependency. Then he began to have long silences. To the therapist's recognition of these silences he responded, "I guess I have nothing more to say," "I talked myself out," and the like. He would sit and stare at the therapist.

THERAPIST: You have talked yourself out of things to say?

PATIENT: Yes, nothing more to say.

THERAPIST: Then you must be wondering whether there is any point in coming to the sessions.

PATIENT: Well, I have been waiting for you to say that. Unless there is something else to do, it was good to get things off my chest. But now it'll only be repetitive.

THERAPIST: Repetitive?

PATIENT: I thought it was already getting too repetitive and boring. I don't know how you could sit there and listen to all these complaints and whinings.

THERAPIST: Besides protecting me from these complaints and woes, do you also wonder what I must be thinking of you?

PATIENT: Well, you must be saying to yourself, "What a crybaby—at this age he still wants his mommy."

THERAPIST: You would not want to be thought of that way.

PATIENT: No, I have been a very private person. People think of me as a very strong person. My friends—well, I don't really have very intimate friends to discuss my intimate life with—but, you know, social friends see me as a very powerful man.

THERAPIST: And you like that powerful man image and don't want to hurt it.

PATIENT: Definitely. I never told anyone that I have an ulcer. I think I did not even tell you that.

THERAPIST: I guess with me as well you may want to maintain at least some of that powerful, independent image.

PATIENT: Maintain some of my dignity.

THERAPIST: You think that you can maintain some dignity only by not talking?

PATIENT: I am not even sure how much I am supposed to say. What does a normal patient do usually? Do they empty out all their dirty laundry here?

THERAPIST: You certainly keep this laundry bag quite firmly tied up with the fear that I might be disgusted with it.

PATIENT: Not just you. I wonder whether I want to see it myself.

THERAPIST: Then you would not only lose my respect but your own self-respect as well.

PATIENT: You know, as we keep talking about the dirty laundry, I don't really have that much. Everyone must have some. But I am extremely demanding on myself. I'll tell you what I am most ashamed of: Would you believe that I am afraid of getting cancer from my wife? Isn't that hypocrisy, that I say I cannot live without her and then I worry that I'll catch her disease?

The patient went on talking about all the precautions he took to avoid catching the disease, also of his fantasies about whom he would marry after her death. With the natural threat of revealing all these unacceptable thoughts, silence becomes a way of maintaining one's dignity, sustaining the wish to be understood without having to say anything.

PART V

ON THERAPEUTIC
RELATIONSHIPS AND THEIR
VARIATIONS

This section addresses the special interpersonal bond between therapist and patient that resides at the heart of all therapeutic endeavors. It is distinguished by a form of communicative intimacy that is unreplicable in ordinary adult relationships. This feature is based on a way of knowing the other as well as anyone can, yet at the same time it is bound by the logistic as well as emotional constraints that can characterize an artifically established interpersonal arrangement. This unusual form of intimacy represents a delimited interaction that transpires entirely within the clinician's office (at least overtly) and is essentially restricted to words and the nonbehavioral expressions of emotion.

The purpose of this unique relationship varies among major branches of psychotherapy: some view it as necessary but not sufficient for therapeutic change or cure, whereas others regard it as a healing medium in itself. Beyond this, the primary type of affiliation that is formed may decidedly differ from school to school. It can also vary from one major diagnosis category to another, and even from time to time with the same patient. Despite conceptual distinctions regarding these varieties of therapist–patient models, in actual practice they overlap. This applies to such prototypic relational paradigms as the transferential relationship, working alliance, and real relationship, as well as specific variations associated with borderline or self disorders, such as a narcissistic alliance or empathic bond.

Whether and when such alliances are established depends on the patient's dynamics and the therapist's techniques. One of the significant determining factors is the capacity for closeness versus psychological distance between the two members. On the patient's part there may be undue dependency upon the therapist or its ostensible opposite, fear of intimacy. Both phenomena have their source in a particular phase of child development. More specifically, clinging as well as its counterpart, fleeing, may be seen as alternative expressions of the same early childhood conflict regarding separation from mother: rapprochement. This also raises the issue of the clinician's ongoing management of attachment and separation as well as frustration and gratification, reverie versus reality. The formation and dissolution of a therapeutic barrier serve to differentiate an "as if" psychotherapy situation from a "real" one, in which unconscious urges for union are satisfied, to a greater or lesser degree. That is, the therapist may even have to merge with a patient for therapeutic purposes—but the merger *must* be only temporary.

Both failure to form a transference attachment and failure to establish an empathic bond can reflect defects not only of the patient but also of the therapist. The failure to form a transference attachment may be viewed as a problem of the practitioner's strategy or technique (for example, the degree of activity or disclosure); the failure to establish an empathic bond more likely resides in a deficit of the therapist (such as his or her incapacity to experience and share the patient's feelings).

The following questions are therefore posed in this part: How is the therapist–patient bond similar to, or different from, other adult relationships? What role do relational factors have in patient change or cure? When and why are different types of interpersonal alliance established within treatment, and what features do these share? Finally, what part may the patient's psychopathology play in the ability or inability to form such alliances? And in direct counterpoint to this, what reciprocal part does the therapist play both in the facilitation and in the failure of the therapeutic relationship?

CHAPTER 18

The therapist and patient develop a communicative intimacy that does not exist in other relationships

WHAT MAKES THE RELATIONSHIP between therapist and patient different from other professional and nonprofessional, medical and nonmedical, artificial and naturally formed bonds? It is intimate, but not in the usual sense. The intimacy between two people usually develops through frequent, regular, or intense contacts; it is marked by the sharing of joint experiences, feelings, and thoughts not usually characteristic of casual contacts or of other formal or contractual arrangements. In contrast, most naturally formed attachments, including family, friendship, and love relationships, may have such intimacy—or at least the expectation of it—as a basic ingredient. But the therapist–patient bond is not based on a filial connection, a platonic friendship, or love, requited or unrequited; it also differs from the more typical tutorial or business partnership, other fiduciary forms of affiliation, such as legal counsel, or even spiritual unions, in which confidences may also be divulged. Despite its temporary status, the bond of psychotherapy contains a special kind of closeness—communicative intimacy—that can go farther than other professional or even personal relationships in its private revelations and breadth of emotions without crossing the boundaries of verbal dialogue. It is also communion through the vehicle of words reaching into the buried recesses of the unconscious.

The role of the therapist is not to become a parent, teacher, friend, or lover, or to actually replace one, although he or she may symbolically become one or more of these. Rather, the therapist supplies another type of relatedness, which has no single prototype in real life. Therefore, the patient's relationship to the therapist is not in reality—although it may often be in fantasy—competitive with parenthood, friendship, or marriage per se; it has its own intimate dimensions.

Communicative intimacy means that the patient is, on the one hand, able to say whatever he or she wants to and, on the other, can be understood without actually saying it. It gives one the opportunity to experience one's most private self in the presence of another. There is no subject excluded from discussion (that is, the range is not deliberately restricted, as when private marital matters are told to one's divorce lawyer, personal medical matters are revealed to one's internist or gynecologist, secret sinful matters are confessed to one's priest, or even all are revealed to a good friend). In return, the therapist is receptive to the patient's confessions, not by matching the patient's revelations with his or her own (as a companion would do) or giving advice (as a lawyer would do) or offering absolution (as a priest would do), but with an implicit message simply of understanding.

Intimacy of communication affects both parties, even though there may be no reciprocal self-disclosure. That is, the therapist does not express feelings of closeness, libidinal arousal, discomfort, embarrassment, shock, or revulsion, if they arise. But although the content overtly travels in one direction only, the intent is still to further mutual communication. In communicative intimacy the task of the therapist is both to facilitate this close communion and simultaneously to contain its therapeutic boundaries. Tarachow (1963) has introduced the term "therapeutic barrier," meaning a technical shield between therapist and patient that represents the invisible partition formed between real intimacy or gratification and its transformation to an "as if" situation. The barrier represents professional boundaries that are nonetheless unrestricted by words and the fantasies and feelings behind them. Communicative intimacy is embedded in empathy, in a way of being with someone. As Spence (1982) has pointed out: "If carried out successfully, the empathic convention allows us to perform a silent translation of the patient's language as he is speaking . . . and, in general, come a little closer to seeing his world as it looked in the split second before it was transformed (and distorted) into language" (p. 113).

As a direct implication of such communicative intimacy, how the therapist responds to revelations regarding some of the most highly conflictual arenas, such as sex and aggression, may be the true test of the therapist's ability to remain therapeutic (that is, intimate through verbal communication). Much has been written about the therapist's nonreciprocation of the patient's erotic feelings and nonretaliatory attitude toward the patient's aggressive affect; for example, the clinician is repeatedly warned not to be seduced by the patient's sexual feelings, or defensive in the face of attacking or angry feelings. But less has been said, or personally admitted, about the clinician's prematurely closing off such subjects due to his or her own reactions to the intensity of the implied or felt intimacy.

In the following case, the therapist attempts to stay with the patient's graphic sexuality without risk to their communicative intimacy. Such evocative material may be both expression of, and defense against, their unreplicable closeness. In either event the special intimacy has no precedent for the patient—or in the life of the therapist, for that matter.

Case Illustration

A thirty-two-year-old woman was experiencing a dependency struggle in her life. Her neediness and excessive criticalness interfered with her work and her relationships with men. After having gone through an initial negative transferential phase in treatment whereby she questioned every qualification, personality characteristic, and technique of the therapist, she settled down to self-searching work. As her early relationship with her father was unfolding, for weeks preceding this eighty-second session the patient had been in the midst of a very highly erotic transference toward the therapist.

PATIENT: You and my father in reality have nothing in common; nevertheless, when I am talking, I am using you and him interchangeably. I know the Oedipus stuff, but you are so unlike each other. I dreamt that we were making love and you were on top, but not like making love, sort of banging at me. It was pleasurable, but I was also crying. You seemed to be oblivious to it all. It is so vivid that even now I feel you against me, your balls hitting my buttocks; I feel the wave of air in between strokes.

THERAPIST: Quite graphic. [The therapist focuses on her way of reporting the dream.]

PATIENT: Because I wanted to experience again the sensation I had in the dream, enormous dilation, almost distended, dripping . . .

THERAPIST: Just to reexperience the sensation? [The therapist still comments on the purpose of her detailed reporting.]

PATIENT: Well, yes. I guess I want to excite you, too.

THERAPIST: Because I was so indifferent in the dream?

PATIENT: Because you are so indifferent, period. I would love to know whether you got a little excited when I was describing my dream. . . . Have you read *The White Hotel?* It is the most erotic, poetic novel I ever read. It is a story of Freud's son, making love to one of Freud's patients, as told by the woman. Have you read it?

THERAPIST: You got scared, not sure you really want to know my reaction.

PATIENT: You mean, changing the subject? I guess I needed some distance, some intellectual distancing, because when I said I would love to know whether you got excited or not, I got terrified of a yes answer. What would I do? Would we jump into bed, make passionate love? But then what? The aftermath—are we lovers, or just a therapist and patient who just made love? What will happen to the therapy? I know you would never approach me. But what if you could? I don't really want to make love to you and don't really want you on top of me. When I was looking at your crotch, what I really wished was just to suck your penis, to sit in front of you, though you could be busy with something else. I'd just be sucking you.

THERAPIST: I could be busy with something else, sort of indifferent to you sucking me. [The therapist omits the word *penis* to generalize the sucking to nonsexual areas as well.]

PATIENT: Not indifferent, in a negative sense, as if you are doing what you should be doing—you know, something else, reading or knitting and at the same time just letting me suck you. It isn't for your pleasure; it is for me. You are just putting up with it. Well, not exactly just putting up. You are holding me, too, maybe caressing but not making your pleasure the center. You must be enjoying it, but not really letting yourself dwell on it. There must be something in it for you, but maybe nothing. For me it feels like you are there just for me. I am all focused on myself. I don't have to worry about pleasing you; it is just understood, that is the way it is. I feel warm and dilated but not only in the vagina, in me, all over hot and wet and dripping and it is not the lubrication. And it feels so good.

THERAPIST: So secure. [The therapist wants to underline the security instead of sexuality, as was displayed earlier.]

PATIENT: I'm secure, full, warm and wet and secure, as if I am perched on my mother's breast.

CHAPTER 19

The patient's patterns of relatedness determine the moment-to-moment course of the therapeutic relationship

ALL PSYCHOTHERAPEUTIC TECHNIQUES are embedded in some form of therapeutic relationship. Unless the therapist can establish an interpersonal alliance and maintain it throughout the course of the therapy, other technical expertise will be of little use. Whether this relationship is considered necessary but not sufficient for therapeutic change to occur (as drive or ego theorists are likely to hold), or is the healing medium in itself (as object relations or self theorists are likely to hold), the human affiliation that is formed takes a pivotal place as it reciprocally affects both therapist and patient. More specifically, whether insight is considered to be the sine qua non of cure as the clinician's interpretations cognitively transform the patient's psyche, or the therapist is viewed as a good and empathic selfobject internalized as a replacement of inadequate parental figures, the two modes of change—the new perspective brought by the verbal intervention and the interpersonal encounter itself—are not easily separable in the total psychotherapy experience. In either event, the therapeutic relationship sustains a significant role, directly or indirectly.

Within this fundamental framework, there are various models for the type of therapist–patient bond that is established. Each major psychotherapeutic school has its own primary conceptualization of the nature of this special tie and of the respective mutative qualities that derive from it. Distilled from different conceptual orientations, some basic variations include the following.

1. Within drive theory, represented by Freud (1912a) and his followers, the interactions between patient and therapist are primarily regarded as regressive manifestations of a "transferential" relationship that is projected from the past. The significant early childhood drives and desires of the patient are unconsciously repeated and relived in vivo with the therapist (in fact, the therapist may induce their appearance) for purposes of search and resolution of the patient's original nuclear conflict.

2. Within ego psychology, a nontransferential "therapeutic alliance" (Zetzel 1956) or "working alliance" (Greenson 1965) is established between therapist and patient. The mutual interpersonal task within this theoretical framework is for the two to join in a realistic collaboration to attempt to draw upon the patient's rational and nonregressive capacities, to jointly develop the patient's ego strength in adaptation to inner forces as well as external reality.

3. Within object relations theory, the therapist becomes a "real," good object to the patient and a current role model for identification. The therapist offers himself or herself as an alternative to, and hopefully better object than, the early developmental figures in the patient's life; by doing so the therapist provides a "corrective emotional experience" (Alexander and French 1946) which acts as a new interpersonal context that replaces, rather than repeats, the past. It also can provide a "holding environment" (Winnicott 1965) of support and safety as a temporary buttress against dangerous or regressive impulses.

4. Within self psychology, the therapist sustains an empathic atmosphere to foster development of stable self and object representations. In this relationship model of a "narcissistic alliance," the nuclear self is crystallized through transmuting internalizations of the therapist. Secure caretaking, via a new empathic selfobject who serves both mirroring and idealizing functions, can compensate for and correct the earlier empathic failures of parental figures (Kohut 1971); this in turn forms the nucleus for inner security and cohesive selfhood.

The formation and use of the different types of psychotherapeutic alliance depend upon making a controversial distinction between the part of the therapeutic relationship that is transferential, that is, based upon displaced desire or wishful fantasy reenacted as if it were real, and the part of the therapeutic relationship that is real, that is, constituting an authentic human bond with a new person. The modes of interpersonal transaction also fall, in Tarachow's (1963) terms, within the range from drive deprivation to drive gratification. The former end is embodied in an assortment of therapist attitudes and behaviors marked by relative anonymity and abstinence, designed to facilitate unconscious fantasy; the latter is characterized by relative responsivity and disclosure, which reaffirm conscious reality. At one endpoint may be found the encouragement of regression, the frustration of drives, and the irrational idealization of the therapist; at the other is the offering of realistic confirmation and mirroring, here-and-now succor and support, and real or symbolic satisfaction.

Within this framework the different types of bond can reside on a subtle clinical continuum consisting of acceptance, concern, and care that extends from therapist neutrality to nurture (based on the degree to which the therapist primarily reflects upon and interprets or primarily responds to and satisfies the warded-off wishes or urges of the patient); and from patient reverie to reality (based on the extent to which the therapist is, or is not, viewed as a distorted figure from the past versus a new person in the present). In this behalf, Greenson (1965) has distinguished three overlapping types of therapist–patient interaction: a "transferential relationship," which is genuine but anachronistic and unrealistic because it is based on old repeated patterns and projections; a "working alliance," which is realistic but not genuine because it is strictly a function, or artifact, of the therapeutic situation; and a "real relationship," which is both nontransferential (reality-oriented and undistorted) and genuine (authentic and true). Across these boundaries, of course, are the fine distinctions between transference (which is relived as if it were real) and the real part of the therapist–patient interaction, which constitutes an authentic human encounter. Tarachow (1963), for example, has noted an aspect of current reality in the response by every patient, in which the individual intensely experiences the therapist as real. As he put it: "You are more real to your patient than you think. When you shake hands with a hysteric, it's a sexual overture. When you shake hands with an obsessional neurotic, it is a challenge. When you shake hands with a paranoiac, it is an assault. Every contact has its own reality" (p. 96).

In light of this, the real relationship is always the medium through which transference reactions transpire. But it has an independent existence as well. The therapist, in the context of professional standards and constraints, allows himself or herself to be seen as such, permitting his or her human features and frailties to be revealed as part of the treatment process. Thus the clinician responds with sorrow to a grieving patient or with pride to a newly accomplished one. A real relationship can thereby be the basis for an "existential alliance," in which the clinician lets the patient know that he or she empathically shares the other's affective pain or pleasure.

On a different level, the real relationship can be used—or more often misused—as a form of "social alliance" (Horowitz and Marmar 1985). The term refers to the inappropriate application of the real object relationship as a type of kinship comparable to that which occurs in ordinary life, outside of psychotherapy. The social alliance creates a friendship, or even courtship, out of the professional pact, and may be marked by superficial banter on the one hand or false signs of great intimacy on the other. It results in a form of nontherapeutic impasse, as the patient (and sometimes the practitioner) deflects the therapy by trying to consciously or unconsciously maintain a real-life relationship in order to flee the working alliance. In another pattern patients may present a different impasse to relatedness: they may cling to the therapeutic alliance because they are terrified of a more regressive transferential relationship.

In the course of therapy, these modes of therapist engagement (transferential, work-oriented, or real—whether therapeutically abstaining, hand-holding, or milk giving—may be utilized separately or together, at times intermittently and sporadically, at other times sequentially to keep a patient on track. These varied *modus operandi* may be applicable to certain patients and not to others; or they may be applicable to the same patient at different stages in the evolution of treatment. Each mode can be used or avoided as the therapeutic responses of the therapist attempt to resonate with the patient's particular level of psychological maturation.

In fact, in understanding the therapeutic relationship, Tarachow (1963) has aptly noted that for both parties there is

> the generic problem of the constant temptation to move close to objects, to have object relationships, to abandon mature ego differentiation for narcissistic and anaclitic object relationships, the temptation to identification, and finally and basically for fusion. The therapist as well as the patient have [sic] a constant struggle against this array of temptations to come closer together. (P. 12)

In light of this natural interpersonal phenomenon, the diagnosis or personality structure of the patient will influence what kind of relationship can be established. Since it is only through an alliance that the therapist may apply therapeutic techniques, first he or she has to make contact with the patient; insofar as each patient has an individual pattern of bonding, it is up to the clinician to identify the patient's pattern and level of relatedness and then to attempt to connect with it. Based on the degree of consolidation of the patient's psychological state and sense of self, for example, the therapist must in turn modulate his or her own attitudes, emotions, and activities to establish and sustain an interpersonal connection with the patient. Because patients vary not only with respect to one another but in their own course of development, the therapist needs to adjust and readjust his or her type of relatedness and self boundaries accordingly.

The therapist needs a large degree of controlled flexibility (as distinguished from uncontrolled fluidity)—to be able to move up and down the psychological ladder of development to fit the patient's needs, simultaneously to monitor regression while testing the patient's potential to advance further. Within a tenuously established or very turbulent relationship, the therapist will have a harder time stabilizing the patient and shifting him or her in a desired direction. In any event, the clinician can never be certain that a particular level of relationship has been formed. There will be fluctuations, manifested in different types of alliance—narcissistic, nonnarcissistic existential, rational, or transferential—as a natural part of the evolving therapeutic course of growth and change.

With a relatively healthy patient, there are several ways in which the therapist may present himself or herself and thus facilitate the establishment of a nonnarcissistic alliance. The therapist may maintain a predominantly reflective presence, identifying, clarifying, and interpreting the unconscious, regressive, wishful world of the patient (a transferential alliance); the therapist may present himself or herself as a realistic, benevolent object allied with the patient's ego (a rational alliance); the therapist may just be with the patient, sharing his or her feelings and thoughts, experiencing their mutual humanness (an existential alliance).

In fact, it has become increasingly recognized that the nature of the relationship that can be formed functions as a diagnostic sign. With individuals who are erratic and contradictory in their interpersonal relations, whose boundaries of self and other are unclear, who tend to split good from bad object representations, or who cling and then withdraw in defensive attempts to fend off true intimacy, the therapist is especially called upon to provide a flexible but stable object. For these patients with deficient self development, the therapist may have to match their narcissistic relatedness by permitting a narcissistic alliance, that is, the illusion of being merged with another person. This kind of alliance will be needed, at least initially or intermittently, to "glue" the patient's self together. In effect, the clinician has to be able to ally, even virtually fuse with, the patient for therapeutic purposes. Eventually, however, it is believed that the patient, by relating to another person who has control over self boundaries, can form a firmer sense of himself or herself, can gradually find out where the therapist ends and he or she begins.

The therapist must therefore bear in mind, perhaps more so than with patients whose self is more intact, that such an alliance is only temporary; his or her own self, or at least part of it, is being borrowed for the occasion. In Kohut's (1971) terms, the therapist becomes a needed selfobject to help the patient regulate self-esteem and feel complete. For therapeutic purposes, the selfobject both forms a necessary interpersonal function for the individual outside of himself or herself and is simultaneously experienced as part of himself or herself. All of us require such objects throughout our lives, although for some people these may be especially critical because of great deficiencies in what the environment has supplied to their internal psychic structure to begin with. In childhood it is the parental figures who provide such experiences, which consist of a combination of mirroring (that is, recognizing the emerging aspects of the child's self and responding appropriately to them) and idealization (that is, providing esteemed role models). Eventually the child can merge with the empathic qualities of the idealized parent or significant filial figure. The child accomplishes this by taking in what is needed from the idealized selfobject through a process of "transmuting internalization," which involves the internalization of functions that the other person (parent, therapist) has and the self (child, patient) needs.

A narcissistic alliance develops with two different but related mechanisms: introjection and incorporation. In introjection there is an indiscriminate taking in of the whole object, bad as well as good. (This is in contrast to identification, whereby the person selectively acquires only certain desired aspects of the object.) With less severely disturbed patients, the introjected therapist can be kept somewhat separate from the patient's self, but maintenance of an ongoing dialogue is unpredictable. In more regressed patients, the therapist is totally incorporated into the patient's psyche; there is an actual fusion. By comparison, for patients who have reached the developmental stage when they do not need to introject or incorporate the therapist, the mechanism for alliance is one of identification with the therapist. That is, the patient's self will become more like the therapist—or, more accurately, what the therapist represents to the patient.

Placed on a continuum, a narcissistic alliance is responsive to the most primitive mode of relating, whereas the transferential alliance is the most advanced as a basis for therapeutic interaction. Each represents an extreme along the developmental spectrum of therapist–patient interaction. Nonetheless, these types of relationship are hardly categorical, insofar as elements of each may be present to some degree in every therapeutic endeavor. The nature of these alliances is also constantly changing in the course of treatment, naturally shifting with maturation and regression. In fact, the therapist must monitor his or her interpersonal activities each step of the way, changing modes of relating, as needed, in order to maintain continued contact with the patient. The following case vignette suggests how both therapist and patient weave in and out of different types of alliance during the course of treatment.

Case Illustration

A forty-eight-year-old man (with the diagnosis of acute paranoia) had had two brief, involuntary hospitalizations. Adamantly opposed to being committed, on both occasions the patient signed out against medical advice, then sued the doctors and the hospital for having detained him without his permission. In psychotherapy he was often explicitly accusatory or implicitly suspicious of others' (including the therapist's) motivations. The following exchange is taken from the twelfth session.

PATIENT: My wife invited this couple for brunch. She knows the wife from work. The two women usually get together often; this time, they decided to include their husbands. I thought I should meet him first before we all got together, so that I could interview him; in case he has something to tell me in private, he could do that without being embarrassed in front of his wife. [The therapist recognizes being incorporated into the patient's psyche, the patient playing the role of therapist with the other husband. The therapist does not challenge or negate the incorporation at this time because the patient needs such fusion in order to remain relatively intact.]

My wife thought that was a crazy idea; who the hell was I? But why should I be put in a position of compromise? I don't usually like being in that role. If the wives are friends, fine. Why bring the men along? I am not going to be friendly with that asshole. I met with him and it turned out that he quizzed me all afternoon. I don't need friends; I told my wife if I need them, I'll find my own, thanks, but don't get me stuck with these holy characters. I mean, who the hell is he to tell me there is no future in real estate? I think it was just a put down of my father. . . . Then he looked at me straight in the eye and asked me where I bought the bagels. I said to him, what difference does it make—are they good or not? Right? He doesn't live in the neighborhood anyway. Then he leaned over to me, and with a soft voice said, "On the corner of Second Avenue and Seventy-fourth Street there is a bakery where they make great bagels!" After he said it he pulled away and gave me that look; you know what I mean. I wondered if he was implying that my father owns the building with the bakery. You know, my father has been so secretive, I don't even know whether I am in his will; I think he owns a few more buildings than he tells me and he'll will them to my sister, I know.

THERAPIST: Is there any way of finding that out, whether the building with the bagel store underneath belongs to your father? [The therapist accepts the narcissistic alliance inherent in the patient's primitive state of relating, but also is seeking a rational alliance. When the patient moves away from reality too much, the therapist brings his ego into the picture in order to balance the irrational thoughts and emotions without confronting the incorporation.]

PATIENT: Oh yes, I'll check it out as soon as I leave here. You know, at times I am wrong and I accept that; I apologize, but not everyone is that way. People will steal, be completely wrong, and never say, "I am sorry." What are they afraid of? Everyone is human and can make mistakes.

THERAPIST: Of course. Everyone is human and can make mistakes. [A rational alliance.]

PATIENT: That means you, too. . . . How about telling me some of your mistakes? [The patient wants to enter a social alliance with the therapist.]

THERAPIST: (Silent, with an inquisitive look)

PATIENT: OK, just one. Tell me just one mistake that you made in your life, that you felt you totally fucked up the whole thing.

THERAPIST: [Silent and wondering why the patient is doing this. Has the therapist gone too far in the direction of the rational alliance?]

PATIENT: Come on, I won't tell a soul, promise.

THERAPIST: Do you wonder whether I made some serious mistakes in your treatment? [The therapist begins to explore the negative transference.]

PATIENT: Come on, I am not going to let you off the hook like that.

Did you tell any big lies and get caught? Did you steal, cheat, murder someone? What is it? Come on, confess one mistake. *(Smiles broadly)*

THERAPIST: You are getting a big kick out of this!

PATIENT: Now, now. Don't you turn this on me again. The ball is in your court. *(Grinning from ear to ear)* Can't you confess one small mistake? Come on, you've got to.

THERAPIST: All right, how about my having you as a patient? [This superficial banter and the hardly disguised aggression of the therapist does not remove him from the social alliance the patient has been seeking; in fact, it delivers it.]

PATIENT: You are kidding! *(Laughs uncontrollably)* Boy, that is funny. *(Laughs)* Boy, you are something—the lengths you are willing to go to not to answer my question. *(Laughs)* That was really a funny joke.

THERAPIST: Do you also wonder whether there is some truth in it? [The therapist recovers from the social alliance.]

PATIENT: Well, if you said that the first time we met, I would have been offended. I think I know you by now, a little bit. Even if there were some truth in it, it is OK. I deserve it. I mean, I give you enough *tsuris* [troubles].

THERAPIST: Especially today?

PATIENT: Yeah, I guess I should not have been putting your back against the wall like that, forcing you to admit your mistake. That was a mistake by itself, another mistake.

THERAPIST: Maybe you wanted a little informal conversation, the kind that friends would have with each other, sharing their mistakes and . . . [The therapist explores the transferential material.]

PATIENT: *(Interrupts)* No, no, I just don't know. I guess it would have been OK if you made mistakes here and did not apologize; then it would have been all right to insist on your facing up to it. But I had no right to ask you to make confessions to me; you are not my patient. So I made a mistake. I do a lot, it seems . . .

THERAPIST: But you also promptly recognize your mistakes and try to undo them, by facing up to them. [The therapist is promoting a rational alliance by praising the patient for accepting his mistakes. At the same time, by using praise as positive reinforcement he is also encouraging the patient to be more accepting of his own mistakes in the future.]

The discussion continues in the next session.

PATIENT: Well, that issue of my father owning the building with the bagel store, I checked it out. Actually, it's funny, the bagel guy is the owner, an old Eastern European guy. He really got very nervous when he thought I might be interested in buying.

THERAPIST: Frightening this poor guy, making him worry. [Here the therapist and patient share a private joke together, the beginnings of a rudimentary existential alliance.]

PATIENT: Yeah! I guess the guy at the dinner party was just telling me that he knows something about bagels; but it has nothing to do with my father or his building or anything like that. Everyone always accuses me of being paranoid; this time they are right. But I'll tell you, it is much better to be a little paranoid than a complete nerd in this world. . . . I can't find a job; my wife is working hard, and my father helps a little. He says I shouldn't count on inheriting money from him because he'll live a long time and most likely spend every penny of it in round-the-clock nursing, that I should be grateful that he will not be a burden on me. So he sent me to this real estate management company for a job interview. This guy was like a Nazi, asking me all kinds of intimate questions, like why did I quit my previous job, why was I chewing gum, did I have a dry mouth, was I on any medication? [In the patient's angry feelings at having been interrogated, the therapist notes thinly veiled references to himself; but again the therapist chooses not to interrupt or bring it to the patient's attention.] Then he says, "Your wife works for our parent company; you are like your father when it comes to picking women. You've got a beautiful wife and a great father." What the fuck does he mean? When my mother died four years ago my wife spent a lot of time helping my father; he was very depressed. I told her that it didn't look good that she was there so much, and I knew that people would think that way. She accused me of being jealous and paranoid. But this guy must know; he is a friend of my father. The two of them must have talked about it. Do they think that I am a cuckold, embarrassing me in public? How dare they! No one gets away with this. Now, what do you say to that? My old psychiatrist used to say this is a paranoid syndrome. Well do you think so, too? Do you think I am crazy or what?

THERAPIST: I think this is the bagel syndrome! [The therapist is again seeking a rational alliance, but this time he is more secure at the prospect of obtaining one, and thus ventures to joke further with the patient.]

PATIENT: Bagel syndrome? *(Laughs)* Not very scientific, Doc. [The therapist gracefully accepts the put-down, knowing that the patient appreciated not being called crazy or paranoid.]

The subject returned in the twenty-second session.

PATIENT: You know, with this bagel syndrome stuff, you created more problems for me. I keep talking with you, even when I am not here. In my head you talk to me and I talk to you, more so when I am lonely. Any time I see or eat a bagel, I get this smile on my face, like this morning. Now people think that I am really crazy. They say, what is so funny? They think I am hallucinating or something. [Again the therapist and patient share a secret, which makes the patient's symptoms somewhat ego-alien. The patient learns to gain some distance by having a sense of humor; now the two are consolidating their alliance.]

THERAPIST: Some troubling thoughts were in your mind during breakfast, nevertheless? [Although the patient is presenting this as a private joke between him and the therapist, he is also reporting an associated thought that borders on delusion. The therapist dares to interpret connections between the patient's reported behavior and possible inner thoughts, even though the patient is still introjecting him. Despite its primitive state, the therapist considers some sense of fusion a temporary and needed measure. It also represents progress from the initial incorporation.]

PATIENT: Yeah, what was troubling me . . . I was wondering why my wife wants to speak to you. You said she could come to our session, but not have a private session with you. I gather you're like other doctors who'll not examine women patients alone for fear that they may get falsely accused, and sue. She always wants to know what we talked about, what you are like, is very curious about you.

THERAPIST: And you were reluctant to tell me about your suspicions of me and your wife? [The therapist emphasizes his reluctance rather than his suspiciousness per se because the latter subject would make the patient too defensive. Focusing on the reluctance can approach the same issue but without the accusatory connotation.]

PATIENT: Right, because you are going to say, "Here it is again, another bagel syndrome!"

THERAPIST: So the bagel syndrome stuff created more than one kind of problem for you, besides the fact that people think you must be crazy to smile all by yourself. But also, it is inhibiting you from telling me your private thoughts. [Here the therapist attempts an interpersonal interpretation. He is still not sure whether the patient has reached the stage of establishing an alliance with the therapist. If so, he can begin to discuss the transferential nature of their relationship.]

PATIENT: Yeah, a little. I guess, now that we talked about it, it is OK.

THERAPIST: [The therapist feels convinced that the patient is able to discuss their relationship, so he pursues it further.] The bagel syndrome came to replace paranoia, only it's under a different name; I am still calling you crazy.

PATIENT: Yeah, what is the difference?

THERAPIST: You sound hurt, angry. [Now that the therapist has gotten the transferential content under discussion, he wants to see whether the patient also can connect some appropriate affect to the subject.]

PATIENT: Angry? Not much. What were you supposed to do? I am obviously paranoid, so you are trying to help me, but you are also a human being. You did not want to hurt me. You are telling me that I am going to do things, wrong things, then really get hurt. But you mean well, I know that.

THERAPIST: Good intentions aside, the hurt is still the hurt. [The therapist explores whether the patient would be able to experience his feelings of pain rather than anger (in order to prevent aggressive projections).]

PATIENT: No, I think you are making too much out of it. I'm a little hurt for being called crazy, that you and I are not equals, but you are really making too big a deal. Now I am getting angry.

THERAPIST: My emphasis is that you got hurt; this puts you in an even less equal situation with me. [The therapist is still exploring the patient's capacity to discuss the transferential aspect of their relationship.]

PATIENT: I guess I get angry when I feel that the other person is really taking advantage of me. You know, the superior role, the more powerful one.

THERAPIST: The other person? [The therapist is exploring the transferential disposition of the patient.]

PATIENT: Yeah, you know, someone, anyone. . . . My father used to pull that all the time. He knew every fucking thing and I knew nothing. He was capable of everything and I was incompetent. He'd attack as long as you would take it; he wouldn't stop. Just hurting me. . . . He never once said, "I am sorry." I would be hurt, cry, and he'd continue to berate me, this time saying that I am a crybaby, too weak, not a man to take the heat, all sorts of shit. He never hugged me after I was so devastated, never thought to say, "All right, OK, now it is over; let me wipe your tears."

THERAPIST: Do you think your earlier anger at me had something to do with my not recognizing how hurt you were, that I continued to berate you as your father did? [The therapist makes a transferential interpretation.]

PATIENT: *(Eyes swelling)* Why didn't he see how hurt I was? Or didn't he care?

Ultimately, if the real object, working alliance, and transference aspects of the therapeutic relationship are properly managed, they become complements in providing reality and empathy, without compromising the role of the transference relationship. The oscillation among different types of therapeutic relatedness may then both facilitate access to infantile needs and judiciously meet those needs. The flexible clinician can thus venture across the relationship spectrum in whole or in part, symbolically or actually, as irrational desires, conflicts, ego defects, and object deficiencies make their pathological reappearance in the patient.

CHAPTER 20

The patient's undue dependency on or failure to get close to the therapist represent two sides of a rapprochement conflict

As THE INFANT goes through the normal developmental phases of separation and individuation (Mahler, Pine, and Bergman 1975), the child's belief in his or her own and in the parents' omnipotence must gradually recede and be replaced by autonomous functioning. Moreover, the thrust of individuation needs to be carried along by an unambivalent energy. But progressing as well as returning to each successive stage is fraught with a combination of desire and danger. Both the wish for and the fear of going back to earlier phases after the separation has occurred are common. Such yearning may naturally occur in adulthood as the patient relives, at least in fantasy, the "symbiotic dual unity" of mother and infant. This is an omnipotent fusion with the maternal object representation, and can even call forth an early delusion of a common boundary between the two physically separate individuals.

Strangely, this urge for closeness may be lacking in children whose symbiotic relationship with mother was either excessively prolonged or otherwise disturbed, particularly when the maternal figure was partly engulfing and partly rejecting. In addition, a fear of closeness and intimacy stems from the same differentiation stage. In adulthood, wanting to be taken care of, to emotionally merge with the therapist, is most frequently seen in female patients and has roots at this very early phase of the development. Conversely, the dread of union tends to be more pronounced in men. As Mahler, Pine, and Bergman further point out:

> The fear of reengulfment by the dangerous "mother after separation," the fear of merging that we sometimes see as a central resistance in our adult male patients, has its inception at this very early period of life. If, however, the mother is too intrusive and consistently interferes directly or indirectly with the boy's phallic strivings, the ambitendent struggle described in the case of girls may ensue in the boy as well and may even give way to passive surrender. (P. 215)

In a sense, the dependent male patient who wants emotional merger with the therapist may be more seriously damaged. These fears and wishes of the third subphase of separation-individuation (hatching, practicing, rapprochement, and object constancy) continue as the individual further differentiates self boundaries. In consequence, fusion or reengulfment remains a threat, which the child must continually fend off well beyond the third year. The ultimate outcome of this conflict may not be resolved even through the maturation of the oedipal and postoedipal phases and can eventuate in a "rapprochement crisis." This is best characterized by "ambitendency," the alternating urge both to push mother away and to cling to her. Indeed, the crisis may make its unresolved appearance far into adulthood.

When this phenomenon resurfaces in treatment, as Roy Schafer (1983) has observed, often such patients fear the empathetic therapist and so attack (or retreat from) what they really long for. When this is examined as a form of resistance to impending intimacy, it may initially appear that the patient is frightened of his or her erotic fantasies. However, if the clinician looks behind these sexual fears to an earlier preoedipal source, that is, to the conflict of symbiotic union with versus separation-individuation from mother, such fears of dependency and engulfment can be traced to a former subphase: rapprochement.

In fact, observations of the rapprochement subphase in infant development strikingly reveal two contrasting behaviors: "shadowing" (staying close behind the mother/object) and "darting away." In Mahler, Pine, and Bergman's words, these antithetical activities of the child

> indicate both his wish for reunion with the object and his fear of reengulfment by it. One can continually observe in the toddler a "warding-off" pattern directed against impingement upon his re-

cently achieved autonomy. . . . At the very height of mastery, toward the end of the practice period, it has already begun to dawn on the junior toddler that the world is *not* his oyster, that he must cope with it more or less on his own. (P. 78)

Case Illustration

PATIENT: *(Walks in, silent and somber)* Well? I told you all about myself. There isn't any more to say.

THERAPIST: Hmm. [The therapist wonders why the patient has pulled back; he had been relatively talkative and self-revealing.]

PATIENT: I guess that is it. I thought about calling and canceling. Then I thought that it isn't polite; I'll come and tell you in person and we don't have to spend the whole hour. Incidentally, the money doesn't matter. It's that there's not much to say. I said enough.

THERAPIST: Perhaps you felt you said *too* much? [The therapist hopes to explore whether the patient feels he has gotten too close.]

PATIENT: I certainly did talk more about myself here in a few hours than I had done all my life. Well, after I left I said, "What is this all about? Why am I talking my head off?" I felt like I was sucked into a situation that I did not intend to be in. You know what I mean?

THERAPIST: Sucked in?

PATIENT: Yeah, like where would this lead to? I was enjoying it while I was talking, but then what? What was it going to lead to?

THERAPIST: Being sucked into something that was not clear. Where would it take you . . . maybe to some dangerous places? [In patients with a central resistance to getting involved, the therapist may need to introduce words that can resonate with the patient's preconscious sensations.]

PATIENT: I am not sure what kind of danger, but this is quite unusual for me to talk about my innermost thoughts and fantasies to anyone.

THERAPIST: You have not talked much about your fantasies.

PATIENT: I knew you'd pick that. It just came out, nothing special. I have no kinky fantasies or anything like that . . .

THERAPIST: Or nonkinky fantasies?

PATIENT: Not really kinky fantasies. . . . But my wife thinks that I am a little too enthusiastic when it comes to oral sex. It's because with the normal way I lose my erection. I don't know, maybe sometimes she gets too dilated, too wet. I can't believe I am still talking *and* I am talking about things like that. I came here just to let you know that I am no longer coming here and you've got me jabbering away again.

THERAPIST: Sucked you in again. [The therapist pursues the fear of engulfment.]

PATIENT: What is the point of my telling you all these things? Now that you know my sexual habits, then what? Are you going to send me to a sex therapist now?

THERAPIST: You would even be willing to go to a sex therapist, just to get out of here. [The therapist could have said, "just to get out of the relationship with me, before you get completely sucked in."]

PATIENT: *(Laughs)* No, I don't believe in that sex therapist kind of stuff. Everyone has their own peculiarity. With me, the vagina is a little strange. I think I have always been a little scared of vaginas; well, not scared, a little hesitant. Look, you've got me saying things that are not even true. Just what excites someone, it just doesn't excite someone else. So, here we are again.

THERAPIST: Here we are again, getting a little close and then getting a little hesitant or scared. [The therapist moves away from the vaginal engulfment issue. The subject must wait until the patient relatively resolves his fears of engulfment with the therapist.]

PATIENT: Am I really scared of getting lost in here? I don't know. I just don't see the point. But why get close? Why even bother to?

THERAPIST: It may not be permanent!

PATIENT: Well, either way . . . it is a little confusing. Do I fear being sucked in, or are you saying that if I am, then I want to make sure that you don't desert me? . . . I can't believe that I have these complicated feelings in me; I thought I was just a simple guy, you know, an ordinary fellow, no fancy psychological stuff.

CHAPTER 21

The therapist's failure to facilitate transference may reflect excessive activity; failure to establish an empathic bond reflects insufficient feeling for the patient

THE CLINICIAN as well as the patient consciously (and unconsciously) responds to the "strange phenomenon" of transference (Freud 1910), in which the patient unwittingly relates to the therapist as he or she once related to significant figures from childhood. Thus the transference inherently carries with it reaction patterns and dispositions, often ambivalent, established and altered during oral, anal, oedipal, and latency stages as well as from adolescence throughout the years of growing up. Although the distortion and idealization that characterize the transference relationship need not be induced, they may be encouraged or discouraged by the therapist's technical behavior—especially the extent to which the therapist is removed and anonymous or direct and interactive.

In addition to sexual (primarily positive) and aggressive (largely negative) transferential dispositions, but in contrast to them, is the potential for an empathic bond. The empathic bond originates in the earliest phases of infancy and remains more or less unaltered through successive developmental stages. The capacity to form such a bond can be considered a fundamental human quality; according to Kohut (1977), "The empathic understanding of the experiences of other human beings is as basic an endowment of man as his vision, hearing, touch, taste, and smell" (p. 144). The empathic bond is manifested as a special interpersonal phenomenon with relatively clear boundaries and a unique nature; it is as universal as transference, but more rational, homogeneous, and simple. Every individual has presumably experienced that bond (however briefly) as an infant and recognizes it immediately when it occurs again. The feelings associated with it are unequivocal (in contrast to the ambivalence of transference): they are always unconditional, positive, and secure.

With the patient in treatment, the therapist may choose to facilitate and use these two forms of relating to greater or lesser degrees: he or she can aspire to maintain a strictly transferential attitude and deal with the inevitable obstacles it brings, or he or she may try only to re-create an empathic bond with the patient and watch it slowly develop. Of course, the therapist may also foster transference and empathy simultaneously or intermittently; they are not mutually exclusive.

Empathy carries two messages: (1) I feel what you feel and (2) you are accepted in feeling how you feel. During the course of psychotherapy, the therapist must continually decide when an empathic response should take precedence over attention to the transferential content, and when the latter must be given priority (at least explicitly). Most of the time transference and empathy coexist and are intertwined. In fact, the need for an empathic bond may be the earliest form of transference; it may represent a predisposition to the most rudimentary relationship. There is an important distinction: the therapist becomes the target of transference by being relatively passive, whereas the establishment of an empathic bond requires "active getting close" on the part of the therapist. The therapist's role is largely a replay of an infant's very early experience. During infancy, the child is in a completely receptive mode; the mother is the one who makes all the efforts to relate, connect, care, and love.

An "empathic failure" (Kohut 1977) occurs when the significant selfobject—parent or therapist—does not respond in the affective way that the recipient may wish or need. Kohut believes that both resistance and negative transference reactions can reflect empathic failures experienced by the patient. Resistance is thought to be the result of the therapist's current actions (that is, lack of attunement with the patient); negative transference reactions are revivals of reactions to failures of empathy from selfobjects in early development (that is, parents' lack of attunement with the child).

The therapist, via an active, expressed emotional presence, engages the patient in an empathic bonding. Although the patient immediately brings to treatment a transferential disposition to be played out, the need for empathy is not displayed until the patient feels secure of its being met. The therapist's repeated empathic sounds and comments are meant to convey reassurance of empathy. Once the patient *feels* the empathy of the therapist, he or she will allow a bond to form with the therapist.

The therapist may need reassurance as well. Havens (1986) has suggested that there are three types of empathy and self-tests for each: cognitive empathy, which is best measured by the therapist's ability to inwardly complete the patient's sentences; perceptual empathy, which pertains to the therapist's receiving sensorily what is communicated; and affective empathy, whereby the therapist experiences the patient's feeling state, first through observations of the patient's voice, posture, and other autonomic expressions as well as speech content, and, second, through confirmed comparisons with the therapist's own feelings.

The two types of attachment—transference and empathic bonding—are significantly influenced by what the therapist respectively does or feels. Insofar as transference distortions are facilitated by the therapist's reflective stance, the failure of establishment of transference may be a consequence of excessive activity on the part of the therapist; by contrast, a failure to establish an empathic bond is not a matter of activity but of emotional contact or connection—a reflection of insufficient feelings for the patient.

Case Illustration

A thirty-four-year-old man was in individual treatment for over ten months following a suicide attempt and hospitalization (a diagnosis of schizo-affective disorder was made). At that time he had swallowed more than thirty acetominophen pills and an unknown number of fifty-milligram Mellarils after being fired from his job. Although he had been functioning rather well until recently, he had just voluntarily quit the new job because his alcoholic wife had left him. Another therapist, who was treating the couple, had anticipated that something like this would happen and informed the husband's therapist.

The patient had cried most of the time during the session; he was agitated and despondent, but reasonably talkative. There were tears pouring from his eyes which he did not even bother to wipe. He looked like an abandoned child, lost and desperate. The ache was so vivid that the therapist could feel it. The patient was silent, just crying.

THERAPIST: How deeply painful! [The therapist's simple emotional expression is stated as a short, exclamatory phrase in a mood-congruent voice.]

PATIENT: She just left me as a worthless thing, not even a note. She wrote my mother that she had to find herself elsewhere. What about us . . . how selfish can you get? She turned out to be a man after all.

THERAPIST: No woman could be so cruel.

The therapist has inadvertently joined the patient in his defense of splitting (good woman/bad man). This is a regressive empathy, an introjection, a primitive mode of identification with the patient. The therapist also rewords the wife's behavior, calling it cruel, rather than selfish. Whereas the patient's wording is descriptive and subjective (as he experiences his wife), the therapist's naming is attributive and subjective (as the therapist experiences her—that she is cruel to *him*). The therapist empathically assists the patient to say how he experiences her, actually feeling the patient's anger toward this "cruel woman." This is not simply cognitive empathy, which completes the patient's sentence, it is an empathy that emotionally translates it. Kohut (1977) has defined empathy in the therapeutic situation as "vicarious introspection" (p. 306).

PATIENT: Deeply cruel; she doesn't even care about leaving all three kids.

THERAPIST: All *four* kids! [Although ostensibly empathic, this is in fact an aggressive statement, a put down, too sarcastic to be received as empathy. The therapist retrospectively wonders why he was vulnerable to such an empathic failure. Was it the fact that he got too close to the patient's experience, as evidenced in his previous remark, and needed to pull away?]

PATIENT: *(Stops crying, looks sheepish, a little smile in the corner of his mouth)* It is very cruel for you to say that. Does it look like I lost my mother? I still have my mother. I took the kids to her. She is a little old, so it is hard for her to take care of us. Furthermore, she has no sympathy for what I am going through; she thinks that I should go to work, period.

As Kohut (1977) has pointed out, failures of empathy are unavoidable—indeed, they are necessary if the patient is ultimately to form a firm and independent self. Therefore, in psychotherapy there need be no connotation of guilt or blame if the therapist acknowledges the limita-

127

tions of his or her empathy; at the same time, it is just as important to make clear that the patient is not to blame either. Some theorists assume that excessive empathy on the part of mother or therapist can be harmful, that as a result of the gratification of drives the ego remains immature and does not sufficiently develop drive control, modulation, or sublimation. But Kohut (1977) instead insists: "I do not believe that many cases of harmful maternal spoiling through overempathy and an excess of 'mothering' do in fact exist" (p. 78).

THERAPIST: She does not fully understand how devastated you are! [The therapist hears the fully justified reference to himself but stores it for the moment. He wants to reestablish the empathic bond first by again feeling the patient's experience, and—perhaps critical here—attending to his own oscillations between empathy and the failure of it.]

PATIENT: No, she says, just go to work and don't think about women. When you have money, they'll come to you.

THERAPIST: Hmm.

PATIENT: My mother never liked my wife and was very competitive with her. I think she is sort of glad to see my wife gone and to show me also that she was right about my wife being no good. Now my mother says that my wife fooled around with other guys.

THERAPIST: How cruel! [Knowing that the word *cruel* was an empathic link in their previous exchanges, the therapist is going back to the same adjective.]

PATIENT: It's like turning the knife.

THERAPIST: You are surrounded by a group of men. [The word *group* is intended to include the mother.]

PATIENT: I thought about trying to find my wife. Then I said, what if she is with another guy? Then I thought I'd kill her, my mother, and you.

THERAPIST: All these unsympathetic people!

PATIENT: And what do I do with the kids? They are young and demanding. I can't take care of them.

THERAPIST: Physically and emotionally it must be exhausting. [The therapist makes this supportive statement as he senses that the patient must also be feeling guilty for not meeting his children's needs, feeling that he is, himself, another uncaring, cruel man.]

PATIENT: I can't kill *them*. They are innocent. I love them. They are no part of this. They are just innocent bystanders. But my mother is certainly part of it, and you are certainly part of it. Not just because you are so cruel! First of all, you're right. My mother also says I am like a baby.

THERAPIST: So you're not just another cruel man, but a helpless one, who needs to be taken care of himself, who is stuck with all these needy kids. [Here the therapist, although not sure of the accuracy of his empathic attunement, tries to help the patient not identify with being cruel.]

PATIENT: Also, here I am stuck with you. I mean, I lose my wife and I get you instead.

THERAPIST: Just as cruel a person. [The therapist knows that the patient is disappointed in an earlier empathic failure, but by emphasizing the negative aspects of the patient's ambivalence, he is hoping to shift the balance toward the positive.]

PATIENT: If I had her, I wouldn't need to be here.

THERAPIST: Not only don't you have her, you also found yourself in a position of needing to be with me, someone who doesn't sympathize enough with you. [The therapist continues focusing on the possible negative feeling of the patient toward himself, as the patient is manifesting no signs of trusting feelings.]

PATIENT: A double whammy. *(Eyes swell)* I don't care whether you think it is babyish or not. I can't help it. I want her and I need her. I don't want to live.

THERAPIST: *(Looks at the patient, in pain, hurting)*

PATIENT: *(Sobbing)* Didn't she love me at all? Didn't she care about me at all? [The patient's affective discharge, his showing more vulnerability to the therapist, implies that the empathic failure has been reasonably repaired and that the work can continue.]

Repeated and unrepaired failures of empathy by the therapist interfere with the development of empathic bonding with the patient. These failures generate enormous rage in the patient and are affective manifestations of the earliest forms of negative transference. However, interpretation of these negative feelings as being transferential—for example, "I wonder whether the rage that you experience toward me is meant for your father" (or your wife, or mother)—would only escalate the negativity. In fact, making such an interpretation, independent of its truth, is another empathic failure.

While the failure to establish transference can be remedied by procedurally and technically decreasing the direction and self-disclosure of the therapist, the failure to establish an empathic bond can be remedied only by genuinely feeling for and with the patient.

PART VI

ON VERBAL
COMMUNICATION AND ITS
DIFFICULTIES

Psychotherapy communication and ordinary conversation are decidedly different in many ways; in fact, one begins where the other leaves off. This section deals with this special communication as a unique form of intimacy ("communicative intimacy"), its therapeutic boundaries and limits as well as its cumulative and creative capacities.

The patient's highly personal and historical information is imperfectly transmitted from patient to therapist; communication is filtered twice by successive screens—through the protective layers of the psyche and across the lens of time. Yet subjective and idiosyncratic experiences, distorted by memory and individual dynamics, eventually become mutually understood and consensual. This raises the crucial matter, in Spence's (1982) terms, of the establishment of narrative truth (created in the present) versus historical truth (occurred in the past), which involves a complex dialectic between presumed facts and ex post facto reconstructions intertwined by the joint search for meaning.

In another critical phenomenon, language is the exchange not simply of words (and silences), but of messages. Insofar as therapeutic communication necessarily becomes a form of linguistic translation, the therapist's verbalizations (interpretations, explanations, and the like) will resonate most if expressed in the patient's language. As the careful clinician endeavors to know and understand the patient's reality, and translate and transform it through the medium of shared speech, he or she must in effect be bilingual.

The question remains, What does the therapist ultimately convey? This section ends on an ironic note: although the crux of dynamic psychotherapy prototypically lies in the reservoir of repressed and conflictual material that must be wrested from the patient's memory, less attention is often given to what the patient does manage to remember. Thus the therapist must speak cautiously—one cannot predict what the patient will never forget!

This section therefore poses the following questions: In what ways does therapeutic communication between therapist and patient differ from ordinary conversation? What are its natural linguistic and emotional barriers to mutual understanding? Can the scrupulous clinician locate the truth of the patient's statements? More specifically, how are historical and narrative data distinguished in the quest to understand the meaning of the patient's verbalizations? What qualities or techniques are recommended for the therapist to communicate most effectively?

CHAPTER 22

Psychotherapy communication can begin only where ordinary conversation leaves off

ALTHOUGH IT OCCURS between two people and is dialectical and communicative, the verbal interchange in psychotherapy bears little resemblance to everyday conversation. Despite some conversational small talk at the beginning of the session, such as "Good morning," "How are you?" and the like, social exchanges are usually circumscribed as a preface to the session proper, and some clinicians consider any such verbal exchange a contamination of the therapeutic process.

At the end of a conversational interaction, another communicative process ensues. The transition is expected not only by the therapist but by the patient, contrary to the belief that the patient would prefer to chat with the therapist as if they were casual friends. If and when ordinary conversation occurs, especially for the first time, it may understandably intrigue and please the patient. But any prolonged or repeated attempts to return to this informal pattern should raise questions in both the therapist's and the patient's mind. Invariably it represents a need or wish—by either party—to divert temporarily or even to escape totally from the therapeutic task.

To monitor the verbal interchange the therapist must recognize that ordinary conversation has certain unspoken rules which markedly differ from the communicational rules of psychotherapy. Tarachow (1963) has gone as far as to suggest that "an ordinary conversation between two people does not at all facilitate contact between the two. In fact, conversation generally sharpens ego boundaries and the two individuals are separated more at the end of a conversation than they were at the beginning" (p. 16). By contrast, psychotherapy is intended to generate in-depth intimacy in communication. These distinctions have both linguistic and interpersonal significance.

Conversation generally has the following features, as contrasted with psychotherapy communication.

1. *Conversation is relatively variable in style but restricted in content.* The spontaneity of both parties gives conversation its vitality and variability. Who speaks, how much, and about what is relatively open ended and highly flexible, even though the broad nature of the content may be restricted to some extent by what is socially acceptable. Although either party may have a hidden agenda, one would be hard put to plan a conversation.

In psychotherapy, the patient has a specific agenda or problem to discuss. It is reasonably premeditated or planned, although aspects of the agenda may change. The therapist's contribution to the interaction is systematic and purposeful. Seemingly spontaneous in terms of the immediate interaction, and individually creative in relation to specific patient responses, it is in fact highly structured with regard to content as well as timing. Freud (1913), who compared the therapeutic process to a game of chess whereby "only the opening and closing moves of the game admit of exhaustive systematic description," suggested that the technical structure and uniform rules are especially evident in the initial and final stages of therapy.

2. *Conversation is a two-way street.* In conversation, both parties may talk about some subject, about themselves or each other, and at opportune moments may respectively speak or respond, occasionally interrupting one another or perhaps talking simultaneously. The relatively equal distribution of talking time generally characterizes conversation and in most instances generates good mutual feelings between conversants. The irregular or uneven contribution of speech or silence is a natural consequence of the failure of conversation.

In psychotherapy, the verbal exchange is intended for a special use and is thus a one-way street, whereby the narrative flow primarily emanates from the patient and the therapist's presence is primarily justified by listening. In Spence's (1982) words, the patient's verbalization is "ad lib" (p. 104), whereas the psychotherapist speaks not according to social convention, but intermittently, as he or she chooses. Relative silences are deliberate, such silence being part of the professional role of "evenly suspended attention" (Freud 1912b) in which the therapist is intentionally nonintrusive. The therapist does not interrupt without a therapeutic reason and restrains from revealing a personal competing agenda or sharing personal problems. The therapist is highly circumspect about speaking and hopes that the patient is equally free. One might even go as far as to say that in psychotherapy the therapist speaks primarily when he or she prefers to and the patient when he or she doesn't prefer to.

3. *In conversation one does not excessively burden the other.* In ordinary conversation, the conversant tends to observe how much the other person can take and to not reveal too much. These limits on burdening are determined by the responses of the listener. Losing interest, changing the subject, or even canceling a future date may indicate that the listener has had too much. These expressions are meant to discourage additional demands.

In psychotherapy the patient is not only allowed, but actually encouraged, to burden the therapist by unloading his or her problems. The therapist does not run away or cut short the demanding person or difficult subject matter. In fact, the therapist's attitude selectively and purposefully asks for expansion of the troublesome topics and personal concerns.

4. *In conversation, persons tend to show the better side of themselves.* In ordinary conversation, the individual tries not to expose his or her vulnerabilities and generally presents only good or acceptable qualities. Whatever self-revelations a person makes are usually relatively safe or given within the context of self-protection. (One always needs to maintain a certain degree of respectability.) For example, the use of humor as a form of self-mockery both reveals something and fends off the full impact of the revelation. Even among best friends, some subjects are kept undiscussed in order to preserve the established equilibrium of the relationship.

In psychotherapy, although the individual still tries to defend against the exposure of vulnerabilities, he or she may be asked to reveal those very "bad" and unacceptable qualities that are most shameful or feared. On the therapist's part, trust and unconditional acceptance set the stage for the person to expose his or her particular vulnerabilities. It is the very nature of psychotherapy that no self-disclosure should threaten the relationship or lead to loss of the therapist's positive regard for the patient.

5. *For conversation to be understandable, it must be embedded in common sense.* By and large, in normal conversation we share the "conversational

postulate" (Grice 1967), which rests on an assumption that the reply of the recipient is directly relevant to what was just said. In conversation, the sequence of responses, and even the questions asked about unclear content, can be fairly well anticipated. Ordinary exchanges are rarely surprising or throw the person spoken to off balance. There is an overall rational order, a logical syntax, connecting thoughts and subsequent responses, naturally designed for relatively easy comprehension of the words spoken to one another. As Victor Rosen (1967) has suggested:

> During most conversations, people assume that the referents of the words, phrases, or metaphors employed are understood in common. The listener either implicitly or explicitly provides the missing links in the verbalized ideas of the speaker. Both speaker and listener often assume that the background information necessary for correctly identifying the subject, object, or predicate of a statement is mutually available. (P. 471)

In addition, although there are different levels of communication, there is usually a relatively recognizable relationship between what is said and what is meant.

In psychotherapy neither responses nor questions are as easily anticipated. As Spence (1982) points out, despite the need to be responsive to the other person in the dialogue and thus adhere to conventional rules of making sense, "The patient's talk must differ . . . from an ordinary conversation—namely, in its freedom to wander" (p. 84). This kind of verbalization in psychotherapy takes its precedent from Freud's (1913) "fundamental rule," which directly instructed the patient as follows:

> Your talk with me must differ in one respect from an ordinary conversation. Whereas usually you try to keep the threads of your story together and to exclude all intruding associations and side-issues, so as not to wander too far from the point, here you must proceed differently. . . . Say whatever goes through your mind. . . . Finally, never forget that you have promised absolute honesty, and never have anything unsaid because for any reason it is unpleasant to say it. (P. 147)

Strange or illogical trains of thought may be elicited, or highly selective ideas or events focused on. Much of the actual interchange may bear little resemblance to ordinary discourse and show no apparent rhyme or reason. In fact, the therapist may encourage those very ideas and subjects that are most difficult to communicate or understand.

It has thus been suggested that Freud's fundamental rule is composed of two contradictory instructions. On the one hand, if the patient shares his or her thoughts and feelings in normal conversation, introspection is lost; on the other hand, if the patient is accurate in conveying his or her ideas via introspection, conversation is lost. That is, if the patient's ideas and associations are really free, he or she will be incomprehensible; and if the patient is easily understood, it can be assumed that some censorship or rearrangement of the original thoughts has taken place. Such discrepancies have led Chessick (1981) to say that "psychotherapy begins where common sense ends" (p. 495).

The qualities of conversation and psychotherapeutic communication discussed here may not represent all typical conversations and all psychotherapeutic communications. Their verbal boundaries can overlap, especially as patient and therapist continue to test the psychological boundaries of their relationship. Certainly the need to receive informal therapeutic help from friends frequently alters the nature of one's exchange with them; comparably, the wish for personal human contact can shape the quality of therapeutic communication toward less traditional paradigms of psychotherapy technique.

CHAPTER 23

Only the unconscious can reach the unconscious

BOTH PATIENT AND THERAPIST begin therapy with a separate reality and a separate language in which to describe it. Nearly everyone who comes to treatment is entrenched in his or her own overdetermined and private universe and moves out of it only gradually. The patient who is in psychological turmoil may be especially susceptible to defensive or characterological entrapment in a protective inner world. In psychotherapy, when it is successful, such subjective and idiosyncratic realities are transformed into a new reality that is intersubjective and consensual. This transformation is accomplished via a form of therapeutic translation that evolves from the mutual language of shared experience. It has less to do with the therapist's and patient's conscious lives and experiential realities than with their shared unconscious life.

To reach the private and subjective world of the patient, the therapist must temporarily and simultaneously regress with the patient to empathize with the patient's psychological state. For the therapist the regression is short-lived, voluntary, and reversible; it is not a manifestation of cognitive or emotional turmoil, unless the therapist is fragile and vulnerable. Rather, the therapist's temporary regression is a monitored one, purposeful and actively generated (therefore capable of being retrenched as necessary); it is meant to establish the base for a state of intersubjectivity with the patient.

Empathy allows the therapist to be tuned into the patient's world. Only by being there can the therapist forge a new psychic reality together with the patient. In psychotherapy, the therapist must learn to get in touch with his or her own unconscious material as evoked by the patient's productions; conversely, the therapist uses his or her own unconscious material to elicit further information from the patient's unconscious. The therapist reprocesses material with two purposes in mind: to help the patient translate it into conscious communication and to make it relevant to the present situation without excessive contamination by the therapist's own idiosyncratic and private subjective world. One learns to shift from one's own private reality and language to the living language of the patient. More specifically, this may mean learning not just a new linguistic vocabulary but an experiential one as well.

As Spence (1982) has put it: "What the patient is trying to describe is being constantly reinterpreted and fleshed out with the [therapist's] memories" (p. 102). By contrast, it is suggested that if the subjective difference between the worlds of the therapist and of the patient becomes so extreme that communication breaks down, then the reality offered by the patient will not be registered (most likely due to the therapist's preoccupation with his or her own conflicts).

However, if the clinician remains sufficiently attentive to the patient, it will be possible to bring about a more consensual reality. The therapist, in effect, must be accepting of the patient's subjective reality, no matter how distorted it may seem, and must not quickly substitute his or her own reality for the patient's. Putting aside the question of whose reality is more valid, challenging the patient's beliefs inevitably leads to self-justifying confrontations, not to a psychotherapeutic encounter. Only after being an empathic participant in the patient's inner world will the therapist be able gradually to formulate a new reality that is intersubjective and consensual. The process is equivalent to learning a new language with the help of one's native tongue.

Case Illustration

A forty-four-year-old diamond cutter had been complaining about rectal pain for two years. He had gone to internists and proctologists and was found to be in good physical health. He was diagnosed as suffering from rectal spasms and given some symptom-relieving medications (such as lubricants, antispasmodics, and Valium), which proved of little help.

Although he was not very psychologically oriented, the patient immediately described his father as being a "pain in the ass." The patient's father had owned a diamond business and took his son in when he graduated from high school, then trained him to be a cutter. As an adult he was still being treated as a child—an incompetent one. The patient felt that he was not as skillful as his father, and he was dependent on his father for the survival of the business.

The patient had been married for eight years to an "inadequate" woman, a marriage arranged by his father. Until his marriage he had lived with his parents and rarely dated, and his few sexual contacts were with prostitutes. The marriage was not consummated for a year and a half, during which time the couple lived with his parents. It was only after they got their own house that they had intercourse, but this was infrequent because he had difficulty maintaining an erection. When he shared this information with a cousin who was a graduate student in psychology, he was told that he may be a "latent homosexual." The patient dismissed this explanation, however, because he knew that he had no sexual interest in men. Eventually the patient's wife became pregnant and gave birth to a son. This five-year-old, who suffered from encopresis, was their only child to date.

The patient's assessment was that he had an unknown, painful disease in his rectum; it would be diagnosed eventually, but by then it would be too late. When the therapist pointed out the "pain-in-the-ass" metaphor in regard to the patient's father, he accepted it as "OK" but followed this interpretation by saying that it did not really help. During the course of treatment he toyed with the therapist's suggestion that he might be squeezing his own rectal sphincter to stop his son's incontinence. He thought about the idea and concurred that there might be something to it; clearly he looked intrigued.

The patient did not appear comfortable with introspectiveness. He was verbally, intellectually, and educationally limited. He usually sat politely waiting for the therapist's questions, to which he would respond briefly. His thinking was pragmatic; he did not remember his dreams; he couldn't free associate; and he apparently did not have a fantasy life. The therapist does best to ask such patients to describe their daily life in detail, no matter how insignificant it appears to be, and to allow himself or herself to have visual images or fantasies until promising trails of thought can be pursued.

PATIENT: You are going to be bored with this. Are you sure you want this in detail? Well, I get up, brush my teeth, shave, take a shower; oh, I forgot, Joe [the son] is usually in our bed; he gets up in the middle of the night and comes to our bed. No matter how many times I take him back, he comes again. My wife says, "Let him be," but that cousin of mine who I spoke with thinks this is not healthy. Anyway, I think that at this point we have lost the battle. The reason I got back to Joe is that he gets up first and wakes me up because he soils himself. I change him, clean him up; then I take care of myself.

The therapist wonders about the patient washing his son, visualizes the scene, including the patient's finger around the child's anus. The therapist tries to regress to his own childhood, but has no comparable memories. He cannot recall his own buttocks being washed; it certainly wasn't his father who washed him. And where is the mother in all this? The therapist recovers from the regression and wonders whether a combination of excitement and prohibition are causing the patient's rectal spasm. He asks himself if he should raise the question to the patient but decides not to. If such queries are made too early, the patient may get offended and defensive at the implicit accusation.

THERAPIST: Washing Joe has been your job all five years? [The therapist is sympathetically seeking more information toward formulating a tentative hypothesis.]

PATIENT: Only in the mornings; my wife does it the rest of the time. She likes sleeping late; she's not all that strong. She's a little immature herself. She was overwhelmed when Joe was an infant. I helped her a lot.

THERAPIST: You finish washing Joe? [The therapist does not want to delve into the patient's relation with the wife yet, which he thinks may be an unnecessary detour; he'd rather stay with the potentially regressive material.]

PATIENT: You really want to do this now? All right, I eat my cereal and get in my car, get to the shop. I am usually the first to arrive. We have an elaborate security system that has to be undone. Do you want to know the code? I open the safe and take out the trays of uncut diamonds.

The therapist dismisses the patient's sarcasm for now; it is not a strong enough defense to warrant an interruption. Instead, the therapist will wait for a possible repetition in the future. Meanwhile the therapist visualizes lots of shining gems in a tray in front of him, and again regresses: he remembers that he had, as a child, a trayful of marbles. He used to put one of them in his mouth, learned the trick of making it look as if he had swallowed it, but really had hid it under his tongue. Others used to get alarmed by that.

THERAPIST: What do you do with them?
PATIENT: I look at their colors and shapes, grade them, calculate how to cut them, the best possible size—you know, I have to decide.
THERAPIST: You look at the stones, examine them, their shine . . . [The visual aspect of the experience is emphasized rather than the linguistic one, since many unconscious experiences are coded visually. The therapist will stay with the sensory domain as long as possible in order to capture the texture of the patient's memories.]
PATIENT: Oh, yes. At times I sit and stare at them for hours. They are fascinating; the more you look at them, the more you see.
THERAPIST: Do you ever put them in your mouth? [The therapist, based on his own past experience with marbles—his own unconscious material—is taking a chance. Although it is seemingly a straight-forward question, confrontation of the patient's unconscious material is implicit. Using his own unconscious to seek material from a pa-tient's unconscious is also an effective way of unfreezing highly defended patients.]
PATIENT: (Visibly upset) Are you crazy? They are worth thousands of dollars. You could swallow them by mistake and they may never come out. (The patient continues to stare at the therapist, highly anxious, obviously troubled)
THERAPIST: [The therapist is thinking of them never coming out and regresses: he tries to remember whether he ever swallowed marbles, but could only remember his mother's warning and concern. He wonders why the patient has gotten so anxious about the question.]
PATIENT: Smugglers of diamonds in the past used to swallow them in one country, then come here and if they did not pass them in a few days they'd have to have surgery. People have been doing other things for a long time now.
THERAPIST: Other things? [The therapist's successful association depends on his own information bank. As the associations diminish the thera-pist must search for more data.]
PATIENT: Why? You want to know all the secrets of the trade? People put diamonds into their cavities—vagina, rectum . . . this is getting tougher. [The therapist wonders how to ask the question of whether he does or did smuggle diamonds by putting them into his rectum. Would that explain his anxiety-loaded reaction to the earlier ques-

tion? The therapist realizes that this is a sensitive subject. There is also a legal issue to be considered.]

THERAPIST: This is getting tougher? [The therapist isn't sure whether the patient is referring to the sessions or the smuggling. He puts that sentence in question form. It is less interruptive than asking the patient what he is referring to. The patient, in fact, may have an entirely different idea. The therapist also does not say, "I don't understand," which tends to generate accused feelings, that is, that the patient is not making sense.]

PATIENT: Well, because of the drug smugglers. Customs officers tend to check the cavities because of them, if there is a suspicion—people don't want to take a chance with that.

THERAPIST: Has that interfered with your business? [There is no easy way of asking: How do you smuggle diamonds now?]

PATIENT: No. We no longer do that; it was a long time ago. I hardly remember coming from Belgium, when my father used to put diamonds in my and my brother's rectums and probably in his, too, I think. Anyway, that was a long time ago; then it was a routine thing to do.

THERAPIST: What was it like for you to carry the diamonds in your rectum? [The therapist is a little surprised with the casualness by which the patient provided this important material. Is this like calling his father a "pain in the ass" in the first session?]

PATIENT: We both hated it. It was very uncomfortable. They were packed, so I wasn't hurting or anything like that, but you had the sensation that you wanted to go to the bathroom. And we were not allowed to go to the bathroom for "number 2," so my father used to accompany us to the bathroom for peeing on the plane, to make sure. Then we'd get home finally and he would remove them. Messy stuff. I get upset as I think about it.

THERAPIST: It was not just a physically painful experience. [The therapist visualizes the scene, even experiences involuntary squeezing of his own anus.]

PATIENT: The physical pain was the least painful part of it, the embarrassment, shitting on his finger; he did not use gloves or anything. I guess he had to do it . . .

THERAPIST: *(After ninety seconds of silence)* These are difficult memories. It must be especially difficult for you to speak ill of your father.

The therapist wonders why he himself used the term "speaking ill," a saying commonly reserved for dead people. Death wishes against his

143

own father? fathers at large? or has he tuned to the patient's rage against his father? But the therapist needs to address the struggle that the patient is experiencing, rather than encouraging him to express more feelings about the subject or to direct them against his father. This is particularly true if the patient has a story of violation to tell, or when it comes to talking about one's parents.

Besides the obvious guilt-provoking aspect of expressing of aggression and hostility toward one's parent, the patient also is in danger of losing a self-identifying object. During the earlier stages of treatment when the relation between therapist and patient is not yet well established, any encouragement of exorcizing of the patient's "bad parents" by allowing the patient to attack them generates a negative reaction to psychotherapy. As Guntrip (1969) has pointed out: "The major source of resistance to psychotherapy is the extreme tenacity of our libidinal attachments to parents whatever they are like" (p. 344). In fact, the worse the parents are, the stronger the attachment, so that the patient fears that the therapist will rob him of his parents. The patient may fear losing even these malevolent introjects without being sure that the therapist will provide an alternative. Even after the patient is convinced of the therapist's capacity to care and that he could be a better parent, the therapist in such a role may generate a sense of disloyalty, thus the retreat from further regressive memories.

PATIENT: What kind of man was he? I know that he wasn't the only one doing that, but why would a father do this to his own sons? My brother is so disturbed by those memories that he does not even talk to my father. He moved out of state; he is a lawyer. He got out of the business and family altogether.
THERAPIST: You couldn't . . . and his finger is still in your ass.

Of course, this is a crucial point in terms of the patient's presenting conflict, as the therapist offers an inexact interpretation. One of the purposes of making such an interpretation, as Glover (1955) suggests, is to allow the partial discharge of drives to occur, thus weakening them and making the work of defense against what remains easier. The inexact interpretation can also be used to test the waters, to see whether the patient will cling, reject, or skeptically and tentatively receive it, so that the therapist can then determine the course of his intervention. The colorful metaphor "his finger is still in your ass" is in synchrony with the content and the language of the session. Its pictorial nature is intended because this patient seems more visual than verbal. The therapist is also sending the message, "I can speak your language."

PATIENT: That is funny coming from you, Doc. You look so proper, but I like it. You are right, and it is all my fault. I did not go to college, and I wasn't strong enough to go do something else, so I checked in with him. I let him run my life.

THERAPIST: You even let him get you a wife. [The therapist feels accepted now and intersubjectively attuned to the patient, thus widening the scope of the interpretation.]

PATIENT: Would you believe it? The other day while we were fighting over a minor thing, I became completely wild. He threatened me that he would just throw me out of the business and have me divorce my wife and give the kid up for adoption!

THERAPIST: He is really pushing his fingers in. [The therapist is capitalizing on the metaphor, to see how much the patient can receive without becoming defensive.]

PATIENT: Up to his elbows. (The patient appears to be in synchrony, ready for more exploration.)

THERAPIST: What would cause him to say such outrageous things? [The therapist asks for more information, and at the same time he uses this opportunity to strengthen their alliance by calling the father's behavior—but not the father—outrageous.]

PATIENT: He wants my son to come to the shop after school. He thinks that is how people really learn the craft. I feel he is too young and should be allowed to play after school. What if he does not want to learn the craft? This is an old European attitude—must a son go into his father's business? Look at me, am I not happy?

THERAPIST: You started at the same age Joe is now? [The therapist, sensing their increased intersubjectivity, can now delve deeper. Is there a parallel in the age at which the conflicts emerged between the patient and his son, and the patient and his father? Is this an age-related reactivation of conflict?]

PATIENT: Yes, more or less. I was the donkey (as they call it now), a passive but not-so-innocent carrier.

THERAPIST: A passive donkey whose innocence was somewhat aggressively violated. [The therapist wants to narrow the subject of innocence to sexual areas, by first establishing a semantic congruity ("passive," "donkey," "innocence"), then introducing related words ("aggression," "violation"). The word *somewhat* was added to temper the interpretation, to give the patient a chance to react to the qualifier in order to absorb the strong substance of the words.]

PATIENT: You mean *totally* aggressive behavior on the part of my father! What else should he have done for you not to call it *somewhat*, to fuck me? *(Very agitated, staring silently for about thirty seconds at the therapist)* I could kill him when I think about all of this.

THERAPIST: At the time, as a child, you primarily experienced the discomfort and your anger was related only to that. [Now that the patient's emotions are heightened, the therapist does not want to encourage tyranny against the father and deplete this energy, but hopes to use it to direct the patient to remember earlier sensations that the therapist suspects were not all negative. This is a theory-driven approach which the therapist uses tentatively; he plans to change the therapeutic course if it is invalidated.]

PATIENT: What does a kid know at that age? We were given responsibilities and praised for them. I was very immature for my age. I did not know much about sex, or things like that.

THERAPIST: In that responsible role, praise must have been enjoyable. [The therapist attempts to get agreement on this point first.] But as far as the sexual aspect is concerned, I guess it wasn't the best introduction to the subject. [Can therapist and patient agree on this second point, too?]

PATIENT: Well, I never considered these experiences to be sex. *(Silent for ninety seconds)*

THERAPIST: [The therapist is wondering whether he pushed the patient too hard. Why is the patient silent? Why is he not looking at the therapist? Should the therapist say something about having pushed? He decides to wait, as the patient looks very preoccupied.]

PATIENT: Now I read about things like that, maybe it is all just nonsense, but I can see from my own son that he wants me to wash his buttocks. Now he is a big boy, he should be able to wash himself but he won't do it, no matter what. And he does not want his mother to do it when I am around, and it takes a long time because he throws a tantrum if you stop. For a kid who soils himself, this is ridiculous! Could he be having pleasure? I thought the Oedipus complex was for the mother. Or is he a homosexual? *(Silent for forty seconds)*

THERAPIST: [Now the therapist wonders whether he should deal with the patient's anxiety in regard to his son's behavior, or to use this anxiety as access to information about the patient's own past. He feels that the latter would be more painful for the patient but that the timing

146

is ripe for pursuing this subject.] Do you wonder whether you had similar pleasure when your father put his fingers in and out of your rectum? [The therapist aims to promote memories based on sensation. He is also explicit so as to prevent shame and embarrassment, trying to make it a natural subject for discussion.]

PATIENT: I have no pleasant memories of it, just the anticipation of discomfort. But I remember that my brother and I used to giggle a lot. Maybe that part was fun, I don't know. But I did not have any spasm at that time, if that is what you mean. Now I wonder whether my father was getting some kick out of it.

THERAPIST: Some sexual pleasure. [The therapist is explicit again, so as not to make it a subject to be avoided.]

PATIENT: I guess, sort of perverse. I read a book where there was a third generation of incest between a man and his family. So I guess it happens.

THERAPIST: The grandfather, father, and son? [The therapist, again by being specific, underlines the theme.]

PATIENT: You mean like ours? Well, with us, it seems to remain on a business and chores level.

THERAPIST: Do you experience any pleasure in touching your son's buttocks? [So far this is the toughest moment. It will test the strength of the relationship between the therapist and the patient and will be an indicator as to how and at what pace to proceed.]

PATIENT: No, but I put my finger into his rectum occasionally to see whether he is impacted. The pediatrician thought that that may be a possible cause of his incontinence.

THERAPIST: Are you more concerned about whether he is getting some pleasure out of it? [The therapist backs off one step, as the patient denies any pleasure with his own activities and returns to the subject of his son.]

PATIENT: Yes, because he seems to be wanting more, and not resisting. With me, it was not easy. My father used to say, "Easy, let go, relax, as if you are going to the bathroom, feel relaxed." But Joe is relaxed.

THERAPIST: *Too* relaxed. [The emphasis sharpens the focus of concern.]

PATIENT: Yes, as if he welcomes it.

THERAPIST: You wish he had some resistance to it. [Because the patient denies any pleasure of manipulating his son's rectum, the therapist decides to drop the route of instinctual feelings for the moment. Any further pursuit would only have strengthened the patient's denial. The therapist now follows the line of lesser resistance—the patient's defenses against his wishes.]

PATIENT: Some resistance, some squeezing at least. He behaves as if he has no sphincter.

THERAPIST: And you are attempting to provide one? [The interpretation of defenses does not require a lengthy preparatory process because they relate to relatively preconscious material, in contrast to instinctual wishes which are unconscious.]

PATIENT: Am I attempting to provide one—how? *(The patient silently stares at the therapist, waiting for an answer)*

THERAPIST: [The therapist is equally silent, looking at the patient with a "You can do it" expression.]

PATIENT: You mean I am squeezing my ass, hoping that he'll squeeze his, too? I do that in the movies; you know, when you see a gangster coming behind the good guy, and he is unaware of it. I begin to turn in my seat.

THERAPIST: To help to protect the unaware and the innocent?

PATIENT: My son certainly has no idea of the meaning of all these things, I am sure. He is just a child.

THERAPIST: You are unwittingly placing him in danger as well as unconsciously attempting to provide protection for him. [This is a partial interpretation of wishes and defenses as preparation for a full interpretation.]

PATIENT: I will never abuse him, but the fact that he wants his backside to be washed over and over again may be endangering him for the future by making himself available for abuse from others. Just that idea that someone can abuse him sexually makes me go completely wild.

THERAPIST: You also used that term "completely wild" in describing your fight with your father. [The therapist uses this semantic connection to reintroduce the father, who is needed for the complete interpretation.]

PATIENT: I don't want my father to have anything to do with my son because he messed me up. I am not going to let him mess my son up. Not that he would abuse him, like that. But he is not a good influence on one's self-esteem; he is critical of everything.

THERAPIST: Your son needs protection, not only from you, but from your father, too? From both generations.

PATIENT: I'll tell you, Joe needs no protection from me, but I know he needs it from my father. Not a sexual protection, just the psychological abuse. Only over my dead body will he have him in the shop.

THERAPIST: You are doing your best to protect Joe. You are fighting with your difficult father to keep him away. You are squeezing your sphincter hoping that he'll squeeze his. In either case, you have a formidable task.

PATIENT: Well, if Joe closes his ass, we'll all be better off.

THERAPIST: [The therapist realizes that they have gradually evolved and reached consensual reality.] The messy soiling will end, the habit of anal manipulation will end, and he will grow up so that he'll be less subjected to abuse from others, including from your father. And then you won't have to fight with your father; you'll be able to relax your rectum.

PATIENT: Gently put. You mean to say that I'll relax, so I won't have these spasms? Well, I hope you are right.

In keeping with their present intersubjective and consensual reality, the therapist now takes the rectal metaphor further: The therapist feels a little "squeezed out" by the patient's somewhat skeptical attitude but recognizes that, for a while at least, he'll be resisting while cooperating, as he did with his father.

CHAPTER 24

Anything that can't be said concisely is best not said at all

THE ATTENTION SPAN of the patient to the therapeutic encounter and to the therapist is limited. Thus, under the best of circumstances, long or multiple messages are taxing. Furthermore, emotionally laden material, especially bearing on the patient's particular psychopathology, is subject to defensive distortion. This distortion takes two major forms: repression (distortion by omission, because the message has been unconsciously forgotten) and misunderstanding (distortion by commission, because the message is remembered but unconsciously rearranged). The briefer and more focused the message, the relatively harder it is to distort (now) as well as to forget (later) what has been said.

To be most effective, the therapist's comments should be short and crisp, free of jargon, and based on the patient's own words and experiential vocabulary. The most useful comments have only one message at a time. There is no need for elegantly composed, elaborate presentations; simple and direct statements or questions engage the recipient better. Brevity helps the therapist to avoid unnecessary corrections and repetitions, as well as to sustain a consistent style that discourages defensive flight into intellectualization or exhibitionism.

When the therapist is unable to state a response (interpretation, clarification, or confrontation) easily and succinctly, perhaps he or she has not completely formulated the statement. In such instances, the

150

therapist's confusion can be transmitted and may create misunderstanding between therapist and patient. In fact, the patient signals that the therapist's message is inadequate. The observant clinician can usually see that the patient's eyes are glazed. When the patient nods affirmatively, it is definitely time for the therapist to stop talking. By then the messages have lost their potential effectiveness. In persistent attempts to deliver such soft-centered messages, the therapist will end up going through all sorts of exhausting maneuvers, only to be trapped. In the clinical situation the therapist often does best to wait until he or she can phrase a point in a parsimonious and incisive manner; the right moment for the therapist may also be, on a preconscious level, a better time for the patient to accept the message.

Apart from producing misunderstanding, an amorphous statement may indicate a countertransferential problem. When the otherwise competent therapist is unable to find a concise, facilitative way of presenting an idea or interpretation to the patient, there may be interference from his or her own conflicted intentions or feelings with regard to the matter at hand. Something seems to be getting in the way. Research on perceptual defense and need (Wolitsky and Wachtel 1973) confirms that an individual's emotional state is far more likely to affect his or her behavior in situations in which ambiguity prevails over clear structure. Therefore, when the clinician does not have a firm grip on how to phrase a statement to the patient, anything he or she says is likely to reflect countertransference feelings.

CHAPTER 25

The therapist must develop a latency of response, then work further to shorten the time

NOT ONLY WHAT IS SAID but when it is said affects how well something is received. There is an old Turkish saying: "Measure a thousand times and cut once." In psychotherapy, the therapist learns how to decipher the meaning of the patient's communications, to understand various levels of message, and only then to reply. In contrast to social conversation, therapeutic communications are not immediately reactive or naturally interreactive; the timing of the therapist's comments is based on very careful listening.

The therapist waits for full comprehension before formulating a response. Timing matters at least as much as content. This pregnant waiting period is the latency of response. To be correct requires anticipating the patient's receptivity at a particular moment. If the message is accurate but the timing is bad, it will have lost its potency.

After having mastered the art of latency of response, the therapist, through experience, needs to shorten that period to a minimum. Ultimately the therapist's responses will be made at the pace of natural conversation, without appearing stilted or calculated. Preparation for this skill is a process that cannot be bypassed if the therapist is to minimize mistakes and misunderstandings.

The context of a message within the therapeutic encounter is another crucial aspect of the therapist's communication. We all know the power of words in everyday life, particularly when they come from those we care most about.

It is at least implicitly understood that the therapist's comments, however simple in appearance, can have enormous impact on the patient. It is the clinician's professional duty to recognize the import of his or her words during every interaction in therapy. Not only the experience of the immediate moment but the integrity of the patient's entire self may be affected by each verbal exchange. In this regard, Jacques Lacan (1977) suggests that the decisive function of the therapist's reply to any single verbalization of the patient is not, as some believe, "simply to be received by the subject as acceptance or rejection of his discourse, but really to recognize him or to abolish him as subject. Such is the nature of the [therapist's] *responsibility* whenever he intervenes by means of speech" (p. 87).

Three years after termination, a patient came for a single session to give the therapist a progress report on her life. She said, retrospectively, that the most important change occurred to her after something that the therapist had said. The therapist, alas, could not figure out what that might have been. He expected some remarkable or dramatic statement; she instead said, "When I was going out with one charming man after another . . . you simply suggested that I should 'look for less charming people.' Now I am married to one and am very happy."

The therapist had no recollection of having said that. Nevertheless, the patient had heard the message and remembered it: she believed in it, made use of it, was happy about it, and kindly gave her therapist the credit years later. Unwittingly or not, the therapist's every word counts. Thus it is important to use restraint; then judicious intervention will likely be taken seriously, sometimes more seriously than the therapist would ever have expected.

PART VII

ON TREATMENT PROCESSES
AND THEIR PARADOXES

Although the patient comes to treatment for the express purpose of being helped, he or she would at the same time rather remain unchanged. This basic ambivalence about the prospect of cure forms an unconscious therapeutic equation for which every therapist must be prepared throughout the course of therapy: "A patient's wish to change is equal to his or her resistance to that change." Likewise, the therapist has an equally dualistic need to accept unconditionally the whole self of the patient while attempting to selectively alter the problematic parts of that self.

It is basic to the treatment process that the patient arrives with a repository of experiences from the past which are necessarily projected, at least to some degree, onto the therapist; these positive and negative transferential dispositions will be there whether the therapist induces them or not. Of course, the practitioner can technically encourage or discourage these dispositions at various points in treatment for therapeutic purposes. Although both positive and negative transference manifestations need to be explored, the therapist must be especially alert and unrelenting with regard to the latter; it is essential not to rest as long as there are any negative signs.

Transferences, for better or for worse, may intertwine with "real" feelings for or against the therapist. Consequently, it is crucial to be able

155

to distinguish genuine from projected affect. Indeed, both the failure to distinguish negative feelings from negative transference, and the failure to distinguish positive feelings from positive transference have undesirable repercussions: in the former instance, the patient can rapidly become enraged; in the latter instance, the patient can gradually feel diminished.

Positive transference has a variety of unexpected perils. Not only can the insidious dangers make their appearance at any stage of treatment, but they may appear as relatively specific phase-related manifestations, such as the patient's premature termination (during the initial stage), sexual acting out (during the middle stage), or prolonged dependency (during the final stage).

Another aspect of the therapeutic process to be discussed is the seeming lack of cohesion in individual sessions, as marked by elusive or untidy connections between beginnings and endings. These can attain coherence and continuity when professionally tied together. Related to these within-session links is a special phenomenon of everyday outside life, the so-called exit line, which is transported into the clinical context; the entrance line is similar in function. These statements frequently lurk at the periphery of each meeting. Rather than being relegated to the area beyond therapy, they are instead examined as a microcosm of the larger universe of significant therapist–patient relations. In particular, the critical interpersonal issues of intimacy and separation are implicated.

This section therefore poses the following questions: What paradoxical processes are inherent in every therapeutic situation? How does the therapist distinguish between "real" versus transferential feelings of the patient, and why should he or she deal with them differently? Although it is usually expected that negative transference can be a problem for the therapist, what are the possible perils of positive transference? And when are they most likely to occur? Finally, as a special example of the positive and negative forces that pervade all treatment, cryptic verbalizations at the very beginning or very end of a session raise the question, What important information do entry and exit lines provide?

CHAPTER 26

The patient will be both eager for and resistant to change; the therapist must accept the patient's whole while rejecting dysfunctional parts

THE DESIRE TO FREE ONESELF from one's symptoms or problems and the paradoxical opposition to this wish together constitute the pivotal struggle of the patient. This is reflected in the enduring observation that all therapeutic practice is characterized by two integrally related unconscious phenomena which simultaneously function as force and counterforce toward patient change: transference and resistance. Briefly, transference (Freud's "transference love"), albeit largely irrational, is the underlying affective bond that forms the basis for psychodynamic work and influences the patient's desire to remain in treatment; resistance is the defensive process that continually subverts and fights against therapeutic progress. In fact, manifold forms of resistance can surreptitiously make their appearance, no matter how overtly motivated the patient appears. Both aspects are inextricable insofar as transference can at any time be transformed into resistance and sabotage its positive powers to sustain the patient in treatment. These dual forces are operating continually as the patient eagerly works toward change or cure while unwittingly wanting at the same time to preserve the psychological status quo. The patient seeks to retain the familiar self.

Also contributing to the goal of health are such factors as the rational and conscious component of the patient's psyche that hopes to feel better through realistic cooperation with the therapist, the part of the person that would naturally like to please the therapist, and the motivating aspects of the individual's need to do what is considered correct or appropriate. The opposing force that resists therapeutic progress may be generated by the unhealthy part of the patient that still needs its pathology and neurotic defenses; those destructive motives designed to displease the therapist by sabotaging treatment; and the wish for other personal benefits that may accrue from being ill, including such secondary gains as getting special attention, being nurtured, or not having to meet the demands of reality. It is critical to negotiate carefully each step toward change, recognizing that the patient's resistance gets accentuated whenever signs of positive effects are forthcoming.

Resistance takes different forms and occurs along a wide spectrum of explicit to implicit, overt to covert behaviors. In a common and easily detectable form of resistance, patients demand to reduce hours; this is an early expression of increased autonomy. However, as Strean (1985) points out, if such patients get the therapist's approval to cut down the number of sessions, "they later feel rejected. Sometimes they view the therapist's acquiescence as a sign that the therapist does not consider the treatment that important or that the therapist is weak and vulnerable. These thoughts often make the client want to quit treatment" (p. 172). Others may simply withhold information within the sessions themselves. In such instances hypercritical patients project their harsh superego onto the therapist, who is unconsciously perceived as a disapproving figure. (Freud's [1909] Rat Man is considered the first example in literature of a patient's withholding information from the therapist.)

Emotional distancing or withdrawing is another effective way of resisting treatment. In more severely troubled individuals, especially when the therapist attempts to get emotionally close, affective withdrawal is quite common. Such defended patients may react to positive affect not as potentially supportive or caring but as a threat that they have to retreat from, particularly when their early experiences with significant figures had been overwhelming or otherwise aversive. These and other forms of resistance are part and parcel of every treatment. In fact, the absence of resistance may be more disconcerting than its presence, for as Charles Brenner (1976) suggests, the patient needs to be a "bad ally" in the therapeutic process. The therapist overcomes resistance not by dodging—that is, resisting the resistance—but by understanding, recognizing, confronting, exploring, and interpreting it, or by otherwise facilitating the expression of any wish or need that the patient has to fail at being a good therapeutic ally.

There is another, perhaps more subtle, aspect of the therapeutic paradox: as much as patients may suffer from dysfunctional thoughts, feelings, or behaviors, they also yearn to be fully accepted by the therapist as they are. Patients need first to be affirmed as a person, to be recognized, understood, liked, or loved. They desire, even unconsciously expect, to be unconditionally accepted by the therapist. Thus the therapist must accept each patient as he or she is, while at the same time becoming allied with the patient's hope to relinquish parts of himself or herself. The clinician can also assume that those around the adult patient, whether parents, other family members, or friends, are usually worried and/or rejecting; they are rarely completely tolerant of the patient's condition. Their overt or covert request for change is usually taken by the recipient to mean that he or she is no good, although he or she may otherwise appreciate their genuine concern. Thus the prospective patient becomes vulnerable, and as a result defensive, by virtue of merely recognizing a need for help.

For example, in patients with depressive disorders, my clinical experience suggests that their frustrated yearnings for unconditional acceptance repeats their early object relationship with mother. From the beginning, the maternal object is expected to love unconditionally and the paternal object conditionally: the mother, with her unconditional acceptance, can generate a sense of self-esteem in the child—independent of all good or bad qualities; the father, with his conditional approval, can generate a sense of mastery in the child—dependent upon his or her accomplishments. Ideally, the child who is unconditionally loved by the mother can then strive to meet the father's conditions and receive his love and approval as well.

Within the context of these particular past parental experiences, it is expected that a depressive disposition (whether characterological depression, chronic mild depression, or dysphoria) will have its start with a mother who is unable to love her offspring unconditionally and for whom the child's physical appearance, habits, and behaviors are thus potentially subject to criticism or conditional approval. During the school years, these critical attitudes may extend to academic or social life, so that each progressive developmental alteration or behavior bears the burden of becoming an additional failure to meet the maternal requirements. The growing adolescent continues to internalize this conditional acceptance, while demands for accomplishment escalate with every new disappointment. The result is a psychological pattern in which the accrual of achievements becomes the only possible source of well-being. Ultimately such individuals, who can never overcome their mother's love-dependent "conditions," may cave in and not bother to accomplish anything. Or they may excessively strive to get the father's approval as a compensatory measure, perhaps even succeeding in spite of underlying depression. Moreover, mothers tend to be conditionally loving especially with daughters: since mother sees her daughter as a direct extension of herself and the target of her own fulfillment, and a daughter in turn is more likely to identify with and incorporate the mother's value system, even small failures may lead to depressive responses long after the mother is out of the picture. Thenceforth the recipient remains in a suspended state of impending depression in relation to the significant substitutive maternal objects in her life.

Once such a patient is in treatment, the practitioner is placed in the precarious position of replicating the scenario by implicitly asking that the patient change (that is, making a therapeutic expression of conditional love), and in fact contracting to bring about change. Therefore walking the paradoxical tightrope requires that the therapist unconditionally accept the patient and let the patient experience such acceptance while simultaneously rejecting in a technical sense the person's dysfunctional aspects.

Each alteration or new adaptation by the patient, however small, requires a painful reorganization of the self which must be recognized by the therapist. As Rogers (1965) has pointed out:

> This painful dis- and re-organization is made possible by two elements in the therapeutic relationship. The first is that the new, the tentative, the contradictory, or the previously denied perceptions of self are as much valued by the therapist as the rigidly structured aspects. Thus the shift from the latter to the former become possible without too frightening a leap from the old to the new. The other element in the relationship is the attitude of the therapist toward the newly discovered aspects of experience. To the client they seem threatening, bad, impossible, disorganizing. Yet he experiences the therapist's attitude of calm acceptance toward them. He finds that to a degree he can introject this attitude and can look upon his experience as something he can own, identify, symbolize, and accept as part of himself. (Pp. 193–94)

In conclusion, two sets of paradoxical forces, one impinging upon the patient and the other upon the therapist, are set in motion as the patient prepares for therapeutic change. In the best of psychotherapeutic worlds, the therapist's dual tasks of accepting the whole person and trying to alter selected parts are ideally in synchrony with the patient's dual desires to change and to remain the same.

Case Illustration

PATIENT: When you say my forgetting our appointment is related to my feeling towards you, it just doesn't ring a bell. I simply forgot to set the alarm clock, that's all. Not only did I miss my session with you, but also I was late to work. You see, it isn't directed at you.

THERAPIST: Do you commonly forget to set the alarm clock? [The therapist gathers information in preparation for a confrontation.]

PATIENT: I wouldn't say that, but it occurs occasionally; how it occurred last Tuesday, I can't tell. If it is related to you or being in psychotherapy, I am really not aware of it. If it is, it must be completely unconscious; I can't be responsible for it.

THERAPIST: Whose unconscious is it? [The therapist confronts the patient.]

PATIENT: Now that you put it that way, obviously it is my unconscious. I still have to take the responsibility for it. It is really amazing. I am really intrigued that I could play that sort of game on myself, I mean unconsciously . . . because I do want to come to treatment. The whole day I was cursing to myself for having forgotten to set the clock. So why did I do that?

THERAPIST: You wonder whether unconsciously you are sabotaging your own treatment, even though expressly you do want it. [The therapist frames the conflict.]

PATIENT: I guess so, but why? Why would I sabotage my own treatment; isn't it crazy? Here I spend a big chunk of my earnings, which I could use for other things, not to mention the time and all the aggravation of traffic. And I forget to set the alarm. What sort of idiot am I?

THERAPIST: You mean what sort of conflict do you have? [The therapist wants to get away from the patient's unproductive self-blame and litany against himself, but searches for the conflictual feelings.]

PATIENT: Well, you are more charitable. Whatever conflict I have, I should still be here. Especially if I have a conflict I should be here, if I want to get well.

THERAPIST: Do you think that is the conflict? [The therapist offers the first interpretation.]

PATIENT: Whether I want to get well or not? I don't think so. I mean I started this. No one is twisting my arm; it is all voluntary. If I don't want to get well, I could just permanently stop coming, period.

THERAPIST: If you are ambivalent about getting well, you may temporarily stop coming. [The therapist confronts the patient with his denial of the first interpretation.]

PATIENT: By missing some sessions? Maybe I want to slow down the getting well; you know what I mean? My wife says I have become more aggressive since I began treatment. I am not sure whether I want to change that way. I am a nice person; I don't yell and scream. I wouldn't want to be that way. So, I guess at times I wonder what I will be like when the treatment is in full progress . . . because I like myself the way that I am; I mean, you know, there are things that I want to work on, like sexual stuff, but by and large I really like myself.

THERAPIST: In that sense therapy presents a danger. [The therapist provides the affective component of the conflict: anxiety.]

PATIENT: Kind of. I was more anxious the last two weeks. Do you think that was related to being afraid of changing, or changes I am experiencing?

THERAPIST: Hmm. [The therapist leaves room for the patient to elaborate.]

PATIENT: *(Silent for about forty seconds)* You know, my wife doesn't mind at all that I am more aggressive, so it isn't her, it is just me. But I do want to become a little more aggressive, not completely change; a little more aggressive and sexual maybe. I don't want to be as nice a guy, just to be pushed around by others; there has to be a happy medium.

THERAPIST: Do you feel that I have been pushing you around to get well, to be aggressive? [The therapist temporarily drops the internal conflict of ambivalence about change and now explores the transferential resistance. When the patient provides potentially transferential material during the discussion of resistance, transferential issues are taken up.]

PATIENT: No, not really—well, maybe a touch. I don't want to follow your script either. Although you never said that you are going to make me a more aggressive and sexual being, I presume you take some pleasure in my victories out there. I don't know, do you? Well, *do* you?

THERAPIST: If I do, you want to make sure that you are not depriving me of such pleasure. [A transferential interpretation is set in motion.]

PATIENT: No, come on. You mean to say that I'll sabotage my treatment just to deprive you of getting pleasure from my success? That is ridiculous. Do you really believe that?

THERAPIST: Hmm.

PATIENT: I mean, it makes no sense.

THERAPIST: No more or less than sabotaging your treatment by not setting the clock. [The therapist brings two unconscious activities together, hoping to make them more accessible to the patient.]

PATIENT: You mean, that my depriving you is also unconscious stuff? Some unconscious I have. Well, it is true that I don't want to be a goody-goody patient to you. You know, I have been like that all my life. I don't want just to passively go along with your scenarios; I do and I don't. At times I feel like I am putting the brakes on while my other foot is on the gas; you know what I mean. Why is that? I am not pulling all my weight, so to speak. . . . My father used to say when we worked together, you should put your shoulder to the wheel, like doing chores around the house. I never really did my best; I sort of gave lip service. I guess I resent the fact that he was always bossing me around.

THERAPIST: In the driver's seat.

PATIENT: Yeah, even though I wanted to help, I resented his being in charge.

THERAPIST: Even though you wanted to go to some destination. [The stage is set for interpretation of resistance.]

PATIENT: Yes, I am sort of a reluctant bride. I want to get married, but reluctantly. Even the things that I liked doing, like going to football games, the fact that he initiated I resented and resisted. [The therapist notices the sexual connotation of the patient's remark, but will use only the dominance/submission aspect of it for the moment.]

THERAPIST: Not unlike our relationship?

PATIENT: It certainly sounds like it . . . though you are not behaving like my father at all. But I am afraid you might, that you'll take over, tell me what to do, what not to do.

THERAPIST: And you'll submit to my demands.

PATIENT: It is interesting that you said that. The morning that I overslept, I woke up with a dream: I was in my high school gym. There was a wrestling match, or many people wrestling with each other, like practice. I was also wrestling with someone. Then all of a sudden I fell face down; this guy was lying on me, trying to turn me over. I can't recall his face, but he kept saying, "All right, you lost, you better submit."

THERAPIST: Any associations to the dream?

PATIENT: No, not much, except what I just said. The word *submit* stuck in my mind. When you mentioned the word, I remembered the dream. I used to wrestle with my father. It was his hobby. He was almost as good as a professional.

THERAPIST: Hmm. [The therapist wonders about the patient's incestuous fantasies.]

PATIENT: *(Silent for thirty seconds)* That is it, nothing more on that.

THERAPIST: Any fantasies from those wrestling days? [The therapist does not really expect any.]

PATIENT: No.

THERAPIST: Any sensual, sexual feelings, or thoughts associated with those memories? [The therapist wonders whether he is getting too impatient.]

PATIENT: No, there was more sweat and pain in the dream, too. This guy was sweating so badly that it was coming down on me like a waterfall. Nothing sexual there either. I mean, I don't think so; it may still be unconscious. *My* unconscious, of course.

THERAPIST: Am I making you sweat here? [Next time the therapist will ask whether the face in the dream was his own or the patient's father's.]

PATIENT: No, no. But I am going to buy a second alarm clock to make it harder for my unconscious.

CHAPTER 27

The therapist never rests in the presence of negative transference

THE MOST COMMON REASON for therapeutic stalemate is unrecognized, or recognized but unpursued, negative transference. Unfavorable feelings of patients, from annoyance to active anger or abhorrence, carried over from significant past figures and directed against the therapist, represent this phenomenon. Although the immature ego of the child seeks and perhaps finds some adaptive way to survive an aversive or dangerous environment, early frustrating and traumatic events that generated these negative dispositions are unwittingly brought into adult life. The patient usually goes on repeating the same way of relating, even though the threatening experiences may cease to be present. As Freud (1937a) observed, "The adult's ego with its increased strength continues to defend itself against dangers which no longer exist in reality; indeed it finds itself compelled to seek out those situations in reality which can serve as an approximate substitute for the original danger, so as to be able to justify, in relation to them, its maintaining its habitual modes of reaction" (p. 238). Moreover, the problem of negative transference can be compounded if the therapist actually behaves like the patient's negative introjects. This may occur unsuspectingly as a manifestation of Joseph Sandler's (1976) "role responsiveness," in which the therapist's behavior stands midway between his or her own tendencies and the role the patient is projecting onto him or her.

To complicate the matter, at times negative responses of the patient are indistinguishable from transferential reactions; for example, resentment may arise for presumably nontransferential reasons, (such as a fee increase, the therapist's announcement of the next vacation). The theoreticians who believe that every response is transferential question the validity of such a distinction. In either event, negative transference, like positive transference, is always present to some degree, but the former is much more difficult to uncover and deal with. The difficulties, which stem from a kind of mutual collusion, have two main sources: (1) patients prefer not to expose and have to face their aggressive feelings, and thus defend against awareness of transference hate much more than of transference love; (2) the therapist, in turn, would rather not be the recipient of such aggression and thus may unconsciously overlook it (whereas the therapist more easily notices—even basks in—positive transference).

Despite the predilection to keep negative transference at bay, it makes its appearance in various forms and guises and in all degrees of explicitness or elusiveness. It can be as obvious as the patient directly telling the therapist that he is too inexperienced, or as subtle as complaining about traffic on the way to the session. At the merest hint of negativity, the therapist should attempt to address it, the major reason being that unexposed, unconfronted, uninterpreted negative transference tends to escalate. Alternatively, exposed, confronted, and interpreted negative transference can at least be diffused, if not eliminated, as a formidable obstacle to the progress of psychotherapy.

Case Illustration

A fifty-six-year-old woman was referred by her internist because of chronic hypochondriacal symptoms and complaints for which no organic evidence could be found. A family history included a mother who was alcoholic and punitive to both husband and daughter and an abused father who had been unemployed most of his life.

PATIENT: Oh, it's so dark in here; why do you keep the place so dark?
THERAPIST: [The therapist remains silent, wondering whether his office is really too dark. Since he does not remember any other patient ever commenting on this before, he receives it from this patient as a negative signal. Nonetheless, he does not react to every negative comment of the patient, and certainly not to the first one. Rather, he

registers the message and listens to the patient's narration, alert to possible subsequent negative messages.]

PATIENT: Anyhow, Dr. Fine suggested that I should come to see you. I must tell you ahead of time that I don't believe in psychotherapy, but he thinks that the pains in my stomach are all psychological. What can I tell you? Here I am.

THERAPIST: Against your better judgment! [The therapist wants to ally with the patient, so he echoes her antipsychotherapy theme.]

PATIENT: Not exactly. [The therapist's intention has obviously had a paradoxical effect; in negative transference, even the therapist's agreement with the patient can be rejected.] I am willing to give you the benefit of the doubt. I am willing to try anything, but psychotherapy I think is my least favorite. I know that lots of people swear by it. But for me, I must say, it is sort of a shot in the dark.

THERAPIST: As if psychiatry being a shot in the dark is not enough, finding yourself in a dark office is hardly reassuring. [The therapist capitalizes on her exact words. Again attempting to ally with the patient, he hopes to at least establish a semantic alliance.]

PATIENT: (Again contrary, but mellowing a little) Well, actually it isn't so bad now as it had been just coming in from outside. I suppose my eyes are getting used to it. [The therapist feels slightly relieved from the barrage of negativism, although he is still alert to it. He realizes that the patient may have momentarily dropped the darkness-of-the-office issue, not because she necessarily feels any better toward the therapist, but because she has perhaps decided to use heavier artillery.] Tell me, doctor, what causes spastic colon?

THERAPIST: Is that what you have? [The therapist avoids answering the patient's question directly because he suspects it may be a trap, that she must have asked this question of dozens of doctors and must know the answer. In the throes of the patient's negative feelings such questions are usually testing the therapist, examining his or her knowledge on the subject as well as setting the stage for arguments. Therefore the therapist gives the patient the upper hand by neither lecturing to her nor replying. He thus disengages from the potential for one-upmanship.]

PATIENT: That is what they say. It is now more than eight years; I tried every diet, medication, you name it. No one really knows what it is, what causes it and how to cure it. I cannot believe that with all the technology they cannot find a cure for a simple disease. They keep shuffling me from one doctor to another.

THERAPIST: And now you are shuffled to yet another one—me, a psychotherapist, of all people, when you already know that I, too, don't know what causes your problem or how to cure it.

Here the therapist ties the institutional negative transference (that is, psychotherapy being her "least favorite") to the therapist himself, knowing that for the patient the institution and the therapist have become extensions of each other. He also makes this transition because dealing with institutional negative transference is fairly difficult to sustain; it tends to get intellectualized, abstract, or impersonal. Furthermore, if the therapist successfully deals with the negative transference of the patient toward himself, the patient may come to feel good about the therapist, while remaining skeptically disposed toward the institution.

PATIENT: Not that I know that you don't know. [Again the patient takes a contrary position, reflecting repeated negativity no matter what the therapist says.] I hope you do; I wish you did, or anyone did. Otherwise why would I come here? Why wouldn't I want to get rid of this illness by any means?

THERAPIST: Unless it serves some purpose.

PATIENT: *(Anger escalating)* What purpose could it serve, except pain and suffering? And no one cares. [The therapist realizes as he says this that although intellectually he is correct in confronting her primitive defenses, emotionally the confrontation may be too harsh. He wonders whether he is becoming retaliatory under the guise of confrontation: Is the patient wearing him down with her negativism? Has she raised enough doubts in the therapist's mind about whether he can help her? Is his aggression related to feeling frustrated in view of her presenting problem? Is he pushing her out so that he does not have to confront his own sense of impotence? This countertransferrential possibility is confirmed as the therapist's mind wanders to the previous patient, who is so trusting and pleasant and always appreciative of him.] No one pays attention anyway; why suffer? You think I am a masochist, that I enjoy suffering? No one does. Haven't I suffered enough?

THERAPIST: And you are suffering here as well.

The therapist hears the patient's complaint that now he, too, is hurting her. This time, however, the therapist recoups and prepares himself not to expect positive feelings from the patient, also not to attempt to cure her hypochondriasis but to try to empathize with her. The therapist thinks that most likely everyone rejects her the way that he may have been beginning to. As the therapist takes this step away from himself, he can begin to listen differently—how terrible it must be for her to want to relate but only to know how to engage others negatively.

The patient spends the rest of the time describing how lonely she has been since the death of her husband ten years ago, telling the therapist that her children don't spend time with her. The negativeness of the patient is temporarily suspended with the therapist's confirmation. But he still needs to be on the lookout because negative transference tends to come back, unexpectedly and quite irregularly, as it does at the end of the hour.

PATIENT: Doctor, you didn't tell me what you think caused my disease.

THERAPIST: Yes, because at this stage that would be a real shot in the dark. Let me first get to know you a little better. [The therapist again uses the same metaphor as the patient in order to further their semantic mutuality. He also sets the agenda for the next few sessions. He lets her know he is not going to tell her what causes her illness but wants to get to know her better. And he plans to stay with this agenda in spite of the patient's frequent protestations (such as "What does this have to do with my spastic colon?").]

PATIENT: Well, this does not really help, but. . . . All right, see you Thursday. *(Both start to walk out)* I still think you could use a little bit more light in here. [The therapist refrains from responding. The patient needs a small victory, which the therapist allows by letting her have the last word.]

It is good practice not to outwit the patient, especially when he or she is on the way out. The therapist certainly does not repeat his previous interpretation, which will prompt the patient to reject it and counterargue. It is never good to end the hour on a tense and disagreeable note.

Of course this patient is still in the negative transferential stage. It's just temporarily abated—one or ten more interpretations will not make it go away. Although the therapist is saying to himself, "We have to deal with these issues," lots of frustration lies ahead for both therapist and patient.

Confronted with negative transference the therapist has to pay special attention not to behave like the patient's "bad archaic objects" (Strachey 1934), the primitive voices of his or her parents. Strean (1985) takes this further to suggest that "as the client becomes aware of the distinction between his archaic fantasy object and the real external object (i.e., the therapist), there is a breach in the neurotic vicious cycle.

The client, having become aware of the lack of hostility in the real external object, will diminish his own hostility. Feeling less hated, the client will hate less" (p. 82).

In spite of the therapist's best efforts, negative transference may pop up quite unpredictably; it needs to be dealt with each time with the same rigor. Negativity is the foremost quality that will compound every issue and problem. As long as the patient is feeling antagonistic toward the clinician, he or she will overtly or covertly reject all interpretive efforts. At such times, simply expressing and discharging the feelings take priority over any interpretation. Once that has occurred, the clinician can begin to address content issues. Considering the efforts necessary to deal with obstructionistic feelings, Habib Davanloo's (1978) concept of the "relentless healer," although developed in a short-term approach, is applicable to any dynamic therapy: it means that the therapist can never rest as long as there is any sign of negative transference.

CHAPTER 28

Positive transference can be perilous and is the main culprit in benign premature termination, acting out, and prolonged dependency

HANDLING THE TRANSFERENCE is perhaps the most compelling and difficult task of psychotherapy. Freud's (1925) own statement on the matter suggests the perils of transference:

> In every analytic treatment there arises . . . an intense emotional relationship between the patient and the analyst. . . . It can be of a positive or of a negative character and can vary between the extremes of a passionate, completely sensual love and the unbridled expression of an embittered defiance and hatred. This transference . . . soon replaces in the patient's mind the desire to be cured, and, so long as it is affectionate and moderate, becomes the agent of the physician's influence and neither more nor less than the mainspring of their joint work. . . . [If] converted into hostility . . . it may then happen that it will paralyze the patient's power of associating and endanger the treatment. (P. 42)

The therapist is inevitably most concerned about the patient's development of negative transference. In contrast, there is a general sentiment by clinicians, often implicit, that receiving the positive transference of the patient is a rather pleasant, preferred position to be in: you can just bask in it unless it gets too hot for comfort and requires interpretation.

The tendency to indulge as long as possible in the patient's benign feelings, devotion to treatment, and exaltation of the therapist is perhaps natural—it is hard to imagine what harm could come from accepting such benevolence. Indeed, in the glow of positive transference everything may seem to be just fine. The therapist tends to relax, secure in the relationship and reaping its benefits, however temporary. Most therapists like this phase of treatment; some get bored, others wary; few are sufficiently worried. As a result, they may be caught off guard more than when negative transference occurs.

I am leading to the fact that, somewhat deceptively, positive transference has its own problems and perils. For one thing, persistent positive transference invariably means that negative transference is lurking close behind; according to Greenson (1967), it is hidden, not absent. In his delineation of the types of resistance in clinical practice, he cites the phenomenon of "frequent cheerful hours," in which "great enthusiasm, and prolonged elation indicate that something is being warded off— usually something of the opposite nature" (p. 69).

Even the prototypical positive transference, in its paradigmatic form of falling in love with the therapist, is usually more irrational and regressive in its treatment manifestations than the comparable phenomenon of falling in love in real life. This extreme form of positive transference, especially in the most erotic scenario of romantic infatuation and passionate yearning for the therapist, is not an unexpected occurrence. Historically, its vicissitudes have been reported since the dawn of psychoanalysis. Mesmer, Breuer, Janet, and Charcot, as well as Freud himself, have amply described the emergence of strong sexual feelings within treatment and the inevitable problems wrought by their presence. Although affairs between therapist and patient were never sanctioned by Freud or his followers, they did occur, and not only in fantasy or wish. However, therapists have often been saved from moral indictment by termination of treatment by the therapist. As a result, the recommended response for the therapist has been explicit since the days of Freud—under no circumstances should such transference be gratified (Freud 1915); these reactions must be interpreted.

But there are less excessive circumstances of positive transference as well, of love and its variations, including idealization and admiration; respect, concern, and trust; and nonsexual or nonromantic dependency on the therapist. These are diverse in their manifestations as well as their intensity at different times and in different patients. In short, both the function of the positive transference itself at any point in the course of treatment and the interpretive technique for such occasions are complex and subtle. In fact, each stage of psychotherapy poses its own positive transference uses and perils. The interpretive task of each phase is therefore based on facilitating its particular therapeutic goals and preventing its impending dangers.

Phase 1. Forming a Therapeutic Relationship (Peril: Flight or Premature Termination)

The initial phase of psychotherapy, which has as its major task the establishment of a therapeutic alliance, uses positive transference as the primary momentum for accomplishing that task. At the same time, interpretation of positive transference must be geared toward protecting the relationship and preventing the patient from fleeing from it. In the context of positive feelings on the part of the patient, Greenson (1967) has observed flights into health and the presumed loss of symptoms without insight. The primary peril of positive transference is premature termination, not due to malevolent feelings toward the therapist on the part of the patient (who naturally needs to flee from such an aversive experience) but rather to the beginnings of intense affection and yearning that waken unleashed wishes for—and fears of—intimacy. Alternatively, there may be an opposite danger, overdependency, as preoccupation with the therapist and overestimation of his or her healing powers feed into the patient's excessive needs for approval, affection, and closeness. However, overdependency is more typically a problem in the final phase of treatment.

Phase 2. Facilitating or Deepening the Transference (Peril: Excessive Erotic Feelings and Sexual Acting Out)

In the middle phase of psychotherapy, which deliberately aims to recapitulate the patient's conflicts to learn more about their origins, the therapist's techniques are geared toward deepening the transference. At this point, the predominant peril of positive transference is excessive or uncontrolled libidinal drives and demands, particularly that of sexual acting out, as heightened erotic feelings inevitably come to the fore. Since actually acting on such desires for the therapist is taboo, the patient may express them elsewhere.

This perilous aspect of positive transference is a frequent accompaniment to an intensification of the patient's unresolved conflicts as manifested in increased positive transference. Excessive idealization and longing for the therapist are juxtaposed against repressed anger at the frustration of unrequited love. Bertram Lewin (1955) has suggested that the distortion that inheres in acting out behavior is inevitably in the direction of wish fulfillment. It has also been noted that as a form of nonverbal communication to the therapist, such acting out not only represents resistance to treatment but expresses a reaching out by the patient toward the desired object (Greenson 1967).

Phase 3. Preparing for Separation (Peril: Perpetuated or Prolonged Dependency)

In the termination phase of psychotherapy, which must attempt to dissolve the therapist–patient bond as the patient prepares for leave taking, the therapist's effort is directed toward fostering independence and undoing the dependency that has developed throughout the treatment process. At this stage, the major peril of positive transference involves the reactivation of entrenched early feelings of attachment. A special danger of positive transference is regression to the infantile maternal bond, to which the patient may at least temporarily return and then be unable to break away from.

Despite progress made in therapy, the final phase is not an unambivalent experience: it often revives separation anxiety and old issues of dependence versus independence from significant persons of the past. The temptation for prolonged dependency is especially compelling in this final phase, which inevitably resembles a mourning process whereby the patient grieves not only over the impending loss of the therapist but also over the simultaneous loss of his or her former self.

Thus, positive transference, as benign as it sounds, can set the stage for a wide range of counterproductive activities on the part of the patient. In the early phase of treatment it may lead to premature (albeit benevolent) termination; in the middle phase it can result in sexual acting out; and in the final phase, it can encourage extended dependency. At one stage or another the patient may not just fantasize about but express libidinal wishes, may regress unadaptively, may become unduly dependent, or may make inappropriate decisions based on false expectations or excessive efforts to please the therapist, all with the positive transference hope of reciprocally receiving the therapist's adoration. No stage is exempt from the potential dangers of positive transference. To the extent that the therapist does not sufficiently anticipate developments that can accrue from the positive transference, he or she is in for an unpredictable therapeutic course.

Case Illustration

The patient was a twenty-eight-year-old woman who sought therapy because of difficulties in her social and work relationships with others, especially men. Her boyfriend had complained of her emotional outbursts and mood swings, over which she felt she did not have full control. The patient also said that she had trouble with her boss, who denigrated her, particularly making remarks about her being disorganized. She spoke of her boyfriend with admiration and her boss with revulsion. As she expressed her feelings about these men, her emotional display was exaggerated, with a tendency toward verbal and affective hyperbole. She appeared to be easily influenced by others, presenting herself as the helpless victim of a bad situation, stuck in external circumstances that were beyond her.

In relating details of her personal life, both current and past, her knowledge, especially of her childhood, was very vague, and she talked about events in her private life dismissively. Her daily activities and interests revealed nonstop telephone conversations, frenetic social activities, and little intellectual curiosity (primarily reading "gossip magazines and love stories").

The following case vignette portrays the vicissitudes of positive transference in the same patient at three different stages in her psychotherapy.

Initial Phase (Session 7)

PATIENT: During the week I often think of you. I'm sort of preoccupied with you, the things we talked about and things you said, how close I feel to you at times.

THERAPIST: How do you feel about your being so preoccupied with me? [The therapist explores the fears of closeness in this phase.]

PATIENT: It's a little strange—I don't remember ever having felt that way towards anyone before.

175

THERAPIST: That sense of strangeness might be a little disturbing. [The therapist also demonstrates a sensitivity to the fact that the patient may feel in danger.]

PATIENT: Yes, frightening. In fact, to be so intimate and close with someone, and also not knowing that person well.

THERAPIST: Is it frightening enough, this sense of closeness, that at times you feel like running away from me? [Here the therapist attempts an interpretation of the fear; he does not deal with the patient's wishes to get to know the therapist better.]

PATIENT: *(Laughs)* Well, like right now! No, I'm kidding, but last week and this week, many times I thought about calling and canceling and I didn't know why, because part of me wanted to come. I guess I do want to feel that closeness, but also am somewhat scared and want to run away. It is not just that I'm afraid of being close to someone, or I mean your being close to me. But what if there is nothing to be close to? What if this is me, the real me, who has nothing behind this facade, nothing relatable? I have no recollections of my being close to my parents. I must have blocked it all out. This may be as close as I ever could come; this might be my limit—after this maybe it is all emptiness. Maybe it's like whoever said, "Down deep I am very superficial."

THERAPIST: And why stay to have it validated? [The therapist is quite active in the initial phase of the treatment.]

PATIENT: Occasionally I think there is something more. I sense that with my son—he is the only one with whom I feel I can give more or I can take more. Why don't I try this with others? I may not be as empty as I think I am. Am I really worried that you will confirm that I am no good, that I am this awful, selfish, ungiving, unloving, unlovable monster?

THERAPIST: And that I would not want to get close to and like such a monster.

PATIENT: When you say things like that, I feel that you won't run away and throw me out. You are saying to me that it is all right if I am a monster, and that in fact I may not be such a monster any-way . . .

THERAPIST: We'll have to stop.

PATIENT: So, I'll see you next week?

THERAPIST: I am not going to run away.

In retrospect, the final response was probably too flippant; such incongruence with the mood of the session often represents countertransferential discomfort of the therapist. Here the therapist is aware of becoming the target of the patient's overdependency on the one hand, and her limited intellect and introspectiveness on the other. In fact, the therapist wonders whether he *should* run away—thus, in his typical defensive pattern (reaction formation) he says, "I am *not* going to run away." On the surface, however, the therapist seems to be trying to reassure the patient that he will be there for her. If it succeeds, such reassurance might undesirably place the patient in a helpless, needy position. At this phase, fostering overdependency, which can be as countertherapeutic as flight, may be considered the opposite side of this perilous transference coin.

PATIENT: *(Laughs)* We'll see. [In fact, she is not reassured.]

Middle Phase (Session 58)

PATIENT: Would you believe that I am beginning to talk like you—and talking about you, too. You are like God. My friends are saying they are sick and tired of listening to me. But anyway, it's funny, they say I don't pronounce my letters the way I used to; I've begun to say *v*'s for *w*'s. [The patient has apparently adopted one of the characteristic features of the therapist—his accent.]

THERAPIST: Hmm. [The therapist's silence here is intended to not contaminate the flow of the patient's speech.]

PATIENT: *(After a long silence)* I guess I'm sort of becoming like you. Yet you are so distant; at times I wonder whether you care at all. I know that isn't fair, even though I feel so close to you as I have never been before to anyone. I don't even know what I want from you, I mean.

THERAPIST: You wish *I* also were close to you. [In contrast to the initial phase where the *fears of* closeness are interpreted, in the engaged middle phase *wishes for* further closeness are identified.]

PATIENT: Well, I know that you care, but I guess that I want to mean something more to you.

THERAPIST: Hmm. [The therapist is much less active in the middle phase of treatment.]

PATIENT: I know that will not be and should not be, but I feel like begging for some love—it is just pitiful. I feel so unimportant, so insignificant. Why would I even deserve such attention? *(Long silence)* [This is a difficult moment for most therapists to resist expressing positive feelings. It would be so much easier to say something like,

"Of course you deserve attention," or the like. But we know what the patient really wants is not the therapist's love; the therapist is just a stand-in for a past figure. Any reassurance will preempt the patient's associations and will direct him or her away from historical connections to early conflicts.]

THERAPIST: Hmm. [Deprivation intensifies the transference, thrusting the patient further into her inner world, which generates regressive memories and fantasies.]

PATIENT: *(Coming out of long silence)* I used to play baseball, to wrestle with my brothers just to please my father. I knew that he'd never love me the way he loved them. . . .

Termination Phase (Session 294)

PATIENT: These days, somehow, you are in my dreams a lot, especially just before I wake up. I am not sure whether they are dreams or fantasies.

THERAPIST: Have these dreams and fantasies increased since we began to talk about termination? [The focus is not on the content of the material (such as wishes, as in the previous phase) but on the timing of the material. The only exception to this rule is historical material related to early separation.]

PATIENT: No, not necessarily. Maybe I began to talk about them more often, although they have always been there.

THERAPIST: So you began to talk about these feelings since we've been speaking of terminating treatment. [The therapist becomes active again in this phase of treatment, but is willing to change the pace as new, legitimate, termination-related material becomes available. Termination is a phase, not a rigid state. Freud (1937a, 218) warned the therapist against setting definitive termination dates as a "blackmailing device" to extract new information.]

PATIENT: *(Noticeably annoyed)* So this is sort of manipulating you?—if that is what you're insinuating. It's like I read about the patient's symptoms increasing toward the end of treatment in order not to terminate it.

THERAPIST: You feel accused and angry. [Every interpretation is a deprivation, especially in the termination phase, wherein the impending withdrawal of the therapist makes the interpretations more frustrating and thus less tolerable. As Paul Dewald (1964) has pointed out, in planning to leave treatment, the patient is being asked to give up an important relationship. So the therapist should not expect thanks; this phase generates lots of ambivalent feelings, not unlike that of a separating adolescent in relation to his or her parents.]

PATIENT: Well, not exactly, just a little irritated with all these innuendos that somehow I don't want to terminate the therapy.

THERAPIST: Just a *little* irritated? [The therapist wants the maximum of affect here. Otherwise, her suppressed hostilities will interfere with the full exploration of their relationship and its resolution.]

PATIENT: I don't know, I mean I cannot just blast you for being so insensitive. [Although the patient's aggression occurs as a reactivation of an earlier negative transference, at this phase it is commonly used as a resistance to dealing with the termination issue. Such aggression is usually prompted by an unwitting action of the therapist which the patient may experience as an empathic failure.]

THERAPIST: For fear that I might have you terminate even sooner. [The therapist again ties the content of the negative feelings with the timing of the termination.]

PATIENT: I really think you are overestimating my dependency on you. You know, I got my degree, I love my job, I am appreciated by my boss, who promoted me twice in one year, I have a good husband and a healthy child, and I am still young. I'm in charge of my life. I can make any changes, if I want to. I have a few friends, real friends, and being with them enriches my life, but I love also being alone. I have become my best friend, in a twist of Walt Whitman, I stand and look at myself long and long to feel so contained. *(The patient seems to be enjoying her confident self-presentation)*

THERAPIST: Surely, you have accomplished a great deal. Maybe just the separation is difficult, even if it is time. [The therapist makes the issue of separation the main topic and again ties it to the issue of time, but he is a little wary and run down by the patient's aggression. Thus, instead of saying, "*You* may be having difficulty in separating," the therapist generalizes and dilutes the confrontation.]

PATIENT: Even if it is time? Whose time are you referring to? I was sent to boarding school at the age of thirteen; I never understood why.

THERAPIST: Before you were ready for it. [The therapist does not address the statement "I never understood why" because that would be too derailing. The issue of boarding school was dealt with extensively in the course of treatment (the patient as helpless victim of her parents and the question whether she had been loved at all). Now the therapist deals with the same subject within a limited focus—only as it relates to past experiences of separation.]

PATIENT: Yes, it was too premature. Whose interest was it serving anyway? I could not even tell this to them.

THERAPIST: Now you wonder whether you are my helpless victim and it is not *your* but *my* interest to terminate. [The therapist may have moved from the past to the present a little too quickly in order to make this separation-related transferential interpretation a primary focus. In this statement the therapist also conveys the idea that the patient was unable to tell her parents but could tell the therapist.]

PATIENT: God knows, you may have a better patient, a more interesting one, a waiting list, something. I know it's crazy. And I know that I also want to terminate. I guess it's too hard to separate from something, or someone, well—from you. I am going through all this song and dance. I don't really mean to. Stop it! Stop it! *(As if she is scolding herself—looks into the therapist's eyes for a long time)* Oh, God! I am going to miss you.

THERAPIST: [The therapist feels the pang of separation. Until this interchange he "knew" that he was dealing with the issue of separation, but now he is experiencing it.]

CHAPTER 29

The therapist may be deceived by positive transference at any stage of the therapy, when the therapist's self-image matches the patient's transferential disposition

AS NOTED ABOVE, positive transference can be perilous to the patient at each phase of treatment. There is also a more ubiquitous danger of positive transference that cuts across all phases: the tendency for the therapist to receive positive feelings of the patient at face value, unilaterally to accept or reciprocate them without delving further.

Even Freud suggested that not all transference needs to be interpreted. He (1912a) was specifically referring to an "unobjectionable" aspect of the positive transference, which he referred to as friendly or affectionate feelings that are admissible to consciousness and that help to strengthen the patient's attachment to the therapist and weaken resistance to change. Indeed, it is Freud's "effective transference" that laid the groundwork for such notions as the "therapeutic alliance" (Zetzel 1956), or "working alliance" (Greenson 1967), which has since honored the rational aspects of the patient's observing ego in mutual collaboration with the therapist. Later conceptualizations have gone further to elaborate upon the curative value of empathic responses to the patient (Kohut 1971), even suggesting that the patient's idealized feelings toward the therapist should not be challenged, particularly with narcissistic patients; they serve not merely to sustain an unthreatening environment but as a way of helping the patient to overcome deep-seated feelings of distrust and rage beneath a damaged self.

However, unquestioned benevolent responses may also signal a hidden countertransferential element—that the therapist is in danger of fostering positive transference to overcome his or her own underlying negative or discouraged feelings toward the patient. At the same time, the therapist may blindly believe that he or she is maintaining an atmosphere in which treatment can continue. Although graciously accepting the ideas that one is competent or well regarded may not be countertransferential, it is easy for the therapist's contentment or pleasure to go unexplored. Strean (1980), for example, has warned that the therapist's wish to be loved is often gratified rather than analyzed in both therapeutic and supervisory situations. Martin Stein (1981) suggests that the therapist is usually unwilling to scrutinize positive transference because this reciprocal benign attitude "is comfortable for both parties." Schafer (1983) has more specifically observed that because the therapist naturally prefers to be regarded as a benevolent and reparative figure, maintaining the positive transference may serve to satisfy a variety of conscious or unconscious fantasies or needs, such as the desires to be narcissistically fed or to feel powerful.

In short, even though the patient's positive views of the therapist may be less overtly problematic than his or her negative views—and are, at least in part, well deserved—their predilection for unexamined perpetuation and analytic neglect can be dangerous to treatment. In short, the competent clinician needs to be specially alerted to those exalted times (however few) when his or her own positive view of himself or herself reciprocally matches that of the contented patient.

CHAPTER 30

The therapist's failure to distinguish actual negative feelings from negative transference will enrage the patient and bring the treatment to a rapid end

FAILURE TO DISTINGUISH between transferential and "real" feelings toward the therapist can have significant implications for the patient's response to treatment. The question arises: How does one tell the difference between the two, if indeed there is any? Even Freud recognized that there can be "new editions" of old conflicts, which are total projections based on exact replicas of the past irrespective of present reality, and "revised editions," which are not true replacements because they attach themselves to actual characteristics of the recipient. Although some theorists, such as Brenner (1976), consider all of a patient's reactions to the therapist as transferential, qualitative differences in the nature of patients' responses suggest that distinctions can be drawn between what has been completely transferred from past significant others and what more likely belongs to the therapist.

As Greenson (1967) has observed, often what distinguishes a transference reaction from a nontransference reaction is not its content but other qualities. The therapist has clinical criteria to denote the occurrence of transference: inappropriateness (which refers to the largely irrational character of the transference response), intensity (which applies to the unusual strength of reaction elicited in the patient), ambivalence (which relates to the shift or split in affect that occurs toward the therapist simultaneously or from one time to another), tenacity

183

(which reflects the resilience with which such feelings tend to persist despite the therapist's actual behavior), and capriciousness (which describes the erratic, and sometimes trivial or frivolous, events that evoke the feelings).

Greenson was referring to the peculiarities of transference in general and did not portray these features further, that is, as they may differentially manifest themselves in positive and negative transference. Such criteria are generally more useful in distinguishing positive transference from positive nontransference feelings, than in differentiating negative transference from negative nontransference feelings. More specifically, no matter how distant and unconnected it may seem, every negative utterance of the patient may reflect his or her feeling toward the therapist. Anger at the boss, irritation at mother, frustration with a spouse, dislike of a friend, and so on, must be carefully listened to. The proximity of the external references as well as the intensity of the feelings will determine the conscious accessibility of the transference. Statements about disliking the wallpaper, lighting, or artwork of the therapist's office are in the immediacy of the preconscious and require gentle (but not too slow) connecting with the therapist.

Freud (1912a) said, "Every conflict has to be fought out in the sphere of transference" (p. 104). That is certainly true for negative transference. But the therapist need not jump immediately to inquire whether the patient has negative sentiments toward the therapist. First, explorations must be directed toward elaborating these situations, exploring the details of the feelings and meanings of these emotions, before the therapist asks whether the patient feels similarly toward him or her. Any premature attempt to make such a connection will preempt the detailed elaboration of affect and prevent the patient's full disclosure of negative feelings. More important, the interpretation may be received by the patient as an unwelcome threat and bring up a defensive need to flee from the therapist or himself or herself.

The therapist tends to be concerned about the development of negative transference by the patient, and once he or she becomes aware of it, invariably begins to worry about the course of treatment. And rightly so, because the misidentification or mismanagement of negative transference invariably leads to an escalation of the patient's primitive rage or aggression. A major consequence is the creation of a potentially uncontrolled impasse of overt or barely submerged wrath; this in turn invariably leads to turbulent acting out, often bringing the session to an abrupt end through the patient's hostile flight from further treatment.

The good news is that the consequences of negative transference are quite predictable; there are also rather simple rules for handling such transference, with predictable responses from the patient. The key, of course, is not to overlook or to identify erroneously the cues of negative transference. With accurate identification the alert clinician can start to openly acknowledge, systematically confront, and interpret them. To allow himself or herself to be a target of anger and aggression—in fact, to draw the fire—is a good beginning.

The bad news is that because negative affect can escalate so fast, the therapist does not have much time to recognize negative transference and sort it from negative feelings, thus it may be necessary to consider both possibilities simultaneously. First, the therapist has to make sure that he or she is not in fact consciously or unconsciously inducing negative feelings in the patient (for example, Is he canceling sessions too often? Is she late for the sessions? Does he end early, not providing object constancy? Does she not listen, or daydream and wander too frequently and too long?).

For example, the therapist may easily provoke "real" negative feelings by any of the following actions.

1. Forgetting or confusing important facts about the patient's life. ("Is your brother younger?" "No, I don't have a brother, I have an older sister.")
2. Asking repeated questions. ("When did you say your symptoms first started?" "I told you, just before I gave birth to my son.")
3. Mistaking names. ("I gather John is in competition with you." "John? You mean Henry?")
4. Not noticing changes in the patient's appearance. ("You say men are not attracted to you; have you thought about making some changes in your style?" "I just had my hair done today, and what I am wearing comes from the Color Me Beautiful consultant, who charged me three hundred dollars.")
5. Not approving the patient's language. ("That asshole Harold, that son of a bitch, that fucking asshole pulls the rug from under me—meanwhile, to my face behaving as if nothing is wrong, as if he is my best friend." "You must have been furious with this two-faced, as you called it, 'asshole' friend.")
6. Implying that he or she does not like or is not interested in the patient. (Examples include frequent glancing at the clock, yawning, getting sleepy, or actually sleeping during the sessions; giving the patient unusual or inconvenient time slots by mistake; double scheduling with another patient; or not offering a regular schedule.)
7. Revealing envy of the patient. ("Both cars are beautiful; I cannot

make my mind up—it is not my usual indecisiveness; maybe I'll buy both." "What an embarrassment of riches.")

8. Getting irritated with the patient's relative lack of psychological mindedness. ("You know you keep saying that again, and again—we seem to be getting nowhere: that I have difficulties with intimacy, that I was never close to my mother. We just keep repeating the same thing again and again." "Well, we can only work with the material you bring in.")

9. Displaying impatience with the patient's resistance. ("No, I really have no special feelings for you. I know that the patient is supposed to fall in love with the therapist, but it just hasn't happened. I don't mean to insult you or anything like that, but you are just a helper; there're no personal feelings of any sort." "This is a well-known phenomenon; there are patients who find it difficult to develop these feelings toward the therapist, which we call resistance to transference.")

10. Expressing annoyance with the patient's wanting personal information. ("Well, what do you do in your leisure time?" "We are not here to talk about me.")

11. Being rigid about charging for cancelations or unscheduled vacation times; overcharging or giving repeated bills. ("Here is your month's bill." "You already gave me one last session.")

12. Making sarcastic remarks. ("I got this pain again all over, in all my joints; well, not exactly. On my left elbow, for sure—do you think I've got Lyme disease?" "I wonder whether your hypochondria has found a new disease.")

Not remembering important dates in the patient's life, maintaining unnecessarily long silences, eating or drinking during the session, answering telephones during the session, self-grooming, burping, demonstrating counterfeit concern, and not shaking an extended hand are other examples of the therapist's behaviors or attitudes that rightly generate negative feelings of the patient toward the therapist. This is not to deny the possibility that such feelings are also intertwined with negative transference. However, mistaking negative feeling for a transference reaction, then interpreting it as such, has invariable implications: it can create enormous rage in the patient. The patient feels unfairly accused, that his or her judgment and perception of reality are questioned. Or the patient may feel manipulated by the powerful clinician, or resent the self-deception of the therapist who erroneously rejects anger that is directed toward him or her. And finally, not to tolerate the patient's negative feelings generates further negativity. As Mahler, Pine, and Bergman (1975) have noted, ongoing mild negativism is essential for the development of a sense of identity. The therapist (not only the patient) must come to terms with its existence and even its usefulness.

In terms of clinical practice, most therapists would perhaps recognize their mistakes and apologize, thus diffusing the patient's legitimate anger. But if the clinician does not apologize, and instead hides behind therapeutic neutrality by asking for the patient's elaborations and fantasies, he or she will end up fueling the patient's anger. The patient may forgive technical mistakes, but not attitudinal ones. (These attitudinal mistakes, incidentally, are primarily countertransference manifestations of the therapist.) One of the common expressions of such mistakes is to immediately redirect the patient's anger, displacing it onto a past relationship where it does not really belong.

Case Illustration

PATIENT: Ah . . . I thought for a minute that you were not listening. I know, this is all repetitive and boring to you. I mean it is a business for you, so how much do you really care? I shouldn't even consider that you would be fully attentive, but I am not sure whether you listen with half attention or not.

THERAPIST: I wonder whether you are accusing me of not being attentive and caring because that is how you felt about your mother.

PATIENT: *(Furious)* Bullshit! Leave my mother out of this. I am talking about *you*. Screw it.

Look, I can't stay here any longer; I've got to go . . .

The critical issue here is that the therapist who generates real negative feelings in the patient only makes the situation worse by interpreting them; rather, the solution is to be searched for in the therapist. This has less to do with technical competence than with personal health and honesty. The therapist who gets repeatedly into negative relationships with patients has to ask: Is this an isolated reaction to a certain patient or patients, or is it a common pattern? Is it then a countertransferential problem to be put to good use? If so, it is remediable with self-examination and treatment. Only under such circumstances can the therapist who has found sessions coming to an untimely end begin to accept that he or she is unable sufficiently to acknowledge negative feelings by the patient which are, alas, not solely transferential.

CHAPTER 31

The therapist's failure to distinguish actual positive feelings from positive transference will diminish the patient and bring the session to a slow end

THE CRITERIA NOTED EARLIER in regard to negative transference versus negative feelings also apply in regard to positive transference versus positive feelings. However, the clinician can usually make better use of these distinctions when dealing with positive affect because such emotions tend to surface less quickly than negative ones. In addition, although there is a risk of treatment stalemate, there may be enough recovery time in a session because it may not come to an abrupt end.

The following paragraphs outline some of the major ways to differentiate transferential from "natural" positive feelings.

1. *Relative inappropriateness.* The patient may express appropriately a sense of trusting the therapist, liking him or her, or appreciating his or her competence, interest, dependability, and concern. But when the patient begins to refer to the therapist in highly idealized and unrealistic terms—as a godlike or heroic figure, infallible, selfless, or the like, often in conjunction with exalted expectations—the therapist can be reasonably sure that these are fantasied attributions and feelings which are both inaccurate and inappropriate.

2. *Intensity of affect.* If the patient expresses extreme positive emotions toward the therapist, to the extent that they preoccupy him or her outside the sessions or preempt relationship with others, or if such affectionate and elated feelings (or narration about them) consume a

substantial portion of the sessions at the expense of content-related material, one may say that the patient's affect has reached excessive intensity, and thus warrants being considered transferential.

3. *Intransigency (or tenacity).* The patient may sporadically talk about his or her good thoughts, fantasies, or wishes with regard to the therapist, especially when justified with content material (for example, appreciatively acknowledging some change in his or her life and attributing it to the therapist). But when these expressions become persistent and tenaciously remain at center stage, never disappearing for any discernible length of time, or are chronically intertwined with content material, they may be considered as intransigent, thus transferential.

4. *Thematic perseveration.* The patient may talk about any personal or impersonal matter, but particularly when it is related to undermining his or her own attributes (the other side of the therapist idealization coin)—that is, undesirable qualities that reflect low self-esteem, such as not being smart or interesting or attractive or sophisticated, or not deserving what he or she has in life (job, spouse, money, success)—the therapist should be especially alerted. If any of these concerns becomes a focus of attention that is repeated incessantly or indulged in exclusively, it falls into the category of thematic perseveration, and is thus transferential. Thematic perseveration is not limited to self-abasement, however. Other thematic perseverations are also transferentially based, easily recognized by the therapist, and considered as a resistance. Self-degrading perseverations (which unduly inflate the therapist by implication) are particularly problematic because they may be misunderstood by the therapist as requiring empathy or sympathy, and may lead to further confusion of the "real" and transferential roles of the therapist.

5. *Obviously identifiable origin of displaced feelings.* The patient may present historical material with such a wide range of experiences and emotions (often ambivalent) that the transfer of these to the therapist may not be easily identifiable. However, at times in the patient's narratives one individual will stand out as highly influential or as the object of very powerful feelings. Both the affect itself and the nature of that earlier relationship, if repeatedly enacted with the therapist, are most likely carrying transferential elements.

Although positive transference is an asset during the initial phase of treatment as a basis for the alliance between patient and therapist, sooner or later it can also begin to be used as a resistance to treatment. Resistance may come in the form of a temporary impasse or even permanent termination. The most commonly experienced positive transference flights from therapy belong to the following categories: *(a)* a patient dreads becoming dependent and is frightened that the therapist may encourage dependency, so leaves while he or she is still independent; (b) a patient appreciates, highly values, and admires the therapist, and feels unequal to the task, so does not return because he or she does not want to waste the therapist's time; (c) a patient begins to fall in love with the therapist and feels embarrassed and unworthy, so does not want to stay around to be rejected; or (d) a patient is sexually attracted to the therapist, and is afraid that the therapist may not find him or her sexually interesting or desirable, so leaves for fear of humiliation. Alternatively, more disturbed patients worry that the therapist may in fact respond to the patient's advances. Or patients of the same sex as the therapist may pose a special problem, the potential for "homosexual panic."

Of course, positive transferential feelings are grist for the mill of therapy. As long as the fears or wishes of the patient are interpreted, they will not become obstacles in treatment; in fact, they can move the treatment to a more advanced stage. On the other hand, interpreting nontransferential positive feelings of the patient for the therapist can leave the patient exposed, diminished, and ultimately depleted. Such a patient is not angry and full of rage but, rather, feels emotionally wiped out and undone because he or she has been slowly but progressively undermined. The patient displays the reaction of a temporarily diminished or defeated self. The session may wind down gradually because the patient has nowhere to go.

It must be remembered, nonetheless, that transferential and real feelings reside along a continuum—there is no pure form of either. The clinician needs to identify the primary motivation of the patient in order to make better use of his or her feelings and to know whether to interpret them or not. This process is especially important in the beginning phase of treatment because the failure of interpretation here has the greatest potential impact—premature termination. In the middle phase, such a failure only interferes with the deepening of conflictual material and regression of the patient. In the termination phase, it unnecessarily prolongs the treatment (but does not destroy it). Thus, confusing the patient's "natural" positive feelings with the transference in these last two stages and making transferential interpretations do no real harm. In the middle phase, interpretation will intensify the feelings of the patient and may reactivate some negative transferences; in the final phase, the therapist's interpretation of nontransferential positive feelings may speed up the termination but leave some unfinished business. Otherwise, unnecessary interpretation in the advanced stages of treatment has no serious consequences; it changes the course of treatment in a limited and temporary way. However, the noninterpretation of positive transference at formative stages substantially changes the course of treatment.

At the same time, the interpretation of reasonable positive feelings of the patient toward the therapist—as if they are transferential—can bring the sessions to an end whereby the patient feels both misunderstood and emptied out and has nowhere else to go. If the patient is not using positive feelings as a resistance, there is no clinical reason to expose them. Thus, it becomes imperative during the first phase of treatment to decide whether the patient simply has positive feelings toward the therapist which should be capitalized on for the patient's well-being, or whether the patient's feelings are a transference phenomenon which should be interpreted to prevent an impasse.

Case Illustration

PATIENT: This is really an important and valuable experience for me. I never had therapy before, and I was somewhat skeptical whether I could benefit from it. I guess I was also afraid to look at myself squarely and make some hard decisions. The greatest fear, though, was to see "a psychiatrist." You know, that caricature of the therapist, not saying a word, just staring at you, cold and distant, emotionally ungiving. It was a wonderful surprise to meet you. You were not like that at all. You smile, you say hello, you respond, you say things. I am really so lucky; I feel cared about and even liked; I don't know. You are kind and gentle even when you ask some tough questions; you make it so easy to answer.

THERAPIST: You are so complimentary toward me?

PATIENT: No, really it is true; that is exactly how I feel. I don't believe you even need compliments. I wouldn't do it for that at all. You seem so comfortable with yourself, with what you do. Complimenting would be like, sort of out of order, so unnecessary.

THERAPIST: How does it make you feel to be so positive toward me?

PATIENT: How does it feel? Oh, I am fine with that, to feel positive toward you. As I said earlier, I just couldn't be luckier; to take and to respect one's therapist the way that I felt toward my father! I respected and liked him very much, too, but it's not comparable. He was my father. I loved him—that was expected. He loved me, too, just a

191

natural relationship. But to find a stranger, a therapist with qualities that one can admire, to really like the person, that is so rare.

THERAPIST: You skipped "to love."

PATIENT: To love, you mean to love you? No, I don't think so. You mean sexual love? I don't think so, I am not aware of it, unless it is so unconscious that I can't get in touch with it. I didn't love my father in a sexual way either. My mother says, though, that I went through what is called the oedipal stage. Apparently I was quite seductive and explicitly sexual with him when I was 4 or 5 years old. I have no recollections. But when I say I loved him, I mean the way the child loves one's parent, same way I love my mother, even more so.

THERAPIST: You said you don't recall your sexual feelings toward your father?

PATIENT: If I have them, they are unconscious; I don't know what to say about it. They are not bothering me, that I could say. If they ever become conscious I'll certainly talk about it. I feel quite comfortable talking with you about almost anything. But I feel like I am disappointing you for not having unconscious thoughts or not remembering them. I feel like I failed you. Is it possible that I am resisting, as you said the other day? I mean, am I *supposed* to have sexual fantasies about you? What is the matter with me? Am I desexualizing everything? Couldn't one just have affectionate feelings? I guess I am still a child; I don't really believe that but . . . *(Remains quiet)* funny, I don't know what I could talk about now . . . like there's nothing I feel like saying. I don't know what happened, but right now I feel empty, I guess. All of a sudden I feel all alone. [For the remainder of the session this sense of emptiness permeates the patient's feelings and she continues to say very little.]

The therapist who does not see any of the signals of transference (identifiable origin, intensity and intransigency, relative inappropriateness, or thematic perseveration), but who still insists on interpreting the patient's "real" positive feelings as transference may be reflecting his or her own problems or vulnerability. Apart from a theoretical commitment to an "everything is transference" position, it is useful to wonder what such a therapist is afraid of—being liked, respected, dependent, admired? Does he or she feel undeserving of all that? Is he or she afraid of disappointing the patient? Is he or she worried about the expression or lack of control of his or her own feelings, wanting to keep treatment on a totally impersonal basis? Does he or she have a problem with modulating intimacy and closeness and drawing boundaries when needed? If the therapist is unable immediately to discern the difference between positive feelings and positive transference, he or she will probably recognize it retroactively, after realizing that the patient has gradually been rendered impotent by a therapist who, through misidentification and thus mismanagement of positive affect, has contributed to that diminution of self and sense of void.

CHAPTER 32

The beginning and ending of sessions tend to be untidy and must be tied together

IN PARALLEL WITH THE DEVELOPMENTAL CONTINUITY of the entire course of therapy from onset (initiation phase) to departure (termination phase), each separate session can be viewed as a microcosm of treatment with its own integrity. Thus the end of each session has a significant thematic relationship to the beginning of that session. The patient may bring up a subject at the onset of the hour, only to drop it until the final moments, unless it is satisfactorily dealt with during the course of the session. Opening themes are not only transferential but reflect a variety of important issues, including present and past historical connections, events within versus outside of treatment, and the like.

However, as Hans H. Strupp and Jeffrey L. Binder (1984) note, at times the major theme of the session may not be so easy to detect. Often the therapist will have to listen for a long time before a salient theme emerges. At other times the patient will be so defended that any significant connecting thread between early and late verbalizations seems broken or lost completely. These authors insist nonetheless that such thematic material is never really gone, but merely recedes from view. It can temporarily elude the therapist, or—perhaps more problematic—get acted out so that the transformation into behavior masks verbal cues to the nature of the conflictual content. But such themes invariably reappear at some point or points during the session, usually in the subtler aspects of the therapist–patient relationship. Thus, untidy or loosely connected sessions are not to be erroneously regarded as wasted or "bad" hours; rather, the material has yet to be carefully tied together.

The diversity and richness of the patient's associations and elaborations, compounded by the direction taken by the therapist, can easily derail the patient from his or her original agenda. In fact, it is quite possible that the overt agenda itself was fake, defensively meant to send the therapist on a dynamic detour.

Nevertheless, attempts to return to the initial material will help make the hour cohesive and will test the falseness or genuineness of the initial agenda. At worst, an artificially induced connection will be made by the therapist, only to be quickly dismissed by the patient. More commonly, concerns, anxieties, and preoccupations of daily life will be addressed as a precursor to or accompaniment of insight, playing an important cathartic or preparatory role to making deeper dynamic connections. At best, the session's beginning and end become integrally linked, and important insights can occur.

The emergence of thematic content is placed in bold relief by so-called entrance and exit lines, as will be discussed next. The patient's initial and final communications to the therapist either forecast or reveal in retrospect the most telling concern of the hour. Specific entrance and exit lines are not only directly meant for the therapist and thus primarily transferential in nature, but address themselves to particular psychological themes of arrival and departure, especially the vicissitudes of interpersonal engagement and disengagement.

CHAPTER 33

Exit and entrance lines reflect the transferential themes of separation and intimacy

---

Exit Lines

THE FRENCH have long recognized a lingering phenomenon of unfinished ideas or words upon leavetaking, repartee thought of only too late on the way out; they refer to the unsaid residue or ghost as *esprit de l'escalier* (spirit of the staircase). After we get past the door, we may regret what we failed to say or be preoccupied with what we should have said. As an extension of this commonplace circumstance, what I am concerned with here is a related phenomenon: what the person *does* say just before departing. In everyday conversation, legal debate, or personal argument, we are all familiar at one time or another with the need, or at least the wish, to make the final pronouncement. Such verbalizations can become memorable utterances of great power, enduringly remembered and repeated as famous last words.

Exit lines have typically been used in the theater as a deliberate dramatic technique to set the stage for subsequent or final scenes by creating a verbal climax. Being given no time to respond to a parting speech or remark, the stunned protagonist (as well as the audience) is left behind in a state of suspended silence—just as the curtain comes down. In the psychotherapy office, the drapes need not descend, but those last

196

strokes of the therapist's (real or symbolic) clock may be a comparable cue of unresolved dialogue coming to a close. What the patient blurts out in those precious minutes may be the culmination, not of what he or she has already revealed, but of what has not been said during the hour itself.

Few therapies, with the express exception of James Mann's (1973) time-limited psychotherapy, address the meaning of time. In short-term treatment a preset and finite framework is now known to affect the emergence as well as the resolution of significant conflictual themes. Unconsciously or consciously there is a heightening of the patient's temporal awareness, an increasing realization that time in therapy, as in life itself, is limited. Even in long-term treatment, whose endpoint is less determined, each session may be a microcosm of the constraints of time, creating an urgency in the patient to make the final moments matter.

In the comparable context of psychological testing, Stanley Appel-baum (1961) found that the last response on a Rorschach test was often the most significant and diagnostically revealing of the patient's psychopathology. Knowing that he or she will not immediately have to face the consequences of parting words can give the patient courage to say what he or she would otherwise not be able to. Whether in theater, testing, or therapeutic situations, such responses are presumably products, at least in part, of the subjective sense that time is running out. In fact, deathbed wishes (such as Jane Austen's "I want nothing but death"), questions (such as King George V's "How is the empire?"), or requests (such as Pavlova's "Get my Swan costume ready"), which represent the person's "last gasp confession or revelation" before dying (O'Kill 1986), may be the essence of the exit line.

Psychotherapy has its own version of exit lines, likewise carefully timed so that there is no immediate opportunity for a return remark by the therapist. In addition, such utterances are often deceptively presented as if they are merely afterthoughts that are not connected to the session. In his treatise on the beginning of treatment, Freud (1913) observed a problematic tendency of this kind, that certain of his patients who were reluctant to use the couch attempted to make an artificial separation between the formal therapy process which occurred lying down and the less formal aspects which transpired upon entering and ending the hour. These patients erroneously assumed that what was revealed standing up would not be delved into. Freud therefore warned therapists to take note of what is said before and after the session proper in an effort at "pulling down the partition which the patient has tried to erect" (p. 139). Since he was primarily concerned with alerting clinicians to this type of defensive behavior, which he regarded as a form of resistance, Freud did not actually analyze the meaning of the particular contents of the exit lines.

In a more recent attempt to explore the clinical occurrence and meaning of the exit line, four case examples indicated its special role as "a defense against the feelings evoked by the experience of separation" (Gabbard 1982, 586). To soften the blow of abandonment, it has been suggested, these times can bridge the hour with the external world. In the patient's attempt to bind intra- and intersession events, the exit line phenomenon may involve, in this view, "a fantasied continued relationship outside the session" (p. 580). As the therapist is abruptly left without sufficient time for an appropriate rebuttal, it may furnish the more specific fantasy for the patient of somehow having triumphed (albeit temporarily). Particularly if the therapist has just announced that the hour is over, the patient accomplishes dual aims: he or she has perhaps fended off the narcissistic injury of being reminded that one cannot stay as long as one wishes, while at the same time leaving a lasting imprint upon the therapist's postsession thoughts. The patient may have bodily left the premises, but he or she lives on in the therapist's mind.

Case Illustration

A thirty-seven-year-old woman, a junior executive, had been talking for several weeks about wanting to change her job, complaining of the routinized and ungratifying quality of her administrative position, which she said was "without tangible results." She also spoke of the unresponsiveness of her superiors and of not having "supportive" peer relationships. The therapist focused on various nuances of her complaints and her need to find new work, helping her to further explore pros and cons of her situation and possible alternatives. The patient could not make a decision, nor could she talk about anything else. The hours continued to have obsessive, ruminative qualities without any sign of resolution.

In the ninth session the patient repeated the same issues. Feeling demonstrably frustrated, on her way out she said:

PATIENT: I may have to revamp my whole life. I told Gerry [her boyfriend] that I'll no longer see him. In fact, I may even have to get rid of all my friends, or so-called friends. [After an exit line that reveals the signs of negative transference, at the next opportunity the therapist does best to raise the issue, whether or not the patient pursues it.]

THERAPIST: Obviously you may have lots of terminations on your mind. Let's continue the subject at our next meeting. [The therapist finally recognizes the transferential implications of all the previous job termination discussions, but realizes that it is too late in the hour to address the subject of termination of treatment because the patient is on her way out.]

The patient arrived at the next session rather cheerful, animated, and even playful. She spent the first fifteen minutes giving the details of a new encounter with a man who was ten years younger than her, talking about how virile he was. The therapist waits for a suitable, that is, content-congruent, moment to interrupt.

THERAPIST: You are quite excited to find this new relationship, especially that it happened just when you were thinking about terminating with Gerry. [The word *termination* is reintroduced in order to set the semantic stage for discussing the patient's relationship with the therapist. The "new relationship" and the excitement about it is mentioned to bridge both content and process.]

PATIENT: Yes, the timing could not have been better. I usually have difficulty in terminating a relationship, unless there is at least a potential replacement on the horizon.

THERAPIST: So, this is at least a beginning of the revamping of all your relationships. [By using the phrase "all your relationships" the therapist is moving away from Gerry and generalizing temporarily, to be specific a little later.]

PATIENT: At least those that have not been useful or good for me.

THERAPIST: Is our relationship classified under that "not useful" category?

PATIENT: Oh? We have a relationship? It seems like I come here twice a week to complain about my life. You listen—at least I presume you listen—then I leave with the same problems. *(All the cheerful facade disappears and the patient's anger and frustration with the therapist come to the surface)* [At times the therapist may be fooled by a pseudopositive facade. He may believe that somehow the negativity has dissipated and may settle down to work on the presented content. But this only generates further resentment that can blow up later.]

THERAPIST: On your way out the last time, you mentioned "getting rid of" some people. I guess I must be one of them.

The therapist intentionally chooses the strongest wording, "getting rid of." Recognizing the negative feelings of the patient and reflecting them back undiluted can help the patient to see that the therapist will squarely face affects and issues and is not afraid of aggression. If the therapist is willing to be harsh on himself or herself, the patient will not escalate the negativism, and in fact quite often will try to soften the blow. Thus, not being afraid to say things, even in an unconventional fashion, sets an example of communication for the patient. Although the therapist chooses the strongest wording the patient used, he purposely does not exaggerate it because he does not want to convey sarcasm, which would belittle the patient and imply that her feelings are unreasonable. Such tactics may generate guilt, anger, shame, or at least defensiveness, none of which are desirable in the therapeutic relationship.

PATIENT: Getting rid of you? Well, I have been wondering how this is going to help me. I have real problems out there. I need support. Maybe from a friend, or . . .

THERAPIST: Or at least from a supportive therapist who will bring about some "tangible results." [By reading the progress notes of the previous sessions, the therapist can bring in connecting words to the subsequent sessions. Even though the patient may not remember the exact words, he or she nevertheless may have a sense of familiarity when they are mentioned within a proper context.]

PATIENT: I don't want to come here and pay money just for supportive stuff. I am above that . . . I hope I am above that. I want to get stronger, be independent, shake this goddam self-pity, the neediness . . .

Entrance Lines

Besides the exit line phenomenon, wherein the patient's statements at the end of the hour reflect heightened transference-countertransference manifestations (Gabbard 1982), there are also intriguing entrance lines. Even if the therapist is not psychologically left in the lurch, I believe them to be equally a function of intensified therapist–patient relations. Specifically, while exit lines tend to be strong expressions of transferential feelings, entrance lines are more subtle defenses against them. What they have in common, however, is that the less the therapist deals with transferential issues during the session, the more he or she is likely to be subjected to highly charged exit and entrance lines. Moreover, whereas exit lines may be aggressive responses in the face of impending *separation*, entrance lines may be passive-aggressive responses in the face of impending *intimacy*. As Tarachow (1963) succinctly put it in his discussion of gratification and deprivation in psychotherapy, "Entering the room and leaving the room are important. Entering is love; leaving is abandonment" (p. 92).

Entrance lines are even more obscure than exit lines in their transferential messages; there is another layer of defensive structure built into their presentation, and the patient is less pressured for time. Also the therapist tends to take the first few exchanges of the hour as expressions of a brief social encounter and usually does not make much of them. It is obviously not appropriate to interpret the patient's entrance lines before he or she even sits down. The entrance is an awkward moment, and the therapist must try to make that transitional time as easy as possible.

However, the therapist should register the patient's entrance lines, using them later in the session when they fit the unfolding material. And it is best to dismiss the usual utterances of routine encounters—"Good morning," "It's a nice day," "How are you?"—without endowing them with additional meaning. The therapist's attitude reflects a welcoming of the patient, as he or she similarly responds casually—"Yes, it is nice," "Fine, thank you"—without indulging these social amenities further.

On the other hand, the following entrance lines may represent transferential feelings, and, more commonly, resistances against them:

- "I almost forgot that we had a session today."
- "The traffic was terrible. I was tempted to turn around to go back home."
- "Sorry I'm late. I couldn't leave the office early; I had a lot to do."
- "It's so difficult to park around here."
- "You look tired. Am I the last patient tonight?"
- "While I was sitting in the waiting room, I was wondering what I should talk about."
- "Let's see. Where were we? It seems that the last session was such a long time ago."
- "Well, nothing is new since our last meeting."
- "Here we are again."
- "It was so good to be away."
- "Did you receive the check?"
- "The patient who just left didn't look very happy."
- "You start so early."

In contrast to negative transference itself, the resistance to transference need not necessarily be interpreted. If the therapist chooses to maintain a low level of transference intensity, he or she can very well leave those resistances alone. Such a decision may be clinical (the intensity of transference may be destabilizing for some patients); may be practical (infrequent visits make transferential-based treatment impossible); may be a professional or personal choice to limit the treatment to a more here-and-now encounter with the therapist and focus primarily on current and outside issues; or may be countertransferential, that is, the therapist's personal reaction to the patient influences the decision to engage a certain patient with more or less intensity. But the therapist who works within transference-based treatment has to deal with these resistances. The entrance lines can give the therapist an opening to such resistances, as the heightened arousal of the initial few moments tends to display both transference and resistance.

Once the therapist decides to do so, the resistance to transference is best handled by interpreting just the resistance, not the transference itself. Say the patient begins the session with: "I almost forgot that we had a session today." The therapist can take one of two approaches:

1. Interpret the transference: "I wonder whether that reflects certain strong feelings toward me? [Transferential interpretations are tentative, preferably in question form.]
2. Interpret the resistance to transference: "Part of you is trying to stop you from coming to see me." [Interpretation of resistance can be assertive without worrying about the patient's reaction because the therapist is allying with him, or at least part of him.]

Mistaking the resistance for transference and interpreting it as such will reinforce the resistance, because the patient is unaware of feelings toward the therapist and is unconsciously defending against them. And obviously there is a dynamic reason for this defense that cannot be bypassed by simply addressing the existence of feelings toward the therapist. If the patient needs to defend against the internal forces, he or she certainly will fend off the outside forces, namely, the therapist's attempts. If the therapist insists on addressing the patient's feelings toward him or her, the patient will ignore, or even ridicule, the attempt. This is one of the impasses in which the therapist and patient may find themselves, in spite of their not wanting to be in it; rift and alienation follow. The patient will think that the therapist is barking up the wrong tree, and the therapist will think that the patient is defensive; both are correct.

Case Illustration

A fifty-five-year-old homosexual artist talked about his sense of isolation, his loneliness, and his depressed feelings. The patient was in the
waiting room for twelve minutes before the session.

PATIENT: *(While walking into the therapist's office)* I almost forgot that we
had a session today. I'm very busy these days. I am behind in my calls
and answering letters. It's just getting to be too much. [The therapist
thinks it is a little too early in the hour to interpret.] At times I am
overwhelmed with people. If they don't call, I feel neglected; if they
do, they seem to be overpowering. It's as if part of me wants to be
sociable and friendly and the other part just wants to hide under my
bed. I met this fellow recently. He is a cute, smart, thirty-two-year-old
lawyer who knows my work. He has one of my earlier paintings, so
he was all excited about meeting "the guru." We had a pizza in my
studio. I was very attracted to him. We ended up kissing and mastur-
bating each other. When I was done, I couldn't wait for him to get
out. *(Laughs)* Doc, do you know what eternity is? Eternity is the time
between when you come and he goes! *(Laughs very loudly)* It's like I
have to determine the amount and the frequency and the nature of
the relationship. Otherwise I feel stifled and angry and do something
to hurt the relationship.
THERAPIST: You "do something"? [The therapist wants him to identify
his defensive patterns.]
PATIENT: Yes, all kinds of stuff, getting drunk and nasty and abusive, not
calling back, canceling dates.
THERAPIST: Forgetting appointments?
PATIENT: I said "almost"; I don't feel stifled by you at all. In fact, you are
very underwhelming. *(Laughs again)* Actually I was looking forward
to the session all morning and then this afternoon I really almost
forgot it.
THERAPIST: As if *part of you* is trying to stop you from coming to see
me!
PATIENT: Against my own judgment, as they say. Am I schizophrenic?
What is it?
THERAPIST: Some internal forces . . .
PATIENT: *(Interrupting)* Unconsciously you think I don't want to come,
but why? It's my decision; if I want to stop, I'll do it anyway. I like
you too, so I guess all these years of marijuana smoking . . .

203

THERAPIST: *(Interrupting before another rationalization takes seed)* Or all those years of determining the nature of the relationship. Or maybe you have the feeling that you do not have full control over that here.

PATIENT: Yes, in fact I feel that you are in control of this relationship, which is not a comfortable feeling for me. Will I be pulled in, or thrown out?

THERAPIST: Loved or hurt?

PATIENT: Loved or hurt? I'm not sure I want either one from you. On the one hand, I don't want a relationship of any sort with you; on the other hand, I do, but how does that develop? What must I do? I hear other patients through the wall when I come early. They seem so engaged with you, addressing you specifically with strong feelings. Do I want that? I sort of envy it. Why can't I relate that way to you? In the last session, before you took a week off, I tried to get close to you. I was determined to be like the other patients. I asked you whether the therapist and the patient had to like each other for the therapy to be successful. You said that it wouldn't hurt, which was fine. I liked that. Then you asked whether I was asking whether or not you liked me. I said no, well, this was like putting my toe in hot water, just testing, not having all my foot in it. Then the wall came down and I went back to my impersonal isolation. I couldn't wait for the hour to be over. Although I missed you while you were away, I also dreaded seeing you.

THERAPIST: So "something" had to be done. [The therapist uses the patient's word.]

PATIENT: Yes, my mind had to do something—conveniently trying to forget the session. Isn't that clever?

The beginnings and endings of sessions are often untidy enough; these exit and entrance lines add additional complications, usually catching the therapist off guard, thus increasing the chances for him or her to make mistakes. Ironically enough, these errors by the therapist also tend to relate to the transference, but on such occasions they are invariably countertransferential.

PART VIII

ON TECHNIQUE AND ITS BOUNDARIES

This section is concerned with the major therapeutic strategies of treatment. It begins with two overriding aspects of being a clinician, each of which in some measure defines his or her technical boundaries. The first axiom pertains to the broader subject of the practitioner's professional versus private agenda. It addresses what is appropriate behavior in and out of sessions and has direct implications for countertransference responses, which can be a problem if brought into sessions unrecognized or not dealt with. The second axiom pertains to the primary therapeutic functions of the clinician within the sessions. In particular, the therapist's role of helper is differentiated from that of problem solver in characterizing the nature of the therapist's commitment to the patient.

These axioms are related in that they share a special complication: each resides at the interface of therapeutics and ethics. However, they differ in the character of their dilemmas: in the former (whereby the therapist may unconsciously extend a personal agenda into treatment), the clinician can in fact be unethical but does not realize it; and in the latter (whereby the therapist consciously abstains from trying to solve the patient's problem), the clinician may come upon conscious questions of moral responsibility. But as the therapist avoids an active stand or solution, he or she is technically above reproach because of the need to share the patient's problem, not solve it.

The remainder of the section begins where the therapist's listening role leaves off and the interpretive one begins. It thus addresses the sine qua non of psychodynamic technique—the carefully calibrated interpretation. General principles of interpretation are presented, followed by other conceptual and technical vicissitudes. The therapist listens at multiple levels, and then must be able to shift verbal strategies accordingly. The patient's psychopathology, defects, and defensive structure will naturally influence what the therapist says (and how it is said); the practitioner must in effect bend his or her techniques under the weight of the patient's problems. As a specific instance of this, "incomplete" interpretations are distinguished from "inexact" ones, although both types are considered to be intrinsically as well as deliberately incorrect. More generally, all cues and responses of the patient must be matched by techniques that are of comparable size or impact, so that the recipient is neither overwhelmed nor untouched by the power of each intervention.

Other matters, such as the different functions and effects of interpretive formulations, are further addressed, including theory-driven versus intimate interpretations, interpretations of symptoms versus interpretations of character traits, and the like. All interpretations are, at bottom, deprivations: "good" ones disappoint the patient because he or she may have to give up a cherished wish or defense, whereas "bad" ones can disengage the patient by exacerbating already shaky self-esteem within a defective self.

The following questions are posed: What are the therapist's primary strategies, and what are their therapeutic versus ethical implications? Beyond the therapist's listening role, what guiding principles suggest how to presume when he or she proceeds to speak? How does the patient's psychopathology or personality structure influence technique? More specifically, what are the functions and the limitations of interpretations? Given that some types of verbal response will be more appropriate and effective than others, what parameters are best for the careful clinician to consider?

CHAPTER 34

The therapist must not have a private agenda

THE THERAPIST, by definition, is in the service of the patient. This means that all of the clinician's activities during the sessions (thoughts included) need to center on how to reach and be helpful to the particular patient. It is the therapist's only appropriate agenda. Winnicott (1965) asserts that in maintaining a "professional attitude," the therapist "is not a rescuer, a teacher, an ally, or a moralist" (p. 162). Apart from being paid for his or her time and expertise, the therapist cannot expect to extract any other personal benefits, with the possible exception of that singular by-product, professional learning and growth.

Nonetheless, most clinicians now recognize that they can have a profound influence upon the patient despite ardent attempts at neutrality and anonymity, and the concept of the therapist as totally impersonal or value-free is in fact a fallacy (Strupp 1974). Although in psychodynamic treatment the uncommitted stance of the therapist has long been a primary requisite, it is increasingly understood to be an aspiration or ideal state, that the subjective values and viewpoints of the therapist are nonetheless implicitly (if not explicitly) transmitted to the patient.

Perhaps the most common private agenda may have to do with social mores, and the therapist may attempt wittingly or unwittingly to interject aspects of these into the hours themselves and to influence the patient's life accordingly. Typical ethical standards or personal preferences that frequently emerge in treatment can include sexual orientation or gender roles; attitudes toward marriage, divorce, extramarital affairs, single parenthood, or dual-career families; and values about work, school, or parental responsibilities. More controversial may be strong sentiments about political or sociocultural matters, from war to the distribution of condoms. As a prime example of this, a review of literature on psychotherapy and behavioral therapy indicated not so long ago that many therapists regarded homosexuality as undesirable, if not pathological (Davison and Wilson 1974). On a more practical plane, the therapist may be obliged to take a conceptual position, implicitly if not explicitly: Is heterosexuality the ultimate goal for the patient, or does he or she wish the patient to maximize the quality of homosexual life? The latter stance, often unpopular, was unexpectedly subject to clinical debate when a behavioral therapist treated a man who was sexually attracted to boys by providing him with methods to transfer that attraction to men (Garfield 1974; Davison and Wilson 1974). However, the presence of individual values and attitudes is not necessarily troublesome—*if* the therapist either can be sufficiently flexible and professionally dispassionate about them, or failing that, can openly acknowledge them.

Case Illustration

A twenty-eight-year-old man, married for four years, had just become the father of a baby girl. Since the beginning of his wife's pregnancy, the patient had been involved with another woman, Jane, ten years his senior. He was wondering what to do because Jane had recently become withdrawn, less available, and certainly not committed to him. He also said that he did not have the desire to leave his wife before she gave birth. Now he was feeling even more responsible but also loved his child. He had always fought with his wife, and there was "nothing pleasant" about their relationship until the birth of their child. At the same time, he yearned for Jane, with whom he communicated well. During the previous weekend, however, he had found out that Jane had been with another man. He felt as if the rug had been pulled from under his feet and that he would go crazy.

PATIENT: Do you think I should give in to my selfish desires and leave my family, so I could have Jane back?
THERAPIST: Have you had other affairs during the marriage? [Although

it may seem incongruent to answer the patient's direct question in this way, the therapist does not believe that a direct response to the patient would be helpful. He also feels that more information is necessary; for example, he would like to find out if there is a pattern to the patient's behavior.]

PATIENT: Yes, a few others. I seem to be wanting and needing more women. I may not be able to stay monogamous. But with Jane, it is really special.

THERAPIST: If you can't stay monogamous with your wife, what makes you think that you'll do so with Jane? [The therapist introduces his own value system by implicitly discouraging the patient from leaving his wife.]

PATIENT: I don't know, maybe I'll not do that, although the other day when I went with Jane to a small restaurant, the waitress who served us was a beautiful actress or something. I gave her my card on the way out. I had written on it in the bathroom: "My sister would not have approved of my trying to pick you up, which is why I am giving you my card. Please try to call." I said to myself later, how could I be in love and do this?

THERAPIST: Then you'll not be faithful to Jane, and the whole scenario will be repeated soon with Jane as well. [The therapist emphasizes the pattern and also points out that the issue is not with his wife or Jane, but with himself. Leaving his wife will not solve his problem. This pattern will be reiterated with different women. The therapist continues to assert his agenda. Even though the therapist may be right in his understanding of the case, nevertheless his unspoken focus is: Do not leave your wife.]

PATIENT: You mean, so why do I want to leave my wife? Well, isn't there any justification, considering all my problems with my wife? We have many problems in communication, so many fights, wouldn't it be better if we divorced?

THERAPIST: Have you ever gone to a marriage counselor together? [The therapist is following the same track, but this time more appropriately.]

PATIENT: No, a few times we talked about it, but we never went beyond that. Do you feel we should both see you rather than me seeing you alone?

THERAPIST: I think it would be useful for both of you to see a marriage counselor to try to work out at least your communication problem, in addition to your seeing me alone.

PATIENT: So, do you have someone to recommend?

The patient easily agrees with the therapist's conceptualization of treatment, and a new reality seems to be forged in synchrony; or is this change just doctrinal compliance by the patient? An examination of therapeutic trends and their ethical implications (Redlich and Mollica 1976) suggests that a "fiduciary" approach, in which the patient places total trust in the physician's ability and willingness to make crucial decisions, is being replaced by a more mutual "contractual" arrangement. Moreover, Carl Goldberg's (1978) exposition on an equitable "therapeutic partnership" between client and clinician points out that the partnership is founded not only on the nature of the power distribution (that is, how *equal* it is), but on the degree to which it is made *explicit*. In either event, in the case just cited the therapist's personal views on the matter of marriage have influenced his attitude toward the patient and his treatment approach. However, the therapist's conscious or unconscious application of his own point of view appears relatively benign. It is primarily in the best interests of the patient, especially insofar as it also represents a socially and religiously sanctioned value of the larger shared cultural context.

CHAPTER 35

The therapist's task is to experience the patient's dilemma, not to solve the patient's problems

T HE THERAPIST, unlike the internist or surgeon, deliberately does not intervene to solve the patient's problems or even advise the patient to proceed in a particular direction. He or she avoids recommending what actions to take, however tempting this may be, such as persuading a patient to dissolve a troubled marriage, encouraging him or her to quit a job, or directing him or her to be more assertive or sexual. For better or worse, the patient usually has received similar advice and opinions from many others, and yet another adviser is often just what the patient does not need. Rather, the therapist purposely steps back and, at least in part, allows the patient just to be himself or herself and to experience his or her dilemma without additional demands or directives.

Furthermore, life's problems are never so simple or straightforward as to be remedied by the therapist's direction or persuasion. The issues and conflicts brought to the psychotherapist are usually complex and multidetermined, the accompanying feelings invariably deeply rooted and ambivalent; they cannot be resolved with someone else's solutions or recommendations, no matter how expert or presumably objective.

Even if the patient continually asks for answers from the therapist and it appears, at least overtly, as if the clinician is prolonging the patient's suffering by not directly responding, the therapist is not simply being sadistic, irresponsible, or unethical. There are powerful internal and

211

external reasons for the patient's maintaining a troubled marriage or being unassertive. The psychotherapist's role is to identify these forces behind the status quo, bring them to the surface for exploration and understanding, help the patient to experience the different valences that are creating conflicts, and share the patient's feelings as he or she and the therapist together search for solutions. The therapist's role is not to try to solve the patient's problems or make decisions for him or her.

It is a difficult task for a therapist to refrain from encouraging the patient to follow a particular path, especially when it appears to be the "right" solution to the patient's problem. Indeed, the therapist may be tempted to take an active role, temporarily or permanently, depending upon the particular patient's strengths and pathology. While not all such acts necessarily constitute direct advice or guidance, some may border on nonneutrality. The clinician may, for example, naturally want to encourage obsessive patients to ruminate less and feel more; to assist impulsive or histrionic patients to think before they act; to give inhibited patients the permission to take risks; to supportively collude with a paranoid patient's skewed view of the universe; to directly challenge (in the manner of cognitive therapy) the depressive patient's assumptions that dwell behind his or her pessimistic view of himself or herself, others, and the world; or for occasional purposes of expedience, act as ombudsman or strategist in helping to fight the patient's family or social battles.

But the competent clinician exercises restraint for good reason: he or she is not being unhelpful, inappropriate, cold, and ungiving for withholding advice or direction. The issue is dynamic: the moment the therapist takes a stand, he or she will disturb the intrapsychic balance of the patient's conflict. The patient's perspective will shift to counterbalance the therapist's position, thus creating an iatrogenic alteration of forces. Anna Freud (1936) advised that the therapist should not crusade for or against the three psychic structures, that he or she "stand at a point equidistant from the id, the ego, and the superego" (p. 28). She was urging the therapist not to become aligned with a particular position— not to campaign for instinctual gratification, or aim to reinforce moderation, or take a moral stance that may foster guilt or shame.

Let's say that the therapist conveys the message that the patient should leave his wife; then the patient's ambivalence, not only toward his wife but toward the therapist, will bring up additional reasons for him not to leave her. Thus the advice and encouragement in fact may perpetuate the conflict and indecisiveness, not diminish it. Furthermore, since the decision did not originate in the patient himself, the action will add other troubles to the patient's psyche, making him feel that in spite of the therapist's help he is not succeeding. Thus he ends up feeling worse about himself, that he is not well understood or that he has failed the therapist. As a consequence, the patient may either try even harder to please the therapist by making decisions in spite of himself (with unknown psychic consequences) or try to avoid the therapist (another countertherapeutic act).

Case Illustration

A young lawyer left her previous therapist because he was too task-oriented and directive, although she may have needed someone like him then (approximately three years before). She made good use of treatment, but was concerned that she might have lost three years of her life. With her former therapist's active direction, she asked for a promotion and got it, became more assertive with her friends, equalized the relationship with her husband, and demanded sexual gratification (which was successfully received). But something was missing. Although she was doing all these things as she was advised, she felt that she had played an insignificant part in solving her problems; she needed another therapist in order to proceed further. It was as if there was no accrued benefit from these accomplishments because they had been artificially acquired—she had compliantly been doing what others wished—in *their* behalf, not her own.

PATIENT: *(Extremely anxious)* I found out that I can do all these things, but do I want to? I am not sure what I want; I seem to be wanting what should be wanted, or what others want, or what others think I should want. So I jump through hoops. Do I want it? Why do they want me to do things? Is it good for me?

THERAPIST: Everyone seems to know what is good for you!

The therapist does *not* say: (a) How come you don't know what is good for you? (Campaigning for the superego would generate guilt, shame, or embarrassment.) (b) Why not find out exactly what you want and go do it? (Campaigning for the id may generate confusion, acting out, and further conflicts.) (c) Well, let's figure out what you really want. (Campaigning for the ego may generate a sense of inadequacy, wrong, or pseudosolutions.) All of these three postures will set the therapist against the patient in one way or another.

PATIENT: How come I don't?

THERAPIST: Somehow, you know, though, what they want you to do and you do it.

PATIENT: Yes, I do, and maybe just to please them. How is it that I am here to please others though, and do I want to please them? And *why* do I want to please them? Does it please me to please others?

THERAPIST: Confusing.

The therapist empathically recognizes the difficult position the patient is in. The therapist does *not* say: (a) I wonder whether under the guise of pleasing others you are expressing different feelings, such as anger. (This is a theoretically biased interpretation, even if it is true. The therapist is far ahead of the patient by campaigning for expression of her "true feelings" toward others. The patient most likely will deny such feelings and feel misunderstood, undermined, or at least preempted.) (b) You must have an internal need to please others. (This superego interpretation tends to put the blame on the patient for needing to appease others for being bad or having done something wrong. The patient would feel accused to have his or her badness confirmed or at least discovered.) (c) By adaptively pleasing others you may be getting what you want, whatever that is. (This ego interpretation reduces the patient to a coping, if not manipulating, being, and may at least shortchange the complexity of the patient's dilemma.)

PATIENT: Yes, it is confusing. Maybe that is what life is all about—to do your chores, get rewarded, and go on doing them again tomorrow and the next day. Then I say to myself that it cannot be. I went to a therapist for three years in order to figure out all this because I was confused. And I ended up converting him into yet another of my directors who tells me what to do, how to do it, how to feel. Then once I discovered what *he* wanted, it was very easy. I spent the next three years doing things that he would approve of. Each week I would go in and tell him my accomplishments, then walk out feeling that I had done my duty to my therapist. My inner confusion is not knowing what *I* want. Last night I couldn't sleep, I kept on thinking about it. I woke up at four A.M. I tried to read, which irritates my husband; he is a light sleeper. So I lay in the bed with my eyes open. I thought about taking a sleeping pill. Then I thought that in another two hours I would have to get up anyway, in order to be here on time. So I decided not to take the pill. I stayed there two solid hours.

214

I tried everything—counting numbers, sheep, relaxation techniques, thinking all sorts of stuff.

THERAPIST: Troublesome night?

The therapist does *not* say: (a) Have you tried self-hypnosis? (That would be campaigning for a more resourceful ego.) (b) You must get sufficient sleep. (Allying with a demanding superego makes the patient feel guilty.) (c) You are the one who is having difficulty all night and meanwhile worrying about your husband's reaction. (Encouraging aggressive impulses ignores the patient's real dilemma.)

PATIENT: Yes, most troublesome. Occasionally I have such nights. Before trials I used to have this anticipatory anxiety; now I know what they want and, believe me, I can deliver. All I have to figure out is what sort of hoops they have for me to jump through.

THERAPIST: Have you figured out what sort of hoops I have? [Again the therapist does not address the patient's ego, id, or superego by saying: (a) Well, we all jump through some hoops in life. (b) Why don't you make some of your hoops and jump through them? (c) Stop jumping through everyone's hoops.]

PATIENT: Not exactly. You don't suggest that I should do this or that; you don't seem to be that interested whether I had orgasm or not when I mentioned we had sex; I somehow don't talk about my daily life here. I am not sure what I do here; at times I leave and have no idea what I said here. My husband asks me how the session was. I say it was interesting; then he wants to know what we discussed, but I have no idea. He thinks that I am holding back because we used to talk about my sessions in depth in the past. So I can't really tell what hoops I have to jump through here; I don't know what they are. Last night when I was awake, I was hoping to fall asleep, to have some interesting dreams. Maybe that is what you would like to hear; I am not sure.

THERAPIST: You want to hand over some hoops to me. [The therapist does not ask about interesting dreams. That would replay the old scenario of pleasing the therapist.]

PATIENT: Yes, so I can jump through and everyone is happy.

THERAPIST: So I'll be pleased, and your anxiety and confusion will be contained. [The therapist narrows the subject because of the patient's tendency to generalize and makes tentative affect/behavior connections.]

PATIENT: To contain my anxiety and confusion, you think that is all I am doing? I designed my world this way just to contain my anxiety and confusion? I mean the marriage and the job, friends, therapy, so that I'll be less anxious? But it never really worked; I mean, it does not work. By pleasing everyone, I become less anxious, but then I am resentful, angry, and depressed, as if I am cheating myself.

THERAPIST: You seem to be stuck between two equally undesirable choices: either anxiety *or* anger and depression. [The therapist only underlines the affective dilemma. The therapist has rejected the following possibilities: (a) Which one—the anxiety or the anger and depression—is less tolerable for you? (This would have sought a more adaptive ego by choosing the lesser evil.) (b) You have been cheating yourself for a long time. (This would have allied with a shame- and guilt-producing superego.) (c) Why don't you just say, "to hell with the job and friends and therapy? (This would have encouraged the discharge of drives or their derivatives.)]

PATIENT: *(Extremely serious and anxious)* So, what shall I do? What does one do?

THERAPIST: No thanks. [The therapist does not succumb to: (a) Why are you so anxious or deadly serious? (This would reduce the patient's ego.) (b) Why do you keep insisting on giving me the hoops? (This would foster a guilt-inducing, blaming superego.) (c) I wonder whether you want to request the same relation with me as the one you had with your previous therapist, in spite of the expressed desire not to. (This would intellectualize the process, rather than affectively engage the patient.)]

PATIENT: No thanks, for what?

THERAPIST: For the hoops.

PATIENT: *(Laughs)* Well, if you are not going to take them, what will I do? I guess you mean that from now on I have to keep them.

CHAPTER 36

The careful interpretation meets four criteria: optimum timing, minimum dosage, concrete detail, and individual focus

THE CLINICIAN can frequently have in mind an interpretive link to the patient's behavior, but it may have to remain in abeyance until the most propitious moment. To receive an interpretation profitably, the patient must be psychologically prepared for it. The therapist can carefully calibrate interpretations by means of four technical principles: (1) optimum timing, (2) minimum dosage, (3) concrete detail, and (4) individual focus. The case illustration that follows represents the application, or violation, of these four principles in the treatment of one patient.

Case Illustration

A forty-two-year-old divorced woman complained of dizziness for about six months. She was checked thoroughly and found to be in excellent physical shape. She was the co-owner of a small business that was growing rapidly and was in the process of opening a satellite shop in a different neighborhood. Her partner was becoming romantically interested in her, while she had a lover about whom she was conflicted because he drank too much. Her children were, in her words, "typical teenagers." She described her seventeen-year-old daughter as "very beautiful," and her sons, age fourteen and eleven, as "athletic and doing OK in school."

Optimum Timing

Temporal synchronicity refers to both the patient's readiness to receive the interpretation at the time and the therapist's recognition that he or she can anticipate little resistance. Reaching this mutual moment often requires lengthy preparation. Failing to calibrate timing invariably has countertherapeutic results: whereas premature interpretations may not be received or may even be rejected, delayed interpretations may dissipate and lose their emotional impact.

With patients who are not very receptive to introspection in spite of a careful preparatory phase of treatment, the therapist may improvise tentative interpretative statements—fully recognizing that the patient is not ready for them and the therapist is unsure of their salience. These are like little signals to the patient's unconscious, to see whether some activity can be generated. The Japanese have a relevant saying: just because the message may never be received does not mean that it is not worth sending.

These tentative interpretations have to be repeated occasionally to test whether they are being at least partly accepted. The patient's initial negative reaction or indifference need not deter the therapist from exercising this technique. As long as the patient keeps returning to the sessions, the therapist may not be completely off track. For example, patients who have physical symptoms or medical illnesses with strong psychological components, because of their tendency to somaticize their conflicts, are generally candidates for this technique. Due to their "alexithymic" qualities (Sifneos 1973)—pragmatic thinking, defenses against insight, absence of ability or motivation for self-examination, and the like—optimum timing may take longer to achieve.

The following is an example of the patient's repeated rejection of interpretations because of their prematurity. It represents a violation of the principle of optimum timing, among others. The patient opens the session with details of recent dramatic changes at work and in her relationships.

THERAPIST: A lot is coming at you. [The therapist attempts to link her physical complaints to the multiple stressors she has cited.]
PATIENT: Maybe it is too much, too fast.

THERAPIST: In fact, dizzying. [The therapist thinks that the patient is in synchrony with him and verbally introduces a term for her physical symptom in relation to her description of her problems, hoping to promote further synchronicity.]

PATIENT: A good friend of mine says that I should simplify my life, not open the other shop, marry this guy, my partner. You know, take it easy. But this guy is so dull. And Frank, when he isn't drinking, he is great to be with. I don't know which way to go, whom to turn to.

THERAPIST: You have been turning to doctors, your friends; everyone is showing you a different direction to take. All of this must be confusing. [Since the patient has ignored the therapist's attempt to semantically connect her dizziness to stresses that she is experiencing, he backs up one step, looking for a less resistant arena; he says, "I understand you. It must be confusing," hoping for an alternative area of alliance.]

PATIENT: Confusing, yes, and I am not sure which one is right.

THERAPIST: You keep turning these ideas over and over in your head. [This time the therapist is less subtle.]

PATIENT: At times I can't fall asleep all night, no matter what I do. Usually I take half a Seconal. Then I am out for a while, but in a few hours, I am up again.

THERAPIST: With those thoughts spinning in your head. [Again, the patient seems to ignore the therapist's attempts, but the therapist keeps coming back each time with a different angle of trying to connect her dizziness with her stresses.]

PATIENT: Yes, as if they are waiting there all the time. I've got to find the way; I must decide. Frank is a little bit of a lady's man. He likes younger women. I can't trust him too much. I'm a little worried that when I get older, he'll lose his interest. I know I am getting older and have put on a little too much weight. I used to be pretty good looking, not as beautiful as my daughter, but still—of course, she is, as they say, a knockout.

THERAPIST: How does it feel to have a beautiful daughter who is growing up? [The therapist temporarily gives up, as he recognizes that his interpretive efforts are not received by the patient. Is it the content of his interpretation that is wrong, or its timing?]

PATIENT: She's also a good girl, a little too naive maybe. When we walk together, all the heads turn, and she wonders whether there is something wrong with her. [The therapist registers her head turning and wonders how to use it.] I'll tell her that nothing is wrong, that people are just looking at her because she is very beautiful. She says,

"Oh, me! I'm not; you are the beautiful one." I hope she'll have better luck with her beauty than I did with mine. Anyway, there is no comparison.

THERAPIST: You really admire her beauty. It turns your head, too. [This is a long shot by the therapist, a slightly desperate attempt.]

PATIENT: Oh, yes, I watch her getting dressed. She is very special. She takes care of her body, too. In my day, we knew nothing. I feel like I wasted my youth. Now it seems a little too late. Frank says that I should exercise. He likes thin women. At times I see him watching Brenda [her daughter] with a different kind of look than he has with me.

Poorly timed interpretations, regardless of their historical or current truth value, have limited utility because they do not temporally resonate with the patient's experience. Occasionally, however, premature interpretations can be repeated at a later point with greater effect. More often, interpretations that are not optimally timed become a one-sided exercise, with the patient remaining passively unreceptive and unaffected, if not even more disturbed at the lack of connection.

Minimum Dosage

Interpretation, to borrow Noel Coward's statement about wit, ought to be "a glorious treat, like caviar, never to be spread about like marmalade." Every statement that the therapist makes must be minimal, but for interpretation, restraint is especially important. James Strachey (1934), for example, believed that for transferential interpretations (which he considered the only mutative ones) to be effective, they had to be governed by the "principle of minimum doses." The rationale behind this had to do with the excessive anxiety that results from the activation of too much affective (id) material. If the anxiety is more than the ego can bear, massive resistance may result. Heavy dosages of interpretation can overwhelm the patient. Only by being slowly released in easily digestible amounts will the interpretation have both immediacy and durability of emotional impact. In fact, a carefully conducted preparatory phase may even make the interpretation itself virtually mute.

The following is an example of a triple-barreled interpretation, which violates the minimum dose principle.

THERAPIST: Is it possible that your physical symptoms are a way of displacing your psychological concerns—your wish to be young and desirable again, your fear of competition with your daughter, or even some attraction to her?

Some therapists might even go on to tie the incestuous wishes and fears to the patient's mother as well as to introduce the transferential dimension in order to make the interpretation complete. Such an interpretation might be theoretically correct, but it would be clinically countertherapeutic, the psychotherapy equivalent of a drug overdose.

Concrete Detail

As much as the therapist offers open statements to encourage a range of personal associations, when it comes to making an interpretation he or she cannot be abstract or ambiguous. In gathering information, the therapist's neutral statements, comments, or questions are intended to facilitate the expression of the patient's private undirected thoughts and feelings, to prevent premature closure, to avoid the imposition of constraints (conscious or unconscious), and to gain as much data as possible. The therapist tries not to direct, divert, or contaminate the patient's authentic material. When enough relatively acceptable material has been accumulated so that the timing as well as the content are ripe for connections, the concrete and detailed presentation of an interpretation minimizes misunderstandings and sidetracking by focusing squarely on the subject at hand.

The following is an example of concrete and detailed presentation. (The therapist at the same time tries to observe the other two principles of optimum timing and minimum doses.) The patient begins talking at length again about how dizzy she has been and how worried she is.

PATIENT: You know, after I left the last session I felt even worse.
THERAPIST: Was there something in our discussion that made you feel worse? [The therapist is nondefensively and concretely asking the patient to make a connection between the treatment and her feeling worse. Instead of "Your dizziness got worse," the therapist says "You felt worse," because focusing on symptoms is nonproductive and sooner or later makes the therapist feel impotent. By focusing on the person, he hopes to engage her. The therapist is oriented more toward the management of relationships than the curing of symptoms.]

PATIENT: Well, you implied that I am jealous of my daughter. I am not at all, not of my own daughter. I'm not even envious. I wish, of course, that I did not age, that I would stay young and look like her. It is just normal. Every woman feels that way.

THERAPIST: You feel, then, that my implication that you are jealous of your daughter is wrong, and that I may not even understand this normal feeling of women to want to look young like their daughters. [The therapist states the patient's feelings and doubts as she has presented them, in concrete terms and precise, detailed fashion. He also gives priority to negative transference, insofar as exploration and interpretation of negative feelings always come before content.]

PATIENT: I don't think men understand women's problems anyway, not just you. Men are always interested in younger women. They may give all that b.s. about the mature woman being very understanding, but the moment a young woman appears on the scene, off they go.

THERAPIST: Are you concerned about Frank's interest in Brenda? [The therapist is concrete. But there is not a single extra word in the sentence to derail the patient. The wording obliges her to confront the issue squarely without easily avoiding or misunderstanding the question. The therapist dropped the transferential pursuit because the patient generalized from him to men at large. It is not forgotten, just tabled for the moment in order to go after the immediate concern of the patient.]

PATIENT: Well, he wouldn't. Even if he did try something, Brenda would never allow him to. At times I get upset when he is drunk and gets a little fresh with her.

THERAPIST: He gets drunk, and then gets fresh with Brenda. He is one of those men who is always interested in younger women. [Again the therapist is concrete and detailed.]

PATIENT: So what do you want me to do, jump off the roof?

A concrete and detailed presentation diminishes the potential for defensive maneuvering and reframes the subject under discussion in a way that in turn requires equally concrete, detailed, and direct responses. Here the patient's desperateness, her suicidal potential, and her choice of how she would do herself in are very revealing. She is also conveying other messages in the same concise sentence. "What do you want me to do?" is obviously accusatory—she feels that the therapist is not being sensitive to her predicament. At the same time, the therapist hears a potentially dynamically significant connection between her suggested mode of suicide and her presenting symptoms.

Individual Focus

Preformed, abstract interpretations are either irrelevant or alienating to the patient; nevertheless, the therapist does not function in a theory-free context. In fact, we need theory to know what to look for, but not necessarily to confirm the template—to look, to find, to lose, to disregard, to discard, but always to learn. The therapist needs to have clinical as well as theoretical competence to decipher the text (the patient's narrative), to convert the patient's troubles and conflicts into clinically readable language, and then to present the formulation back to the patient for confirmation. Jonathan Culler's (1975) statement on reading a text as literature is a similar phenomenon:

> To read a text is not to make one's mind a *tabula rasa* and approach it without preconceptions; one must bring to it an implicit understanding of the operations of literary discourse which tells one what to look for. Anyone lacking this knowledge, anyone wholly unacquainted with literature and unfamiliar with the conventions by which fictions are read would, for example, be quite baffled if presented with a poem. His knowledge of the language would enable him to understand phrases and sentences, but he would not know quite literally, what to *make* of this strange concatenation of phrases. He would be unable to read it *as* literature . . . because he lacks the complex "literary competence" which enables others to proceed. He has not internalized the "grammar" of literature which would permit him to convert linguistic sequences into literary structures and meanings. (P. 113)

There are a limited number of conflicts that human beings may have and share, and there is also a correspondingly limited number of conceptual templates for each. But the indiscriminately generalized application of such templates in the form of interpretations generates intellectualization and distancing in a therapeutic setting. The therapist must also gather enough pertinent, private information from the patient to make the interpretation applicable exclusively to that individual.

In the following session, the therapist makes individualized interpretations. The patient begins by complaining that the psychotherapy is actually making her dizziness worse.

PATIENT: I couldn't get out of bed yesterday. I was so dizzy. It is just getting worse by the day.

THERAPIST: By the session . . . [The therapist makes the complaint more specific to treatment. His statement also opens up again the discussion of negative feelings.]

PATIENT: Yeah! This is really not helpful. I come here, talk about all kinds of things that have nothing to do with my dizziness, and go home feeling awful. What is the point of all this?

THERAPIST: Not only did your dizziness get worse, but you also feel worse by coming to see me. [The therapist makes the interpretation specific to their interaction, that her feeling worse is related to seeing "me," not just any therapist or coming to therapy in general.]

PATIENT: Well, you put in my mind all kinds of thoughts, like I'm envious of my daughter, whether she and Frank are having an affair. You know, it is not right. I go home upset and watch them suspiciously. It is bad enough that I am sick, but now you've got me worried about all these things. Men, I think, think differently; you guys have dirty minds.

THERAPIST: On Monday you said that I did not understand your normal concerns as a woman. Now I may be misunderstanding your distress by wrongly attributing it to your envy of Brenda and, with my dirty mind, raising questions about her relationship with Frank.

The therapist is specific about the day and the individuals involved. He also adopts the patient's vocabulary, the word *envy*, which he himself never used. He does this for several reasons: first, one does not argue with the patient; second, *envy* may be the correct word anyway; third, even in the middle of negative feelings, the therapist seeks commonalities, and language is often a convenient basis. The therapist accepts the patient's accusation of men having dirty minds, but brings it specifically to himself.

PATIENT: It is too much. I got into a big fight with Brenda after I left here. She walks around in her underwear. I told her many times, "The boys are grown up; Frank is here." She behaves like no one sees her. I grew up very modestly. My mother would have died if I did half of what Brenda does.

THERAPIST: Out of shame? [The therapist wants to bring a specific affective component to her distress.]

PATIENT: Shame, embarrassment, anger. What is she flaunting? I really don't know what's going on.

THERAPIST: Brenda seems to be flaunting herself, and you are not sure how to handle her; you're feeling embarrassed and angry. And helpless. [The therapist, concretely and in detailed fashion, presents the patient's particular dilemma, and introduces *helpless* to prepare the patient for interpretation. If she accepts the helplessness, the therapist will make the interpretation, as that will signal the optimum timing.]

PATIENT: Yeah, completely helpless.

THERAPIST: Do you at times feel so helpless that you feel like jumping off the roof? [Individual specificity is here geared toward how to kill herself. The therapist does not generalize about hurting or killing herself. The therapist is less worried about the patient's probability of suicide than attempting to tie her complaints of dizziness to the potential mode of suicide.]

PATIENT: I thought about it a few times. But just the idea of going to the roof frightens me. I am afraid that if I did, I would lose my balance and fall off anyway, even if I changed my mind.

THERAPIST: You would lose your balance and get dizzy? [The therapist introduces his preconceived template now, confident that it is well timed and feeling in synchrony with the patient.]

PATIENT: Do you think that is why I am always dizzy?

CHAPTER 37

Theory-driven interpretations are impersonal and alienating to the patient

T HE THERAPIST usually comes to practice with certain theoretical knowledge, and there is always the temptation to categorize the patient by it and to expect the patient to confirm preconceptions. Thus the therapist may identify the patient's problems with a preformed interpretation, such as, "The reason you are always getting involved with unavailable men is that you still have not recovered from your early childhood yearnings for your father." Such theory-driven statements can have a prefabricated quality. Patients often dismiss such abstractions because they feel reduced by them. The therapist may gain the apparent acceptance of a formulation from a patient who is trying to please him or her, or simply by doctrinal compliance, the implicit suggestibility based on belief in the therapist's power (Ehrenwald 1966). The results are the same—the patient at best becomes intellectually "aware," without any change in symptoms, problems, or behavior.

If the therapist, instead of making explicit a theoretical bias, were to pursue an area of conflict with specific questions geared toward eliciting collaborative evidence for his or her theory, the therapeutic process might be potentially more persuasive but also more subversive. Questions might be: "Do you think your interest in older men has earlier roots to it?" or "Why do you think that an inaccessible man is sexually more exciting to you?" At least through such questions the therapist would gain additional material with which to work. It was his astute teacher Charcot who taught Freud (1914a) to "look at the same things again and again until they themselves begin to speak" (p. 22). As the attentive clinician gains more and more detailed data from the patient about himself or herself, the events of his or her life, his or her desires and fantasies, particular repetitive patterns naturally emerge out of the material itself. Eventually the theoretical becomes personal, the impersonal turns intimate.

Case Illustration

An outstanding and talented eighteen-year-old college student, a promising actress and pianist, had been suffering from bulimia for the past four years. Despite MAO-inhibiting medication as well as twice-a-week individual psychotherapy, she appeared to be getting worse. Previously she had been in combined group therapy and individual therapy with another therapist, but dropped out of both treatments within a few months.

The patient was three years old when her father left home. After he left she was raised by her mother as a single parent. The mother, an actress, was herself quite immature.

The therapist began to work under the theoretical premise that the psychological aspect of the patient's bulimia was not sexually related pathology (as in anorexia, whereby the girl is conflicted about becoming a woman). He believed, rather, that the bulimia was related to earlier stages of development. He considered the weight and body preoccupation as a somatic equivalent of obsessive thoughts, and the cycle of overeating and vomiting as the compulsive equivalent of a discharge of anxiety—in total, an act of restoration of her psychosexual disequilibrium, a desperate attempt to make herself feel and confirm her realness.

In recent sessions, the patient had reported a series of shoplifting incidents.

PATIENT: Again I shoplifted and walked out of the department store with two pairs of underwear. I don't even need them; it is crazy.
THERAPIST: As if you had no control over it?

The therapist is surprised by her stealing and shoplifting; it does not fit in any way—to his theory—she is not an immoral person. The therapist also wonders why the underwear specifically, especially if she does not

227

need it. Maybe, after all, there is a sexual dimension to this, not easy to decipher. Nonetheless he sticks to his theory of an incohesive self and asks a theory-driven question regarding possible loss of boundaries and control. He wonders whether her behavior is due to excitement or rage, or some kind of uncontrolled impulse.

PATIENT: I do and I don't feel a loss of control. In fact, the more I feel in control the less controlled I become. Do you understand? [The patient apparently recognizes the therapist's confusion.]

THERAPIST: Something goes out of control when you are in control?

PATIENT: Exactly, as if I should not be allowed to be in control.

THERAPIST: A sense of uncontrol comes to you from somewhere when you are left to your own devices. [The therapist is now asserting his theoretical orientation that her self gets fragmented when left alone without any outside control or reference points.]

PATIENT: It's a little unreal, as if I am watching myself living, you know, as if I am watching myself on TV or in the movies. I am designing the scenes, writing the script, I am so much outside of myself. The other night, I am with this guy and we are making out. You know, I am kissing him and all of a sudden it's like I am watching over my own shoulder and laughing at the absurdity of the situation. Why am I putting my tongue in someone else's mouth? I am not even sure what should happen or what I want to happen. I close my eyes and I don't even know who I am, never mind who he is.

THERAPIST: Part of you is out there commenting on you and your behavior. [The therapist wonders, is she taking a healthy distance, or is she dissociating?]

PATIENT: Yes, a running commentary on myself. It is sort of amusing.

THERAPIST: What sort of commentary runs through your head in binge-ing and vomiting? [The therapist has confirmed the presence of a sense of unrealness when the patient feels out of control, and also of an ongoing, parallel process of observing herself and commenting as she behaves. He is now looking for a connection between these two phenomena and her bulimia.]

PATIENT: When I binge, I am certainly out of control. When I vomit it is just a need. I have no running commentary about that, in fact, that part of my mind disappears and I can't even think.

THERAPIST: Just the compulsion to act? [Now that the patient did not pursue the unrealness-of-self route, the therapist retreats to explore the compulsivity part of the theory.]

PATIENT: I cannot stop myself. First I feel like a huge, empty black hole that I have to fill. I feel utterly depressed as I eat, and as I fill my stomach I feel even emptier. Even when I am aware of internal distention I still eat, and then I have to vomit. Afterwards I feel hopeless, just feel like nothing—absolute nothingness.

THERAPIST: During the internal distention and vomiting do you feel more real? [The therapist is back to the fragmented-self theory.]

PATIENT: I am painfully aware of my nothingness. When this guy tried to kiss me down there, you know, I felt so disgusted. He wants to give me pleasure, he says, but I don't get my pleasure that way. Why would he want to do that? I feel nothing. I wonder whether I am a lesbian; my close girlfriend asked me that. I have no idea. The thought of sexual intercourse freaks me out. I want to, but I can't do it. I mistreated this poor guy so that he would go away; but he doesn't. In fact, the worse I treat him, the more he clings to me.

THERAPIST: Hmm.

The therapist considers that maybe after all this, the bulimia is related to anorexia, just another variation of the theme, not wanting to be a sexually desirable woman. And the symptoms are defensive, a smoke-screen. Now that lesbianism comes into the picture, the therapist tries to connect sexual problems, bingeing, vomiting, and stealing. The patient said earlier that she does not do well when she is in control. Maybe all this is a request for the therapist to take control. The therapist feels less confused by this formulation, but wonders whether he is forcing the issue of control just to comfort himself.

PATIENT: I like women's bodies. I know I am more interested in women, not necessarily sexually. I think the woman is more interesting anyway. With guys, I don't know why I get possessive and demanding. Maybe I should have been a nun. Yesterday, my father was very upset because I used his credit card to buy lots of clothes. It was just boredom; one day I went on a shopping spree and it felt good while I was buying. When I came home I wanted to throw away all my old stuff, start from scratch.

THERAPIST: A really new self. [The therapist thinks that the patient's narration is deteriorating, becoming somewhat circumstantial. Maybe the control needs to be exercised by structuring the subject.]

PATIENT: Real or unreal, I want to be different . . . like an actress, I want to play different roles. I have the talent; I know I can get any part I want. At school they all think I am a very gifted actress, but I feel like everything is too much. My father is very worried that I might commit suicide. He brought his fiancée along to visit me. She is a little older than I am. We all had dinner together. I liked her and we have become friends. She said she was bulimic once herself and felt suicidal when she was a freshman and that it'll pass. She had to have all her teeth capped because they were rotten with vomiting.

THERAPIST: How do you feel about getting such a young stepmother? [The therapist temporarily gives up the earlier theories and now desperately seeks to catch a new thread that could unravel her story.]

PATIENT: It is neat. My mother is also dating a guy, an older guy. Do you think I might be jealous? She could never replace me. During the dinner I ate very little. I was anxious, but I don't know why. I felt like I was sitting at the next table and listening to our conversation.

THERAPIST: You disassociated yourself from the situation, to make it less real. [The therapist is back to the realness issue.]

PATIENT: The whole thing is just strange. I think I hate him, not because he is with this woman; she is OK. Actually, I don't really hate him. I don't even know exactly how I feel toward him—my feelings are very intense and I don't know why. But what's the use of talking about it to you, anyway?

THERAPIST: Do you feel like removing yourself from me?

PATIENT: *(Laughs)* Yes, I would like to sit in the waiting room.

THERAPIST: I thought you were there all along. [The therapist's attempt to find a subject around which they could have a therapeutic or working alliance proves to be unproductive. Each thread he tries to catch seems to slip through his fingers. He recognizes that his comment has a hostile edge; perhaps his confusion is coming through. Now that the patient has begun to present transferential material, the therapist again attempts to engage her.]

PATIENT: I hate sitting here and talking. What good can come out of this?

THERAPIST: Have we touched some real feelings? [*We* here is a little too optimistic, premature even, as a wish on the part of the therapist.]

PATIENT: Such as what?

THERAPIST: Reexperiencing intense feelings toward your father.

PATIENT: My feelings are sort of screwy, scary sort of feelings, not just of my father. Whenever I feel so intensely, I immediately bring down that wall. I am no longer present. You said "disassociated"; I guess that is the word. It is not a good feeling. I feel removed, not fully in control, suspended. I binge not to have an oral orgy, as the books say, but just to change that feeling, to stop it.

THERAPIST: That intense feeling of an internal black hole? [The therapist wants to assist the patient to articulate the feelings that precede her dissociation. He wonders whether all her bulimia symptoms are affective equivalents.]

PATIENT: It's hard to describe, a deep pain. It actually hurts. I can't locate where in my body, but it hurts.

THERAPIST: How awful! [Can the therapist locate an empathic thread?]

PATIENT: I would do anything not to feel that.

THERAPIST: You think all your bingeing, vomiting, stealing, and dissociations are all attempts not to feel that horrible pain?

PATIENT: I don't know. None of them helps anyway. They just distract me from it momentarily.

THERAPIST: How confusing! [This is not genuine empathy because it is more a reflection of what the therapist feels than what the patient may be feeling. The therapist wonders why he still finds it difficult to be empathic. Because he could not fit her into his previous conceptualization of psychopathology, couldn't relate to her well transferentially, and couldn't establish a working alliance, he does not know how to proceed to share her feelings. But why is he so confused?]

After the session, the therapist lies on the couch and begins to reflect on this case, why he should remain in suspense between his theory and utter puzzlement. He is still convinced that the patient is arrested at the earlier stages of psychological development, in which intense feelings are experienced and not contained, and the patient has a sense of coming unglued. A child at that stage tends to use obsessions and compulsions to provide some internal order and structure, feeling frightened to be left alone to maintain control over his or her own self.

The patient misinterprets the internal cues of a sense of emptiness as coming from her body and fills it with food. The obsessive-compulsiveness that once reasonably kept in check her internal disorganization is no longer sufficient as an adult. At least as a child she had some degree of parental protection in the forms of limit setting, punishment, and so on. She has none of that left now, including the fantasy of a parent in control, which she may have had as a child. Furthermore, the child may not be as sensitized to the internal feeling of being unglued. But as one gets older, the feeling becomes much more frightening. As her sensation of psychic emptiness does not go away, she fills it to the point of actual discomfort and sickness, and undoes it by vomiting. The act of vomiting is just a complication or consequence of the preceding feeling and behavior.

The therapist considers stealing, lying, and similar behavior as a way of decreasing this internal tension (though paradoxically it may seem to be exciting, a search for tension), just to "feel" when experiencing emptiness. The sexuality is only a reflection of a naturally unfolding maturational process. Her sexuality (or lack of it) and the confusion about it are manifestations of the same maturational lag. Despite these theoretical hypotheses, the therapist wonders whether he is missing something. Perhaps he should not try to understand her so quickly and temper his own pressing need to do so. He has not yet reached that point beyond impersonal theory; worse than that, his discouragement is no doubt interfering with his capacity to be empathic. In Levenson's (1983) words, the therapist must learn to tolerate such "ambiguity as a way-station to truth . . . " (p. 103) as he attentively waits for the patient's material to speak personally to him.

CHAPTER 38

Every interpretation is incorrect on some level

INTERPRETATION MAKES USE OF the special skill—or art—by which the therapist deciphers the latent meanings of the patient's narrative and translates them in a way that can be comprehended and accepted. Interpretation can point out hidden historical connections between present and previous behaviors, between feelings for the therapist and those meant for significant others, between instinctual impulses or desires and defenses against them, and between conscious thoughts and unconscious wishes. By extrapolating from the manifest material of speech as well as associations and dreams, interpretations need to decode disguised symbolic language and to reconstruct lost experiences veiled by memory. They must be converted into meaningful terms that are relevant to the individual patient in the immediate moment.

Although many therapists strive for the so-called correct interpretation, all interpretations fall short on two counts: for *intrinsic* or unintentional reasons, that is, by the very nature of the interpretive act as an artistic rather than scientific translation of events; and for *technical* or intentional reasons, that is, because the therapist varies the degree of interpretive correctness according to the patient's receptivity. For intrinsic reasons an interpretation cannot be perfectly valid because there is no method by which to prove its truth; at best an interpretation is an educated guess. This thesis suggests that each interpretation is inherently a creative construction; it cannot be 100 percent correct because one can never prove an account of the past, nor can one be certain of past links to current experience. In using technical incorrectness the clinician may propose an incorrect interpretation or intentionally withhold a "correct" one. That is, the therapist adjusts what and how much he or she says based on the patient's capacity to receive the whole truth.

The scrupulous clinician may naturally want to search for the best interpretation, which is often presumed to be the one that is most objectively correct. Yet, although this standard is a common goal or ideal, it is often applied excessively and is actually impossible to accomplish. Interpretations, whether "correctly" based on the discovery of the repressed past or simply new constructions, are, as Serge Viderman (1979) argues, creative activities with powerful impact on the shaping of the patient. An interpretive formulation with the transferential power of persuasion behind it acquires a semblance of its own truth. Thus an interpretation that is not precisely true may still attain personal value and usefulness for the patient.

Taking this line of thinking further, it appears quite possible that the therapist's interpretation (no matter how historically correct) generates its own theory, independent of the accessible or inaccessible facts. This is because any interpretation of a particular meaning cannot be scientifically observed or proven. As Kenneth Gergen (1981) has pointed out:

> The symbolic meaning of observables is, either on the level of mundane discussion or on the broad theoretical level, not open to objective verification or falsification. There is no observable referent to which the investigator can reliably point. The meaning of human action is dependent on the observer's system of interpretation. *The observer must bring to the event a conceptual system through which behavioral observations may be rendered meaningful. There is no means of verifying or falsifying a "mode of interpretation."* (P. 335)

Thus, what Adolf Grünbaum (1979) calls Freud's "tally argument" (p. 465)—that to be effective an interpretation must tally with what is real in the patient—needs to be reassessed. But how does the therapist know what is real to the patient? Viderman (1979) suggests that the interpretation may become true for the first time just by being said, that both therapist and patient by their mutual communications are jointly forging an explanation. In this regard he believes that the therapist invariably functions more as a poet than as a historian. He goes as far as to argue that an interpretation need not necessarily connect to the patient's past in order to be therapeutic. Instead it acquires narrative truth simply in the process of emergence. A new mutual discovery is thereby set in motion as each interpretation jointly unfolds.

Making a conceptual distinction between "historical" (based on real past) truths of interpretation and "narrative" (immediate, newly constructed) ones, Spence (1982) suggests that narrative truth attains its own special potency and subjective significance; it becomes convincing by virtue of how many details of the case it includes and the way in which these details are presented. It is a "linguistic creation" that attains its own value by being sayable and coherent, both reshaping and organizing what the patient is experiencing. The more self-consistent the narrative is in unifying the patient's thoughts and feelings, the more adequate the explanation is. Timely preparatory interpretations resonate with what is genuine to the patient and invariably generate associative material. In this way both therapist and patient implicitly validate the relative correctness of the therapist's interpretation.

The incorrectness of interpretations can have negative as well as positive implications. Unfortunately, the clinician cannot be certain whether his or her interpretation is correct on the evidence of his or her own confidence or of the patient's explicit agreement with it. Furthermore, the patient may wish to please the therapist or may want to avoid a confrontation, or for other reasons (such as a tendency for compliance, a fear of rejection, the need to feel that progress is being made) may patently agree with the therapist's statement. The patient may nod or say "Yes" or "I guess so" or "You must be right." But this kind of consensus is often short-lived. After such apparent agreement about a particular situation, the patient might remain silent or change the subject. Presumed understandings thus become partly or wholly "misunderstandings." Having subliminally recognized that the interpretation is not getting a full response, the therapist may keep elaborating on the original statement. Yet, elaborate reconstructions may not only be incorrect but set a bad precedent for the following session. The patient becomes less active, expects the therapist to deliver similar insights, forms the habit of being on the receiving end, and does not learn how to process information independent of the therapist.

The patient may hold on to an inexact interpretation because it fends off a more painful truth (Glover 1955). From this point of view, deliberately devised "incorrect" (apparently exact or incomplete) interpretations by the therapist, which protect the patient by judiciously withholding some part of the total, are not less significant. Such inevitably incorrect interpretive substitutes may even become especially compelling because for the patient they are in concordance with an understanding of his or her self that is less disturbing than that demanded by a more complete or correct formulation.

On the positive side, however, acknowledging that "correctness" is not only an idealized standard but an inflexible one can be advantageous to both therapist and patient. By understanding that an incorrect or inexact interpretation is not necessarily a defensive substitute that will be deleterious to the patient, the therapist may be able to vary the truth of an interpretation for therapeutic purposes. The clinician can use the incorrect interpretation as a way of reaching the patient who is too fragile or defended to hear the whole truth.

In the final analysis, like the glass that is both half full and half empty, the most correct interpretation is also inevitably, and even intentionally, incorrect. This is in keeping with Spence's (1982) conclusion that "all interpretations are more creative than otherwise" (p. 173), whether by the inherently erroneous nature of interpretation as a linguistic translation or by design, as the therapist flexibly filters the facts for the reception of the patient.

CHAPTER 39

The therapist's technique bends under the weight of the patient's weakness

To HAVE TECHNICAL PURITY and an uncompromised therapeutic stand is the dream of every therapist. The therapist's ideal is to identify the patient's conflict and interpret its content (whether transferential or not), without worrying too much about the patient's capacity to accept the interpretation—his or her ability to withstand, tolerate, or absorb the impact of the material presented. But the ideal is a luxury that requires the rare patient who is psychologically highly developed.

Quite frequently the therapist must be seriously concerned that an interpretation may harm the patient. In fact, the therapist may have to stabilize the patient by strengthening ego functions (giving information, offering support, providing object relations, and the like) both before and while carrying out any kind of interpretive work. In short, the therapist has to alter his or her technique to accommodate the psychological strengths and weaknesses of the patient.

Once having established a supportive base, the therapist still may not be able to use "correct" interpretations because the patient remains too fragile to receive them. In such cases there are certain options: (1) the patient may be offered a presumably true, albeit *partial*, interpretation, which attempts to approach the historical truth without quite reaching it; or (2) the patient may be offered an acceptable but *different* interpretation as an alternative explanation. Glover (1955) was the first to distinguish these options, calling the former an apparently exact, or incomplete, interpretation and the latter an inexact interpretation. The former type may be considered a part of the natural course of psychodynamic technique, as the therapist adjusts the degree or dosage of information given the patient. The incomplete interpretation is regarded as a typical step in therapeutic strategy, whereby the clinician helps the patient get closer to the deeper unconscious recesses in increments that are easily received; as such, it is simply an abbreviated version of the truth. The inexact interpretation, on the other hand, may resemble this process insofar as it also attempts to control the depth of interpretation, yet it is not only quantitatively but qualitatively different in immediate purpose: it is a deliberate substitute for the correct interpretation. The two types of imperfect interpretation may even be viewed as antithetical: one steers toward the truth, while the other moves away from it. Tarachow (1963) has described the manifestations of the inexact interpretation for both therapist and patient:

> An inexact interpretation is offered as the definitive meaning which, in the opinion of the analyst, actually falls short of the unconscious or infantile truth. The analyst has judged that the complete truth would be dangerous or intolerable to the patient. The patient seizes the inexact meaning eagerly because it helps him continue to repress the truth, and with the newly offered belief, in effect, form a new symptom. . . . The real focus of the problem remains repressed and is replaced onto the given interpretation. (P. 45)

The inexact interpretation could—for better or worse—provide the patient with a "new explanation" as an alternative to the "true explanation." Glover's own concern, however, was with its negative implications. He believed that the inexact interpretation would be erroneously used as a defensive replacement which might do the recipient more harm than good. By fitting in with an understanding of himself or herself that the patient prefers to believe because it is less harsh or disruptive than the truth, the inexact interpretation may become especially difficult to undo. In this sense, the therapist, wittingly or unwittingly, colludes with the patient in perpetuating a falsehood—or, at best, a white lie. What both varieties of interpretation have in common nonetheless is that they are always backed by strong transference authority.

It can be suggested in this regard that perhaps Glover was being too optimistic about the role and relevance of the ideal "exact" interpretation, believing that there is indeed such a thing as a real truth for the therapist to find. At the same time, he probably was too pessimistic about the deficiencies and dangers of the inexact interpretation. In effect he exaggerated the impact at each end of the interpretive spectrum.

What is being posed here instead is that inexact as well as incomplete interpretations can have *positive* therapeutic effects. Each is differentially designed to protect the patient from an intolerable truth and is deliberately meant, to some degree, to support the patient's defenses. In Glover's (1955) terms, they relate to "the amount of psychological truth disclosed to the patient. Or to reverse the standard . . . classified in accordance with the amount of deflection from psychological truth, or by the means adopted to deflect attention (away from it)" (pp. 559–60). While the two types of interpretation vary in detail and accuracy, in the incomplete interpretation the therapist is more hopeful that the patient will eventually become ready to receive the "whole" truth or some facsimile thereof—it is just a matter of time or preparation. The inexact interpretation, by contrast, is designed to repress the truth indefinitely and thus is applied solely to solidify the patient's adaptive defenses. Therefore, it is helpful for the clinician to recognize these dual options. Both the incomplete and the inexact interpretation can function as a suitable substitute for the complete interpretation, according to the individual patient's capacities and weaknesses. While neither precisely corresponds to a particular event of the patient's past, deviations from the truth can still be useful in creatively permitting new therapeutic material to emerge.

Case Illustrations

Incomplete Interpretation

A forty-eight-year-old depressed man remained in a marriage in which he had fathered two children, although he felt no passion or affection for his wife: they were not intellectually compatible (she was far better educated and severely critical of him), had no mutually shared family experiences, and had no outside activities or interests in common. But in spite of his wishes and better judgment, and even her implicit encouragement, he was not able to leave her. He also felt very attached to and highly responsible in his job as a salesman, a position he had held for over twenty years. Like his father (also a salesman), he worked long hours to support the family. As a youngster he had been obliged to take care of his two younger brothers, since his mother had died when he was eleven years old.

PATIENT: I like the sense of coming home after work to a place where it is warm and comfortable, safe. She's never been a good cook, but there is always food. I watch TV at times, read at other times, and then I go to bed. I don't even talk to her about my job, but the fact that she is there is somehow comforting. I don't quite understand it.

THERAPIST: You wonder whether you are simply dependent on her? [The therapist does not interpret the patient's feelings or behavior, but comments on the patient's own wonderment; the interpretative meaning is implicit.]

PATIENT: I am a little embarrassed to say that, but I guess I am. I wonder what I am afraid of, just a sensation, a feeling of needing her without any evidence that she'll fulfill any of my needs. I don't let things go, I get attached. Obviously I have some deep-seated problem that goes way back. Maybe I should come to see you more than twice a week. I don't know.

THERAPIST: You think your attachment to your wife is somehow related to losing your mother at such a young age? [In this incomplete interpretation, which connects a current to a past event, the therapist avoids the full transferential interpretation of the patient's becoming and wanting to be dependent on the therapist.]

Interpretation of a specific thought, feeling, or behavior is aimed at undoing it. The therapist acknowledges the patient's dependency on his wife and implies that he may have been dependent on his mother as well. Then, in question form, the therapist suggests that these two may be related, in effect bailing out the patient by saying that his dependency need is understandable because he had lost his mother at a young age, that anyone would have ended up having such a problem; it is quite natural. Thereafter, as the patient expresses his need to become dependent on the therapist ("Maybe I should come to see you more than twice a week"), the therapist does not interpret this by saying, "I wonder whether you need to be dependent on me," but offers himself as a dependable person during this difficult period for the patient.

Incomplete interpretations are used as a limited or interim technique. The therapist attempts to gratify temporarily the transferential dependency of the patient, at least in part, because the patient currently needs this support. Although interpretation of transferential dependency as well as its childhood roots would constitute a "complete" interpretation, here the therapist considered the patient too needy to be deprived of that dependency through interpretation of it.

At some point later in treatment, however, the dependency issue will become the focus of their exploration. Exploration may include whether the patient can rely on the therapist, his feeling unsatisfied or over-dependent upon the therapist for nurturing, whether the therapist will die or leave him, how the dependency issue is affecting the therapeutic process, and, finally, how the patient deals with the termination of treatment. Understanding of a triad of transferential themes—the patient's frustrated dependency on his mother, pathological dependency on his wife, and transferential dependency on the therapist—would represent the complete interpretation.

Inexact Interpretation

A forty-year-old accountant was living with his widowed mother, who insisted that he see a psychiatrist because she worried about his social isolation and frequent quarrels with business associates and neighbors. The patient was alternately apprehensive and aggressively suspicious; he was hyperalert and penetratingly observant, but quite unfriendly in his attitude, almost always responding with a biting smile. He held rigid ideas about people, the world, and psychiatry, and vigilantly anticipated bad intentions on the therapist's part. In contrast to his highly developed perceptiveness and a special sensitivity to being "put down," he lacked proper judgment, which usually got him into trouble with his many bosses in his frequently changed jobs. His excessive suspiciousness crystalized around some short-term and circumscribed delusions, such as a man thinking that the patient was a "faggot," or a "Mafia" boss trying to get him killed. He refused hospitalization and medication during these brief periods of psychotic decompensation.

During the sessions the patient spoke clearly, with deliberateness and carefully designed sentences and disclaimers. His listening rarely focused on the manifest content of what the therapist was saying; instead he was intent on what the therapist "might have meant," always vigilantly seeking to seize important clues from any statements and searching for hidden purposes in the therapist's attitude. At times he ruminated over the therapist's casual utterances for days.

PATIENT: I woke up from an awful dream, all in a sweat. I usually don't dream much, or I don't remember. Anyway, it was real scary; this man

241

is chasing me. Maybe it was you. I'm not sure. He has a big knife. I'm running just a few steps ahead of him; then I fall down. I feel the knife entering, but the knife isn't hurting. In fact, it isn't a bad feeling at all, strangely pleasant and playful. Yet I get up, still running. I trip again, and again I feel the knife.

THERAPIST: Scary! [The therapist does not ask the patient's associations to the dream, thus beginning to take the patient away from the possible exact interpretation.]

PATIENT: Boy, was it scary! Even now I feel the fear. What do you think that means? Why should you be chasing me with a knife? You're not that type. You're actually a very soft-spoken person.

THERAPIST: Do you fear that even though I have this soft-spoken personality, underneath I may be able to hurt you? [Here the therapist intentionally avoids the possible homosexual meaning of the dream and steers the discussion toward an exploration of aggression.]

PATIENT: You never know. I guess, as they say, "Watch out for the quiet waters." Not that you would try to kill me or anything like that. I can take care of myself. You haven't seen me being aggressive.

THERAPIST: Are you concerned that you may hurt me?

PATIENT: No, you had the knife, not me. You were attacking me. I wasn't attacking you. I was the one who was scared, not you. [Since the therapist's inexact interpretation got too close to other unacceptable urges (namely, murderous thoughts), it obviously was not inexact enough.]

THERAPIST: Scary and also disturbing. In here you want to trust me. [The therapist backs up a few steps to the fear or trust issue, where the patient is relatively comfortable.]

PATIENT: I can see the headlines: "Man knifed by his psychiatrist." Can you believe that? Well, it was just a dream.

Every incomplete or inexact interpretation to some extent short-changes the patient. The only consolation is that using such interpretations is a necessary measure, sometimes only temporary, until the patient is ready to face the "therapeutic truth" without the dilutions and distortions of incompleteness and inexactness.

CHAPTER 40

All interpretations are deprivations: good ones bring disappointment and bad ones cause disengagement

INTERPRETATIONS SERVE SEVERAL OVERT AND COVERT, specific and nonspecific, functions. The major function is to provide the patient with otherwise unavailable information about his or her mental life and behavior, offering the prospect of insight into oneself and the source of one's problems. Less directly, as the primary communication link between therapist and patient, the act of interpreting may also affect the patient by transmitting empathy, concern, and care. More and more clinicians recognize that interpretations' nonspecific effects of reinforcing the therapeutic relationship can preempt their specific effects of pinpointing psychodynamic events. How an interpretation is made helps to convey a message of emotional acceptance that ameliorates the painful content of the interpretation. At the same time, the substance or spirit of interpretations may technically as well as symbolically serve as rewards or punishments, supplying positive or negative feedback. Thus the entire interpretive act inevitably comprises a complex and often double-edged emotional exchange: giving the patient something (such as reconstructions of missing memories or repressed events) while taking something else away (such as earlier fantasies or desires).

Thus, by their very nature interpretations are never intended simply to gratify the patient. Rather, *all* interpretations are *always* deprivations, regardless of what is interpreted, because the therapist is to some degree depriving the patient of childhood illusions, which have been armor against adult reality. As Tarachow (1963) put it:

> The patient wants to keep all his infantile wishes. There is a perpetual battle between patient and therapist, the patient guarding his defenses and his infantile wishes and the therapist attempting to rob the patient. More often than not the patient is unwilling to make the effort of renunciation which you are demanding of him. (P. 101)

While learning something new about himself or herself (which often means having to relinquish a cherished idea or behavior and risking the unknown in its place), the patient is simultaneously giving up a part of his or her old self, or at least a piece of its protective cover. Therefore, the person usually experiences a loss, a dysphoria, with each accepted ("good" or useful) interpretation.

But the nature of that dysphoric reaction changes if the interpretation is "bad" or not useful, that is, presented as a literal or concrete conclusion rather than as an open proposition that leaves room for personal elaboration. For example, to tell a patient who is angry at his father that he really wants to murder him so he can have his mother to himself is an exaggerated instance of the misuse of the theory of the Oedipus complex. In indiscriminately applying this time-honored "nuclear concept of the neuroses" (Freud, 1916–17) as if it were a standard formula into which the individual is forced to fit, the therapist has destroyed the utility of the theory; the therapist has also traumatized, alienated, or otherwise psychologically injured the patient. Both the theory and the patient have been diminished.

The generic interpretive statement is a form of interpretive overkill. The glibness of an overused interpretation and the Procrustean way in which it is presented to the patient may be not only conceptually inappropriate but personally countertherapeutic. As Spence (1982) points out, an interpretation—even offered as an undocumented assertion—can gain narrative truth value by being plausible, familiar, reassuring, and useful, or by enabling the patient to discover and construct new meanings on the basis of the statement. Since the misapplied interpretation often meets none of these criteria, it attains the status of neither historical nor narrative truth.

More specifically, in the good interpretation that is carefully tailored and timed to the patient's particular problem, the patient is deprived and disappointed but still engaged; in the bad interpretation, the patient feels differently deprived—alone and disengaged. In short, the bad interpretation has brought with it a sense not merely of frustration and loss, but of desertion. The residue of the unacceptable interpretation is greater devastation at having been left in the lurch—the patient has lost the therapist as well as a part of himself or herself. In the accepted interpretation or reconstruction, which according to Freud (1937b) "is only effective because it recovers a fragment of lost experience" (p. 268), all is not really gone. That is, although the patient usually experiences some degree of deprivation with each correct interpretation, he or she is not left totally bereft.

Moreover, because the Procrustean interpretation creates a feeling of forced or final closure, it is not as potentially therapeutic as an inexact or incorrect interpretation. Because the inexact and incorrect interpretations can be applied in accordance with the patient's needs and deficits, they leave the self intact.

An interpretation's "truthfulness" (which may be an illusion to begin with), however potentially liberating, will not protect the patient from its depriving effect. Thus, the expected outcome is, at least in part, disappointing if not depressing. The moment a genetic interpretation is made, the focus will shift from the present to the past (that is, to losses of the bygone era), and if a transferential interpretation is made the focus will shift to the context of the therapist–patient relationship (that is, to its limitations and unfulfilled expectations). Thus the impact of both types of interpretation is inevitably dysphoric.

From a clinical point of view, interpretations by the therapist can be more metaphoric. They may be geared not only to finding the facts (truths) together, but to creating a new story between therapist and patient. Each fact in therapy, according to Paul Ricoeur (1977), must first be "capable of being said; second, it must be said to another person; third, it must represent a piece of psychic reality; and fourth, it must be capable of entering into a story or narrative" (pp. 836–43). This conjointly created context protects the patient from being at the powerless receiving end of the literal, rigidly imposed interpretation. Instead the patient is an active participant, in effect a cocreator of the therapist's interpretation.

Case Illustration

A twenty-one-year-old, good-looking gay male college student came to treatment "to tame my aggression" and "to be more productive." He appeared bright, articulate, and witty, and he was a good storyteller. In the sessions, he was always entertaining and seductive, but he did not really relate to the therapist. He presented himself as unambivalent about his sexual orientation, and in the first session he made it clear that he was not there to become heterosexual. Before he would make a commitment to treatment, he quizzed the therapist extensively about his belief system (including whether he considered homosexuality to be a disease). His incessant aggression (sarcasm, verbal games designed to put others down) was not well received by his friends, and he was not doing well academically despite his obvious intelligence.

PATIENT: I was in the bathroom [where casual sex occurred] this week at least ten times. It seems like I can't get enough. The impulse, or is it obsession—I obviously need it. I am excited, but it does not last long. I am back there again. It is a vicious cycle, though. It is fun, then I can sit down and do some work, but in a few hours I again feel the urge. Am I just promiscuous? Are they all? I mean the place is teeming with gay guys, like crabs in a low tide, all jumping on each other.

THERAPIST: All of your sexual activities seem to be designed to keep you from relating to another person. [The therapist gives a literal interpretation without waiting for the right moment for the patient's participation and has not left room for the patient's elaboration.]

PATIENT: No, this has nothing to do with a relationship; it is raw sex, just plain sex. [The patient rejects the interpretation.]

The same theme carried into the next session.

PATIENT: (Walks in, serious and irritated. Before he sits down, he begins to talk) I resented the statement that you made the last time, that my promiscuity is a way of not relating to people. I have not been able to go to the bathroom. I am really unhappy, as if you took my toy away. You spoiled the only thing that I enjoyed in life. I mean, what else is there but study, study, and go to the therapist, go to the therapist? Thanks a lot! I always looked forward to coming here, but today it was depressing to even think about it. I used to look forward to it, when it wasn't all dead serious. You seemed to be a human being and I could be funny, whatever. Then you dropped that on my lap. I wonder whether you consider my jokes and lighthearted stories as avoidance of relating to you, too.

THERAPIST: I may have spoiled the fun outside and in here as well. [The therapist accepts the blame.]

PATIENT: Yeah, I feel awful.

THERAPIST: You suffered two losses simultaneously. [The therapist acknowledges the patient's losses.]

PATIENT: I'm depressed on the one hand, angry on the other; angry at you, I guess, for having been the cause of this. I am not even sure how justified that is.

THERAPIST: Well, I have caused you those two losses. [The therapist allies with and supports the patient's reaction to him.]

PATIENT: Why am I afraid of intimacy? I mean, the pure sexual pleasure aside, is it true that I get bored with people because I am afraid of getting close? You asked me the other day when I was very close in the past. You know, I couldn't think of anyone specifically. [The patient is a little more ready now to acknowledge the therapist's interpretation, to begin to broach the subject of fear of intimacy.]

Because of the depriving quality of interpretations, psychotherapy brings some disappointment at best. The only way a patient can tolerate this process better is to feel like a contributing partner in the construction of each interpretation, buffered by the trust and empathic presence of the therapist as a cocreator. What disturbs patients most is not the impact of the interpretation itself, but that the therapist has left him or her feeling utterly alone and traumatized in the process of finding the "truth." Thus, besides offering an expression of empathy, an interpretation purposefully should fall short of completeness in order to include the patient in the process. This allows him or her to keep working as an active collaborator. Insofar as the patient must never be made to feel abandoned, one of the ways the therapist can redeem himself or herself is to acknowledge his or her own part in the excessive deprivation, then go a few steps back to examine the possible countertransferential reasons (such as counteraggression, fear of seduction, intellectual competition) for the bad interpretation.

There is no better index of the acceptability of the interpretation than the patient's having associative material to it. Ironically, improvement of symptoms, which may be no more than a flight to health, is considered an unreliable index (Kris 1947). The worsening of symptoms is equally suspect because that may be related to a negative therapeutic reaction (Freud 1923). Moreover, the direct utterances of the patient after he or she has been offered a construction afford very little evidence about whether the therapist has been right or wrong; instead, indirect forms of confirmation must be used. As Freud (1937b) concluded, only the further course of therapy can confirm whether the interpretations have been serviceable.

The real impact of the interpretation on the patient is measured not in knowledge he has gained but in emotional resonance. As Brenner (1976) points out, the chief effect of interpretation "may be that the patient feels discovered, accused, humiliated, praised, encouraged, rewarded, seduced, or rejected" (p. 49). This statement illustrates the importance of not putting too much emphasis on the presumed theoretical accuracy of any interpretation as a preformed truth, because interpretations in actual clinical practice are primarily creative.

Anticipating the patient's reactions to an interpretation helps to determine overall planning for interpretative work. Literal interpretations would cumulatively leave the patient utterly hopeless and depressed, alienated from the therapist, and disappointed in the treatment as well as in himself or herself. To endure such a sense of separateness and aloneness, often accompanied by sadness, requires great ego strength. Fragile patients may find it especially difficult to tolerate this sadness and may turn to acting out or decompensation.

In adults, the damage is often difficult to undo because the therapist, having generated a feeling of alienation, at the same time loses the capacity to influence the recipient. Once the patient experiences this acute sense of separateness and disengages from the therapist, the relationship between the two is no longer the same, no matter how strong the original bond was. Therapists who have unfortunately made a bad interpretation are like mothers who have to reestablish affective bonds after separation from a child. As Mahler, Pine, and Bergman (1975) have pointed out, the "mother after separation" is always a danger.

CHAPTER 41

The interpretation of symptoms may dissolve resistance, but the interpretation of character traits may generate it

BECAUSE MOST SYMPTOMS ARE EGO-DYSTONIC and there-
fore at least in part unacceptable to the person, patients tend to be
relatively well disposed to getting rid of them. Many factors, of course,
may interfere with the full cooperation of the patient in this effort. The
primary factors include sustaining symptoms for the relative stability of
one's psychological state, the self-defining role of symptoms as recognizable parts of one's self, and symptoms as preventive or substitutive
measures (it is believed, for example, that certain psychosomatic symptomatology serves to mask other underlying conditions such as depression [Lesse 1974]). In addition are the secondary gains of illness, such as
getting special attention or being exempt from having to fully meet the
demands of reality. Both primary and secondary gains may at one time
or another generate resistances to treatment. Although interpretation of
the dynamics of the symptoms or of the primary gains tends to dissolve
resistances, the interpretation of secondary gains can harden them.

Since secondary gains are related to characterological traits, interpretations of them, like interpretations of characterological traits themselves, are not welcome. Because these ingrained patterns of reaction are
generally ego-syntonic regardless of how dysfunctional they may be,
any confrontation of them is at high risk of being taken by the patient

as a personal attack; he or she will try vigorously to fend it off. No amount of evidence can persuade the patient to join the therapist's side against his or her own characterlogical traits. Moreover, if such interpretation is accepted under duress or due to excessive compliance, a depressive reaction will frequently follow. Thus the therapist's skill lies in examining maladaptive traits without severely reducing the patient's sense of self or self-esteem.

Nonetheless, most interpretations of characterological behaviors tend to shake the person's very sense of being. And when the self is under such attack, interpretation is rarely perceived as helpful. Even merely identifying the tendencies toward secondary gains can be treacherous. To tell a woman who always gets involved with cruel and sadistic men that she derives some pleasure from it or that there is a need for punishment may be strongly resented, if not totally denied. She may apparently accept the interpretation with a tongue-in-cheek remark: "Then I guess I must be a masochist." And if the therapist then pursues the masochism path, he will find no collaboration from the patient. The patient's statement was meant as a form of dismissal, an act to prevent the therapist's further interpretation, not to encourage it. In fact, what the patient appears to expect from everyone, including the therapist, is the rebuttal, "Oh, no, you are not a masochist at all. You are just an innocent, well-meaning, good person; the others are bad people." Ironically, however, the patient herself will neither believe nor be satisfied with that. If the therapist actually says it, the patient will lose confidence in him or her.

Therefore, in the preparatory phase to interpretation, what the therapist must do first when faced with characterological maladaptations is to try to make these entrenched ego-compatible qualities ego-alien. During the initial phase of treatment, the therapist strives to relate to the patient without any confrontation of these character traits. Then, once enough distance is generated, he or she can start to treat them as if they are symptoms.

Case Illustration

A forty-three-year-old woman, a successful academician and the mother of two girls, ages seven and eleven, sought help because the older daughter had minor learning disabilities and was not doing well in school. A school psychologist had diagnosed the child as having mild chronic depression, which was attributed to the relationship between her and her mother. (The psychologist's formulation was that the mother was too demanding in light of the child's capacity to perform and that due to the mother's disappointment the daughter felt unloved.) The patient's request for professional advice about how she could be helpful to her daughter was prompted by the psychologist and by her husband, who blamed her for the daughter's depression.

PATIENT: Yesterday we had a family session with the psychologist: me, my husband, and my daughter Wendy. They all dumped on me. Wendy says that I don't love her the way I love Susan [the younger daughter]. My husband claims that I don't pay enough attention to the household, that I'm too busy writing my books, and that I'm not home enough. According to him, my younger one is going to be in trouble, too, if she isn't already. The psychologist asked whether I was neglecting my husband and whether his complaints about my attentiveness toward the children were another symptom of our marriage. So I felt very upset. How is it that everything is *my* fault? Learning disabilities are supposed to be a genetic condition, although neither my family nor my husband's has had such problems that we know of. Wendy was difficult from day one. She did not sleep well and was cranky. She was colicky and would cry incessantly. You name it, she had it. I did my best. [The patient says there is nothing wrong in her behavior, it's only that she's unjustly accused. The problem is not with her but with the child who does not do well and with a husband and a psychologist, both male, who think mothers are to blame.]

THERAPIST: You were upset after the family session. [The therapist is not interested in the patient's upset mood as a symptom to be interpreted, but rather wants to explore the mechanism by which the patient gets herself upset. Are there some self-accusations that could create an alternative perspective in the ego? And how can he get her to be self-reflective?]

PATIENT: It's so unfair. I have to work all day and then come home, make dinner, help the girls with their homework. And this kid does not study, so it's nonsense that she has a learning disability. I get angry at her for not studying, not because she doesn't get all *A*'s. [The patient is still defending her characterological traits, that she is not a demanding person.]

THERAPIST: You are upset for being unfairly criticized and misunderstood. [The therapist is understanding on both accounts, but the emphasis is still on the patient's being upset, and he is searching for

251

the nature of the upset in order to move from complaints to self-exploration.]

PATIENT: I am just as upset about things like her not studying, as the way she is, MBD [Minimal Brain Dysfunction], whatever it is. Believe me, I can take lots of abuse as long as she does well.

THERAPIST: Those unfair accusations would have been tolerable, if they had led to her performing better. [The therapist is trying to find an avenue for alliance, even a narcissistic alliance.]

PATIENT: Exactly. I received a call last week asking me to meet with the principal of the school; he wanted to talk about her performance. I was humiliated. They showed me her grades, and she is doing worse than the previous semester. I even hired tutors to help her with her projects. My parents were never called to school for this kind of thing. [The patient has tears in her eyes. She says, "I am right, look at the evidence. I was a good girl as a child and I still am now."]

THERAPIST: It is very painful. [The therapist is hopeful of eliciting her depressed affect by being empathic.]

PATIENT: No, I am enraged. I could have killed her! I came home and she was watching TV. I shut it off and shook her by the shoulders. I had to stop myself. She was unphased. She called me all kinds of names and left the apartment. [The patient does not follow the therapist's path and refuses to get close to her pain; instead she expresses rage to justify her escalating aggression.]

THERAPIST: She humiliates you with her school performance and does not even realize it. [This comment, which is empathic on the one hand and an alliance "against others" on the other, is preparatory in nature; it is geared to highlight the importance of performance for the patient.]

PATIENT: What else am I supposed to do? Then I am blamed as the reason for all this because I don't love her enough. [The patient feels justified, but finally introduces the issue of not loving Wendy.]

THERAPIST: You are blamed for not being a good mother. [The therapist introduces the larger issue of motherhood.]

PATIENT: Exactly. But look what I have to work with. Other mothers have these smart, lively daughters, good students, interesting children. It is easy to be a mother to them. [The patient is still resisting any hint that there may be some truth in all these accusations, that she can blame herself for a minor thing at least.]

THERAPIST: It is easy to love such kids. [The therapist purposely does not confront the patient with the fact that there may be some truth in the statements that she doesn't love her older daughter. The therapist cannot join the husband and the school psychologist in accusing her. He is again investing in a narcissistic alliance.]

PATIENT: Of course I love Susan, because I have no problems with her. She does what she is supposed to do and she is likable. What does Wendy do to be likable? She makes no effort at all. Even my husband comments that she always looks angry, but he still blames me. Now she has been putting on weight. He claims that I have not been supervising her well. [The patient is giving more reasons why she is right.]

THERAPIST: So you have this overweight, angry child who is failing in school, and you are expected to love her and be a good mother. [The therapist continues the narcissistic alliance.]

PATIENT: I mean, it isn't that I don't love her. I do, but I wish I didn't have to be responsible for her performance. [The patient finally says I love conditionally, but still there is nothing wrong with that.]

THERAPIST: Because you are judged as to what kind of a mother you are based on her performance. [The therapist says that by certain criteria you are judged as not being a good mother, which you don't like.]

PATIENT: My mother keeps saying that I should do something about her. What did she have to do when I was a child? I did not need any help with my schoolwork. I gave them no trouble. How could she have failed as a mother with me? [The patient still says "I am fine," resisting any attempt to be self-reflective.]

THERAPIST: And you feel that you have failed as a mother. [This is the therapist's first attempt to see whether the patient can take some distance from her characterologically defensive attitude of being wrongly blamed and begin a self-evaluation.]

PATIENT: I'm beginning to feel that way. Of course, my husband thinks so, my mother thinks so, and my daughter thinks so. [The patient accepts the therapist's statement grudgingly.]

THERAPIST: And maybe this is the first time you have ever failed in your life? [The therapist is empathic, but is also solidifying the recognition of failure.]

PATIENT: I was an excellent student, a good friend, a good daughter. I was always at the head of my class. I was the first to publish, the youngest one to be tenured. I married well and never had any problems. Maybe I should not have had children, because even with my younger daughter I get impatient. I want my children to behave like adults. My husband says I want them to behave the way I did, that is all. I read about the mothers of mentally retarded kids or even criminals, how they are dedicated to their children, how much they

253

love them. To me that's just hard to believe. I could never do it. I see these young mothers oohing and ahing over little infants who look like monkeys. I can't stand it. [The patient is self-revealing without being very self-reflective.]

THERAPIST: It must have been hard then to take care of your daughters while they were infants. [The therapist is looking for confirmatory information without being accusatory.]

PATIENT: No, I didn't take care of them; my mother-in-law did. Until they began to walk and talk, I had very little to do with them. I guess that is unusual. I just don't like infants. Maybe that's why I wasn't made to be a mother. Maybe I'm just too selfish, too concerned about the way things look to others. [This is the first time the patient makes a self-accusatory statement.]

THERAPIST: The way things look to others. [The therapist neither confirms nor rejects the patient's idea about her motherhood, selfishness, and so on, but asks the question to expand this potentially self-critical arena. The patient has begun to identify dysfunctional parts of her character.]

PATIENT: You know, for her to be successful, go to the best schools, be the most popular child, go to the best college, and have a good marriage. You know.

THERAPIST: To follow in your footsteps. [The therapist hopes to make her narcissism ultimately an ego-alien trait.]

PATIENT: Well, it wouldn't hurt. But, then, why do I want her to follow me? Why am I so invested in that? At times I say, "Leave her alone, that's her problem," but somehow I can't seem to contain myself.

THERAPIST: You can't contain yourself? [The therapist emphasizes the ego-alien part of herself (the inability to contain herself in spite of better judgment) in order to have a baseline; he also wants her to elaborate on this ego-alien dimension so that he will have more material to work with.]

PATIENT: When I see her lounging around, not doing her homework, I say to myself, "Shut up." I feel like I'm going to strangle her, but I bite my tongue. It only works for a few minutes.

THERAPIST: You wish you had enough control to take some distance from her. [Now that the therapist has identified an ego-alien behavior, he wants to establish the counterbalancing part of the ego—the control.]

PATIENT: My husband seems to have enough distance. I don't have to be so embroiled in this. Not only do I wish I had more control over myself, but also at times I wish I was like other mothers. Even Frank says I have a hard edge to me, that I am a taskmaster like my father.

THERAPIST: Like your father. [By repeating this the therapist is seeking more data on the subject. He has begun to formulate the case that some masculine identification exists. These characterological traits may be causing problems for her daughters and her husband. Is the patient wishing that she had fewer masculine traits?]

PATIENT: Yes, he is a real taskmaster. They say, like him, I accept people conditionally. Who accepts or loves people unconditionally? Mothers are supposed to. Well, if that's so, I am obviously not a mother.

THERAPIST: That the female parent loves unconditionally and the male loves conditionally? [The therapist introduces sex differences.]

PATIENT: I don't know. You're the doctor. I can't understand how some women love unconditionally. My husband's mother is that way. Mine, I'm not sure. I met all her conditions anyway. What was there not to love? *(Flippantly)* So I'll be the man. My husband should be the woman.

THERAPIST: At the same time you wish you were more like other women. [The therapist explores the conflicted wishes.]

PATIENT: Yes. I am neither a man, so that I can do the man's job, nor do I seem to be this tender, caring, soft, all-accepting, all-loving woman.

THERAPIST: Not an easy spot to be in. [The therapist already has data about her ego-alien characterological traits, so addresses the establishment of an empathic bond.]

PATIENT: Very difficult.

THERAPIST: And your older daughter isn't making it any easier. [The therapist is putting the conflict into a daily context.]

PATIENT: No, she isn't. I guess that is why I get so upset. She makes me feel completely incompetent.

THERAPIST: And rubs your nose into it.

PATIENT: I guess that is why I get so enraged. It's a reaction so out of proportion; aggressive male behavior, Frank says.

THERAPIST: And your dilemma, whether you are supposed to be like a man or a woman.

PATIENT: I always knew that I didn't want to be the typical woman— cooking, cleaning, taking care of the kids, like my mother or my older sister. I wanted to be in charge, like my father. Then as a good girl I had to do what was expected of me, get married, have children, whether I wanted to or not.

THERAPIST: Whether you could be or not. [The therapist sharpens the dilemma.]

PATIENT: It never occurred to me. I did what I was supposed to do. Being such a goody-goody, look where it got me.

THERAPIST: That you are stuck in this mother role and not doing so well.

PATIENT: Maybe that is the word—*stuck*. This problem isn't going to go away. It isn't like I could have an abortion. They'll be there all my life, testing me every step of the way, showing me that I am not a good mother.

THERAPIST: Do you think some of the rage that you experience toward your daughter is related to this sense of being stuck in this role of mother/woman, where you don't feel you fully belong?

PATIENT: It must be. So what should I do? Is analysis what I need? I mean, is there a chance—does it work at this age?

CHAPTER 42

Minimum cues should not be met with even minimum confrontations

AS THE OLD SAYING GOES, "Any fool can tell the difference between high noon and midnight; it is harder to know dawn from dusk." Psychotherapy is conducted in the gray zone that comprises the subtlest and most hidden underlying issues that are rarely the immediate focus of interactions between patient and therapist. Although obvious matters of everyday life can occupy a great deal of session time, in the midst of this seemingly arbitrary verbal exchange the actively attentive therapist can find minimum cause for therapeutic use. Some of these are well known and part of the psychopathology of everyday life (Freud 1901); they generally include verbal content-oriented cues, such as parapraxes (like forgetting names or slips of the tongue) as well as nonverbal indicators, such as aspects of eye contact or facial expression; blushing or blinking; physical position, posture, or movements; and even the witting or unwitting choice of attire.

Other cues can be specific to a particular patient. One patient, whenever she was angry with the therapist, would not take her coat off during the session; another, who feared getting too close, would physically move his chair away from or toward the therapist depending on their psychological distance; another, based on whether he wanted to work seriously or dilute the session by "having a chat," would respectively choose to sit on the couch or the chair; still another patient would chew gum during the session when she was trying to make it more informal.

257

Other patient-specific cues, especially those that emerge gradually as process-oriented clues to the patient's psyche, may be harder to detect. These can include the following:

1. Avoidance of the present: the patient may incessantly indulge in the past as a focus of attention at the expense of any current material.

2. Avoidance of the past: the patient may inundate the sessions with daily activities as seemingly urgent and pressing issues.

3. Avoidance of both past and present: the patient may exclusively focus on the relationship with the therapist in seemingly well-informed, serious, psychologically sophisticated fashion but without any connection to past or present events in his or her own life.

4. Avoidance of the therapist: the patient may eagerly and enthusiastically talk about everything, past and present, in a highly cooperative fashion—as if the therapist were not there.

To detect these other minimum cues the therapist must, obviously, be perceptive and listen attentively. Commonly, however, it is not his or her perceptual ability or attentive power that is failing the therapist, but his or her own psychological need *not* to notice minimum cues. Such personal needs may belong exclusively to the therapist independent of any particular patient—for example, fear of facing certain conflictual subjects (sexuality, aggression, intimacy, illness, death, and so on); difficulties in experiencing and tolerating strong feelings (not wanting to be confronted with the patient's aggression); or attachment to his or her own values or blind spots (such as the need to believe that all mothers are good or that all divorces are bad). Or the psychological needs of the therapist may be specifically triggered by, or related to, a certain patient; failure to notice clues would in such a case be countertransferential.

The clinician's perception and recognition of the patient's minimum cues are just the beginning; responsiveness and proper use of them follow. These cues have to be handled very sensitively. Since minimum cues have their source in unconscious material, the fact that they emerge and become obvious does not make them conscious. Thus the therapist does not grab the opportunity, seize the slip or gesture and confront the patient with it in the hope of exploring related unconscious material. If anything, such confrontation may make the patient feel caught doing something wrong—discovered, if not stripped, without his or her consent. Nothing makes the patient more defensive than the therapist's bringing direct attention to these minimum cues. The patient feels accused or made fun of by the therapist. The following vignettes illustrate three common reactions when the patient is directly confronted with minimum cues.

1. *The patient may dismiss the whole thing.* A patient was in a highly dependent relationship with his wife.

PATIENT: I am in the middle of all this work, and my mother calls to remind me that I have to pick up our daughter at 3:30 from school and then take her to . . . what is that quizzical look?
THERAPIST: Did you hear what you just said?
PATIENT: No, what did I say? I was telling you that my wife called me to pick up our daughter.
THERAPIST: Did you say "my wife" or "my mother"?
PATIENT: Oh, did I say my *mother?* I make that mistake quite often; I meant my wife. Anyhow, so I am supposed to take our daughter to her skating class, then go back to work for an hour, and after that go and pick her up again.

Further confrontation, that is, asking the patient whether he was avoiding the discussion of the slip, would harden his defenses and further alienate him from the therapist. What the therapist needs to do is to register the mother/wife connections in his mind and begin to explore and collect more material about them over many sessions— their characteristics, their relationship with the patient, the patient's wishes and demands, his fantasies and realities, his needs and frustrations. One day the patient may pick up his slip himself and say, "I guess I want my wife to be like my mother was" (or in reality was not): a perfect mother.

2. *The patient may be offended.* A fifty-seven-year-old divorced man, a latent homosexual himself, was quite unhappy about and preoccupied with his son's homosexuality.

PATIENT: *(Excited and agitated)* I don't understand the homosexuality. I mean, what do they do to each other? How a man can kiss another man on the mouth—how disgusting; then they suck each other . . . *(blushes).* My God, what kind of pleasure is that?
THERAPIST: You blushed when you were describing the details of what homosexuals may do to each other.
PATIENT: What, you think I get off on this, you mean some kind of pleasure? No sirree, you got the wrong man; I'm no homo!

If, instead of confronting the patient, the therapist had registered the excitement and blushing in terms of understanding the patient's need to reject homosexuality, it would have been easier to explore later the patient's sexual world, including his very early experiences. In the next session the patient responds to such exploration.

PATIENT: You wonder whether I had any homosexual relationship my-self? Well, not really. Once I was kind of a busboy to this rich old guy who lived alone; he would treat me nicely. He had a big library. He would sit me there, leave me there for a long time alone in complete privacy. He had cigarettes and drinks there, and he would suggest that I read some of the books. He was a very classy guy. After a while he would knock on the door, wait for me to say "Come in," and enter with his elegant robe and sort of parade in front of me. I must have been sixteen or something. He always stared at my crotch. I remember having an erection. I couldn't figure that out. I knew I wasn't homosexual; why then was I having an erection?

THERAPIST: It must have been confusing.

PATIENT: Yeah, I would look forward to going to his place and was also very anxious, wanting to stay away. Mind you, I was just a kid, never had sex with women. Then I decided that it was really dangerous; I stayed the hell out of his place.

THERAPIST: Finally frightened enough to draw the line?

PATIENT: I don't really know what he wanted me to do. The old son of a bitch, I wonder where he is now.

THERAPIST: He is there just knocking on the other door.

PATIENT: (Chuckles) Ha! You mean the homosexuality now, coming at me from a different door, my son? My son says: Why are you so upset, obsessed by that, when 15 percent of the population is gay? Am I really obsessed by it? Do you think that this story that I just told you, my experience I mean, has something to do with it?

THERAPIST: You wonder whether you still carry some feelings left over from those days that may be coming to play in your reaction to your son's homosexuality?

PATIENT: I don't know; maybe it is true that many of my friends have homosexual kids. Why is it that I am so . . .

3. The patient may become self-conscious. A middle-aged married woman, whose husband was having an affair with a younger woman, was denying the fact that it happened and could not express her anger and depression. But whenever she talked about her husband, she would blink her eyes frequently, to the point that her eyes would stay almost closed.

PATIENT: I cannot believe that could happen. We are such a team. He still looks into my eyes with such affection and love. I love him, and I know he loves me. This young thing is most likely a passing fancy of a middle-aged man; she couldn't mean much to him. Then why is he spending that much time with her? It really makes no sense. I wish someone like you would tell him to stop this idiotic stuff. Meanwhile, my stomach is in knots. I have no appetite. I am always anxious for no reason.

THERAPIST: Are you aware that whenever you speak of your husband you close your eyes?

PATIENT: I do? Only when I speak of him? How strange! What other bizarre things do I do, Doc? Now let me see—I am trying to keep my eyes open when I speak of him. Oh, God, now I don't even know what to say. This is like that story of an old man with a long beard. Once someone asked whether he slept with his beard under the sheet or over it, he could no longer sleep. OK, let's try again—my eyes are open, now let's talk about this so-called affair. You let me know if I close my eyes. Do I cross my legs when I talk about the affair? [Although the last sentence became very important later, the rest of the hour was unproductive.]

Instead, the therapist may just quietly register this minimum cue of the patient's closing her eyes whenever she talked about her husband's affair and explore the questions of getting old, her attitude toward her husband's disloyalty, her fear of losing her husband, and her loneliness. Her not wanting to see would then be only a part of the larger agenda, and placed in that broader context instead of being singled out for special mention. In a later session the therapist does not confront her cues.

THERAPIST: You wish I could stop that nonsense of his.

PATIENT: Yes, instead of talking with me, you should be talking to him. Instead of me talking about it, he should tell you what is going on. I told him of your suggestion to see a marriage counselor—he just brushed it off.

THERAPIST: You also wish this whole thing never happened.

PATIENT: That is all I need now! I am almost fifty years old. I spent all my youthful years with him; now I could be easily deposed. This anxiety that I mentioned—what is it, Doc? I never had this before. It is like something caving in in me. I am in a panic.

THERAPIST: Hmm.

PATIENT: It seems like all my internal organs are shaken. I thought I had some power in our relationship. Now I feel so reduced that I feel like I have nothing to say in this whole matter. I am sort of an innocent bystander, just waiting out her fate.

THERAPIST: How painful!

PATIENT: *(Crying)* What did I do to deserve this? I have been a good wife, a loyal wife. I cooked for him, ironed his shirts, took care of the kids. How unfair! I am dreading the idea of not having him home again. I can almost hear his car pulling in, his footsteps, his calling me "Geous"—it is short for *gorgeous*—like he is slipping away from me and taking all this away.

THERAPIST: How sad.

PATIENT: *(Sobbing)* I am so unhappy. Oh, I'm so unhappy. God, I don't want to live; I am feeling so awful, like part of me is torn away from me. God, I wish this whole thing was just a bad dream; I'll wake up and everything will be the way it was. Oh, please God. That bitch, I could kill her! Doesn't she see that the man is married? With all the single men around, why is she going after my husband? *(With eyes open)* It's a shame that he would throw away his twenty-four-year marriage for that young hussy.

The minimum cues of avoidance of past or present are often the most difficult to detect because on the surface the patient seems to be working hard and complying with the therapist. Thus dealing with such avoidances is an especially sensitive matter. For example, confrontation of avoidance of past or present will make the patient feel criticized, that he or she is not being a good patient, has disappointed the therapist, is not doing the right thing, and ultimately, is wronged again in life and in treatment. The therapist who does not appreciate the nature of these avoidances (defensive/adaptive) will confront the avoidance, invariably hurting, confusing, or angering the patient because of being made vulnerable in the presence of the therapist before he or she is ready for such confrontation.

Case Illustration

A forty-year-old man, whose much younger wife left him because of his "drinking problem," talked incessantly about his pain, depression, and sense of loss. He said virtually nothing about his mother having left when he was three years old or about being raised by his aunt. The eighth session continues in the vein of all the rest.

PATIENT: I am just devastated. I walk around confused, I can't focus, I don't listen to people. Soon I am going to lose my job. Everyone says, "Stop thinking of her." I have not even had a single drink since she left. I don't even enjoy drinking anymore. I don't enjoy anything.

THERAPIST: Speaking of thinking about her too much now, you know, you also talk too little about your past.

PATIENT: Are you implying that I should talk about my mother's leaving us? But the pain I have is just about my wife. You are also saying that I think too much of my wife. The past is past. I can't bring my mother back. What is the point of talking about the past when my pain is in the present? To me it sounds like you are trying to divert me. People say I should take a trip to Europe, but I would like to go with her. I called her late last night. She was furious with me. I wanted to discuss a few things. I've got to find some way to bring her back. Do you think that I should go over and beg, tell her that I stopped drinking? I know what you are going to say—the feeding the pigeons theory: if you go after them they go away, and if you sit still they will eat out of your hands. But I cannot sit still. Can't you understand that?

The therapist, instead of explicitly urging the patient to talk about his past, can try to understand the patient's need *not* to get in touch with historical pain in order to maintain some stability in his psychic state. The reassuring atmosphere provided may allow the patient to become more vulnerable without falling apart, thus to become more able to start talking about the past. Empathy and understanding are the therapeutic roads that would lead to a more trusting relationship and to the patient's willingness to regress to past memories and associations.

THERAPIST: How depressing!

PATIENT: I ache for her. How could anyone be so important? I lived with her for six years. But now it seems I cannot live without her. I am so aware of her absence, as if nothing else matters—a strange pain, I can't even cry.

THERAPIST: Like no other pain you ever had!

PATIENT: No, I don't think so. I don't remember well, but there was my mother's leaving us. I know they took us to my aunt's house. Both my sisters were crying; I wasn't. I did not believe that she could leave us; I thought, later on she'll show up and take us home. But she never did. I kept waiting, every day sitting by the window, imagining her coming, visually almost hallucinating, her opening her arms to hug me. Then I would hear my aunt's voice—she was a stern woman—"Are you still daydreaming there? Boy, you think too much of your mother, think a little bit about something else."

Although all content-related minimum cues, when confronted, may lead to further defensiveness on the part of the patient, one way or another undermining the therapeutic relationship and the progress of psychotherapy, all process-oriented cues, minimum or maximum, eventually will need full and in-depth confrontation. Nonetheless, all cues from the patient have to be treated with great caution. The finer the cues, the greater the necessity for discrete and gradual handling.

PART IX

ON CURATIVE AGENTS AND THEIR DECEPTIONS

This part emphasizes that the therapeutic process of psychotherapy is an inherently time-consuming phenomenon that cannot be condensed without changing the essence of the endeavor or the outcome for the patient; there are no shortcuts, no "microwave" miracles. The reasons for this are manifold. They include the natural evolution of the therapeutic process itself, which means the amount of time required for the therapist–patient relationship to develop fully as well as to dissolve; the human and professional limits of the clinician in getting to know another person in depth; and, finally, the psychological barriers of the patient in both achieving and resisting change or cure, however defined. The role of the therapist as a translator of the patient's problems is particularly important insofar as he or she is bound by verbal language as an imperfect medium for learning about another person's actual experiences; it takes time to deal with the gap between what is said and what is meant. This problem is compounded, of course, by temporal considerations of life history and memory in reconstructing, or constructing anew, the world of the patient from the outside in or from adulthood back to infancy.

Certain criteria of positive therapeutic progress are explored in these chapters as true versus deceptive events. The so-called good hour may have as its ingredients special moments, turning points, or sudden insights. For example, a eureka-type knowledge of self rarely endures, however potent it appears. The therapist should be wary of the possibly misleading nature of insight.

Just as outcome cannot be discussed without knowing the starting point of treatment, so the success of psychotherapy depends largely on the assets and limitations of the particular patient. Furthermore, it is only through a maturational process of becoming more vulnerable within the confines of therapy that the patient can become less vulnerable within the boundaries of self.

The therapist naturally plays a part in the patient's ultimate psychological health. On one level, both practitioner and recipient hope to arrive at a meeting point where the two are partners, or "equals," at least in their respective ability to healthily separate from one another. This goal raises the issues of identification, internalization, role modeling, and other relationship phenomena as agents of therapeutic change.

The following questions are posed in this part: What are the major mutative factors and criteria of outcome of psychotherapy? What limitations upon progress inhere in the therapeutic process itself? And how are the participants themselves, separately and together, implicated in the creation of change or cure?

CHAPTER 43

Good moments and sudden insights may deceive the patient and derail the therapist

FOR THE PSYCHODYNAMIC THERAPIST, insight is often considered to be the sine qua non of cure. Therapeutic insight has been defined as "the process by which the meaning, significance, pattern, or use of an experience becomes clear—or the understanding which results from this process" (Harper 1959, 163). A good moment, good hour, or turning point in psychotherapy is frequently associated with some particularly powerful or mutative insight of the patient which has results from mutual exploration and interpretive interventions. However, as Rosalea Schonbar (1965) has succinctly concluded, "Not all change is attributable to insight" and "not all insight leads to change" (p. 78). Some interpretations are nonmutative and even unnecessarily painful. These may be either insufficient (that is, having no impact) or inappropriate (that is, having too much impact) for certain types of patients.

There is yet another scenario about which the clinician needs to be warned. Grand realizations about the self may be exuberantly presented by the patient and turn out to be false reports. Understanding acquired from the therapist may seem to have had a potent enlightening effect on the patient, when in fact the change is not true or enduring. Most likely the patient's motivation is not self-knowledge but gratification or defense.

At various times during the psychotherapeutic process the therapist is naturally the pleased recipient of what appear to be good moments (or good hours), sudden insights, and turning points on the part of the patient. The practitioner may initially have to decide by instinct whether these verbal or affective pronouncements are truly therapeutic experiences or are deceptive displays of positive progress. As in the case of medicine, the cautious clinician should be wary if the prescribed treatment works faster than expected or is otherwise remarkable in its effects. In the "deceptively good hour," according to Ernst Kris (1956), it is appropriate for the therapist to be suspicious: a variety of misleading phenomena may masquerade as insight. Three garden varieties include the following.

1. *Insight that arrives full-blown as an illuminating experience.* This eureka-type phenomenon is usually manifested by too much lucidity too soon. It generally occurs in place of the more desirable but often more subtle experience of self-understanding that transpires in a drawn-out and emotionally attenuated form. As Arnold M. Ludwig (1966) has observed:

> The sudden tidal wave of illumination or enlightenment is rare compared to the numerous small ripples of insights which are experienced and intellectually assimilated over a long period of time. Moreover, therapeutic insights tend to be circumscribed and specific to certain problem areas than the profound and general eureka experiences, such as those described to occur during religious conversion or revelation in which the "whole truth" suddenly is revealed. (P. 315)

Most often, this kind of presumed insight serves the patient's purposes of winning the therapist's praise or approval. It usually has a libidinous motive of earning the clinician's love, or in more severe psychopathology, of achieving a form of symbiotic union. It may even be accompanied by an infantile fantasy of primitive merging. A clue to its false nature typically inheres in the timing of its occurrence, however. It tends to become most evident in the positive transference phase in which there is maximum attachment and dependency upon the therapist. Depressed patients, for example, may be especially susceptible at those times when they most need to assure themselves of an outside person's praise and approval in order to feel good about themselves.

2. *Insight that is offered in the service of gaining independence, or otherwise divorcing oneself, from the therapist.* Perhaps at a later stage in treatment, a kind of pseudo-self-analysis may occur in which the patient has in

effect replaced or surpassed the therapist. Behind this impressive show of insight often lurks the desire to prove to the therapist that he or she is no longer needed. It can have both competitive and hostile elements, reflecting negative transferential or rivalrous feelings. Although the patient may appear capable of going it alone, this type of insight is also misleading, a defensive ruse designed for the clinician to believe that the patient is farther along than he or she really is. This may be a variation of the so-called flight into health, in which the relinquishing of symptoms occurs not because the patient has truly resolved his or her particular neurosis, but rather as a defense against further probing into painful, unconscious material. The patient's symptoms may not disappear, but the ostensible insight serves as a comparable excuse to prematurely flee the therapeutic encounter.

3. *Insight that derives from a monolithic or single model of experience.* This involves a facile or simplistic transformation of events on the part of the patient with hopes that they will seem more convincing than they deserve to. These insights often have a rotelike quality, mimicking the therapist. The patient in effect has unconsciously tampered with the data to make them sound right. Sometimes the patient begins to act like the therapist, or at least like a caricature of one. This phenomenon may occur in patients whose sense of themselves and their boundaries is especially fluid, or in those who are characterologically not psychologically minded (such as alexithymic patients who tend to somaticize their problems). The correct vocabulary may be present, but the illuminations are glib and superficial. A telling clue is that these self-reflections immediately reproduce the therapist's interpretive statements as if they were the patient's own. Such insights, alas, usually stay on the surface.

Deceptive insights are rarely therapeutic. They appear in the service of cure, but are actually used for the patient's gratification or self-protection. They may temporarily satisfy the patient by bringing him or her closer to the clinician, or serve defensive purposes to protect against the pain of insight. Appelbaum (1976), for example, has pointed out the "dangerous edge of insight," by which is meant the heightening of anxiety and other disturbing feelings consequent to increased awareness. This negative aspect of insight was formulated from experience with patients who were unable to withstand the new information about themselves and went on to lose the gains they had made.

Case Illustration

A thirty-eight-year-old professional woman who had previously been in therapy decided to return for treatment with a different therapist after a long hiatus. Based on prior experience in psychotherapy and familiarity with psychological jargon, she tried to be a "good" patient (by reporting dreams, free associating, and the like) who had many successive "insights." However, upon closer inspection, these were actually pseudo-insights that formed a barrier against any genuine or sustained exploration of self.

PATIENT: I just came from visiting my mother. She is getting old; all the time I was there she complained of headaches. She always did. You never know with her what is real and what isn't. Not just headaches, everything, what is the real fact about anything is hard to tease out. She says she loves me. Does she? I cannot really tell. When I was a child she used to say, "You are pretty, but not beautiful; smart, but not intelligent." One day she'll say, "You are a nice girl"; on another, "You are full of rage, you could kill." I was not sure what to believe, what all that meant—was I a good or bad girl?

THERAPIST: Hmm.

PATIENT: I don't have a good sense of myself. It makes me so dependent on others to define me that it is just pitiful. For a little love and a compliment, I'll do almost anything . . . I was about to say something; it just slipped my mind. Damn, I wanted to free associate.

THERAPIST: You are trying very hard here, too. You want so much to free associate, to be a good patient, to be a "good girl."

PATIENT: Yes, I guess I want to be loved by you, too. Oh God, I am so insecure, so pitiful with all this. I want you to think that I am the best patient you ever had, that I'll be able to remain in treatment, not terminate, you know . . . I can't seem to free associate, but I did have this dream. The other day, I had a dream about the treatment. I was talking to a therapist; it was supposed to be you, but it did not look like you. I was talking to "Dr. K." I cannot remember what I was saying, though. I know you are going to ask my associations. Well, why did the face of the person not look like yours? Maybe that is why I forgot the material.

THERAPIST: Earlier you mentioned that you could have spoken better to a female therapist.

PATIENT: Well, of course, that is what it is! Now that you mention it, the face in the dream was a female face, and now it is coming to me as we are talking. Well, all that stuff, the other day, wondering about my sexual orientation; the innuendo whether I had some masculine traits. I was furious at you.

THERAPIST: Maybe that is why the therapist's face in your dream did not look like mine.

PATIENT: Maybe I wanted another therapist; yes, it makes sense. *(Long silence)* Now I've thought of something. This just reminded me of my childhood, when I used to cut out my father's head in old pictures and replace them with famous people, like actors. I guess I am never happy with what I have. I wish my parents were different, more educated, rich. As a child, I used to talk about my parents with all kinds of made-up stories. I still do. I gave them entirely new identities.

THERAPIST: And trying to generate some identity for youself?

PATIENT: Yes. I am so amorphous, I can easily make up an identity, but all is fluid. *(Staring at the therapist)* But you did not ask me more about the cutting the heads off my father's pictures. I guess it is sort of a castration fantasy. You are right, maybe I am masculine, maybe I hate men, I want to castrate them all. Did you see that movie, *War of the Roses*, when she bit his penis? Everyone in the theater expressed some shock or pain, some sympathy for him; I was laughing my head off.

THERAPIST: Now, does replacing my head in your dream have a different meaning?

PATIENT: You mean castrating you? Of course . . . I must have sexual desire and anger toward you. I feel, if you have sex with me, I feel it might define me, that I am desirable; then I would be angry that you would be lying, that I am not really desirable.

THERAPIST: You are never sure whether to believe in me or not, or what to believe.

PATIENT: Yes, in that sense you are like my mother, maybe you say things to make me feel good, but I don't trust you. Then why do I cut out my father's head rather than my mother's? Is it a displacement of hostility? Because in fact she was the castrating one with all those pseudocompliments that I was just pretty, not beautiful.

THERAPIST: While all the time having headaches?

PATIENT: Oh God, oh God! Yes, yes, cutting her head off. Oh yes, oh yes. That very act of killing her would give me some sense of realness, a real act, undisputably real, a base, an identity, the bad girl; bad, but nevertheless a solid identity.

The therapist had to spend several hours undoing this session.

CHAPTER 44

The success of psychotherapy can be attributed to the patient, and its failure to the therapist

THERE ARE MANY WAYS TO DEFINE positive therapeutic outcome. The most famous goal perhaps is Freud's *arbeiten und lieben*, to work and to love. One may view the success of psychotherapy in terms of the patient's overall maturation, better social adjustment in marriage or family, development of an internal sense of peace, increased creativity, and the like. As demonstrated by Mary Smith, Gene Glass, and T. I. Miller (1980), more than seventeen hundred objective and subjective outcome measures have been used in the research literature on the effectiveness of psychotherapy. No doubt the patient's initial condition has a great deal to do with outcome. Although the correlation is by no means perfect, and goals may be deliberately less ambitious for the most disturbed patients—generally, the more severe the psychopathology, the greater the distance to be traveled on the road to health, however defined.

The more disturbed the patient is, the greater the demands on the therapist are. One of the by-products of this fact of clinical life is that the psychotherapist may tend to seek "good" patients, those who are well motivated, psychologically minded, articulate, introspective, and intellectually and interpersonally or socioeconomically advantaged. The ideal patient has even been given the tongue-in-cheek diagnosis of

YAVIS syndrome—young, attractive, verbal, intelligent, successful—an acronym that connotes highly selective patient criteria.

Criticisms of this tendency have noted the unconscious or conscious elitism in the selection of patients, and the ideal is no doubt overrated and stereotypic. Nonetheless, how the patient functions at the onset of therapy cannot be ignored. An assessment of functioning is an integral part of the evaluation process. A traditional list of the most important patient requisites includes high motivation, because the patient must persevere in the face of the demands of time, money, and the inherent pain of exploration; the ability to form a relationship, so as to both connect with and detach from another human being in a trusting and intimate bond; the capacity for insight, which requires introspection as well as the ability to articulate thoughts and feelings; and ego strength, to oscillate between observing and experiencing, reality and fantasy, and to be able to defer gratification. These characteristics apply especially in the screening of candidates for long-term treatment.

Peter Sifneos (1984), for one, regards as a priority of brief treatment the deliberate preselection of appropriate candidates. His patients must have a specific circumscribed complaint (the ability to focus is seen as evidence of ego strength), have had during childhood at least one meaningful relationship, be able to interact flexibly with the evaluator, have the ability to recognize that his or her problems are psychological in origin, and show motivation for change. Other subsequent criteria have included the capacity for introspection and the willingness to give a truthful account of difficulties, the willingness to explore and to experiment, the capacity to make a tangible sacrifice, and finally, having realistic expectations of the outcome of treatment.

Not only must the patient believe in the therapist and have confidence in his or her powers to heal, but even the most talented therapist needs some assurance that the patient has intrapsychic assets that can be continually drawn upon. All therapists may find themselves not only choosing good prospective patients, but applying that selection process throughout treatment as a natural part of assessing progress and ultimately deciding when it is time to terminate. For no matter how skillful the therapist, psychotherapy success still is largely dependent upon the initial selection process.

Psychotherapy is also a function of patient–therapist fit. Therefore, for any clinician, who the patient is will influence ongoing therapeutic synchrony. This refers to how receptive the patient will be as well as to how the therapist feels about the patient, not only initially but throughout their mutual interaction.

The actual or anticipated part that the patient plays in the success of therapy is matched by the therapist's part. The therapist not only facilitates progress but sometimes defeats it. According to a survey of practitioners and researchers in the field (Hadley and Strupp 1976), unrealistic tasks or goals based upon false assumptions about the scope and potency of therapy are the most frequently cited cause of negative effects in psychotherapy. Reasonable positive expectations, of course, are regarded as a requisite for producing therapeutic effects in all psychotherapies (Frank 1961). But misleading impressions may be at least temporarily imparted by every therapist when the wish to instill hope in the patient and the omnipotence granted in return become intertwined. Especially needy patients may get the erroneous idea that therapy and the therapist can solve everything. This notion can perpetuate inappropriate aspirations and intentions that are invariably detrimental to therapeutic outcome. Such tendencies, however unwitting, can be compounded by the therapist's failure to discuss, describe, or even acknowledge the need to set goals with the patient at various junctures during treatment, or by the setting of goals that are lofty or obscure.

Particular problems arise when individual aims explicitly or implicitly exceed the patient's capabilities, promising speedy progress that cannot be realized because the patient actually requires longer treatment. Another unfortunate situation occurs when the patient has actually accomplished certain aims, yet the therapist revises them to prolong treatment (because he or she is unwilling to terminate). In this behalf Greenson (1967) has warned that any form or aspect of therapy that makes the patient an addict to it and to the therapist is undesirable. In such an instance the patient may demonstrate certain strides within or outside of treatment but is nonetheless unable to leave the therapist, or the therapist is unable to tolerate the potential loss.

These scenarios raise the crucial issue of the role of countertransference in cure. It is the clinician's responsibility to control or deal with his or her own unconscious feelings in treatment. Any improperly managed countertransference (perhaps even more so than improperly handled transference) can lead to a stalemated process and a negative outcome. According to Robert Langs (1982), who believes that "unrecognized countertransferences are the single most critical basis for therapeutic failure" (p. 132), countertransference that is either uncontrolled—or, worse, unrecognized—will result in a "misalliance cure." By this is meant the patient will obtain an uninsightful relief of symptoms due to the reciprocal psychopathology of patient and therapist. In unconsciously identifying with the patient's mode of conflict resolution, the clinician's countertransference can unwittingly offer the patient patho-logical gratification, superego sanctions, or stronger defenses that may well provide temporary relief. But these mutually deceptive effects are neither truly curative nor adaptive for the patient.

The therapist's responsibility for negative results is assumed here. Whether that is appropriate depends on how wide a net is cast in defining and understanding countertransferential phenomena. If counter-transference inevitably occurs in whole or in part with every inter-change, as Langs suggests, one may have to ask: Does each therapeutic silence or intervention also contain elements of countertransference? Do all unconfirmed interpretations contain the rudiments of countertransfer-ence? At bottom, do countertransferential influences have a power that overrides all of the therapist's good techniques and intentions? And do they always leave a "destructive imprint" that cannot be undone?

It has also been proposed, however, that the clinician's capacity to recover and rectify a countertransferential situation can itself be poten-tially therapeutic. By mobilizing the patient's resources in the therapist's behalf, a series of new, constructive introjects is generated, to the benefit of both members.

Even if the patient has not been carefully screened for potential and countertransference need not be accorded such primacy, the careful therapist must still be advised to look at outcome twice: once in terms of the patient's part and a second time in terms of the therapist's contribution. To go beyond this, one might say that despite the natural temptation to be self-congratulatory when the result is positive and to blame the patient for poor outcome, the therapist must also, alas, reverse that process: to look to the recipient for his or her clinical successes and to himself or herself for clinical failures.

CHAPTER 45

Only when the patient becomes more vulnerable within treatment will he or she become less vulnerable outside treatment

A CRUCIAL MARKER of the progress of treatment is that the patient increasingly exposes his or her frailties, but is not hurt within the therapeutic context. Both the patient and the therapist survive and should even get stronger. This temporary deepening of vulnerability in the therapist–patient relationship is different from other suffering endured in the process of psychotherapy, although it, too, may get worse before it gets better. For example, the patient may find out some painful truths about himself or herself and his or her past; the patient may get depressed or anxious, or may have an exacerbation of symptoms. Or the patient may feel more intrapsychic strain than is tolerable as he or she learns about the origins of problems—being cut by what Appelbaum (1976) refers to as the "dangerous edge of insight." The patient may even end up making life decisions that are neither immediately gratifying nor best for the future. The therapist cannot grant any guarantees against such hurts; in fact, the therapist anticipates that they will occur and has to help the patient to budget for them.

Yet the therapist does need to secure the patient against the special vulnerability that may ensue in the patient–therapist relationship. This particular vulnerability may take the form of narcissistic injury, humiliation, being rejected or not liked, or feeling exploited. These may be not only the expected temporary frustrations and distortions, but also the unintended harms that may unwittingly endure.

The patient can become self-revealing and can expose all of his or her weaknesses and peculiarities only if previous attempts to do so were positive; failing that, the patient can gradually be reassured that he or she will not simply endure each exposure but will be understood, if not appreciated, in the process. Although the therapeutic relationship reiterates the parental configuration, with all its problems and unresolved conflicts, the therapist is in reality *different from* one's parents. Alexander Leighton, Raymond Prince, and Rollo May (1968) have succinctly depicted this crucial aspect of the total therapeutic process: at its core, psychotherapy "itself, or some parts of it, constitutes a symbolic reenactment of something which went wrong in the past and which is now being set right . . . therapeutic activity is concerned with making this [reenactment] come out on the side of the patient. . . . The patient does it over again . . . without the mistake" (p. 64).

Each level of self-revelation that is accepted by the therapist creates another secure platform for the patient to build upon, thereby allowing himself or herself to regress or to advance further. Every regression or alteration in prior functioning inevitably makes the patient more vulnerable, and thus generates additional material for psychotherapy and greater potential for the patient to transcend the past. The presence of a trustworthy therapist secures the progress of therapy by permitting the patient to gradually expose increasing amounts of that vulnerability. Thus, by shedding his or her defenses and allowing both bad and good aspects of self to be revealed in the presence of the therapist, the patient can gradually attain mastery over his or her problems and, in turn, gain greater inner security. Ultimately, only by being allowed to become more vulnerable within the treatment atmosphere will the patient be able to become less vulnerable within himself or herself.

CHAPTER 46

Therapy, like all relationships, is time-limited

ALTHOUGH PSYCHOTHERAPY may be theoretically timeless or "interminable" (Freud 1937a), the natural termination date is based upon the ending of the specific relationship between therapist and patient. It is therefore time-limited, but not in the traditional sense. Natural termination is based on the concept that the duration of psychotherapy parallels intrapsychic development. Thus, in the course of treatment the transferential dependency and idealization of the therapist, which is likened to an infant : parent configuration, is gradually replaced by a more realistic, egalitarian, and independent configuration of adult : adult. Having begun with a complementary but asymmetrical or "tilted" relationship (Greenacre 1954), both therapist and patient must stand symmetrically in maturational relation to one another. More specifically, having mutually bonded for purposes of treatment, they must become comparable in their respective readiness to separate.

Thus the therapeutic boundaries of psychotherapy are ultimately determined not by a prearranged or externally imposed end-setting arrangement but by the changing nature of that particular bond, its intense attachment and eventual disengagement. Freud (1937a) considered artifically setting the termination time a "blackmailing device" which does not "guarantee to accomplish the task." He believed that such a definitive termination date might itself generate an induced urgency wherein "while part of the material will become accessible under the pressure of the threat, another part will be kept back and thus become buried" (p. 218).

Others (Mann 1973) have suggested that the issue of time for the patient goes beyond the question of actual termination of treatment, and that it is in fact countertherapeutic *not* to have a preset time limit. The rationale here is that an open-ended, indefinitely long treatment creates the feeling that engagement is timeless. Thus it can become an iatrogenic factor in unduly prolonging the therapeutic process. The therapist may make a countertransferential contribution to the time factor, whereby his or her own dependency needs and libidinal urges or fantasies are more likely to be aroused in a protracted or elusive time frame.

The broader implications of termination dates have to do with therapy as a microcosm of the finite outside world: developmentally the child views time as eternal, whereas the adult gradually recognizes his or her own finitude within the boundaries of time. By contrast, in treatment without temporal constraints the patient, like the child or the immature or disturbed adult, never fully faces the reality that time—in therapy, as in life itself—is limited. Thus maturation in psychotherapy, as a parallel measure of maturity in the outside world, becomes a matter of finally facing one's mortality and the loss of others. In the light of therapeutic termination it also means a heightened sense of one's self as one relinquishes parts of a former self. Here an end-setting arrangement can technically be construed, literally as well as figuratively, as a real impending deadline that signifies that time is running out.

During the course of psychotherapy, time represents the focus for facing the past, mastering the present, and forging the future. With or without temporal boundaries, it is the evolution of psychological or phenomenological time, not actual time, that becomes the crux of successful completion of treatment. When the patient in effect reaches the same stage as the therapist in therapeutic growth and maturation, natural termination occurs. This means that the patient has given up most magical fantasies, unrealistic aspirations, and infantile distortions about the therapist's powers; it also means the patient can see the self more realistically, neither as all-powerful or perfect because he or she is "cured," nor permanently insecure without the presence of the therapist. At the same time, the practitioner has to deal with his or her own attachment and psychological development vis-à-vis the particular patient. The therapist, too, needs to both engage in and gracefully disengage from their temporary bond. In effect, both therapist and patient must become more equal, not in real demographic dimensions nor necessarily in values, attitudes, or accomplishments, but in their psychological relationship to one another, their respective interpersonal development.

Case Illustration

PATIENT: June thirtieth is just three weeks away. I have these mixed feelings of sadness and exaltation. Only a few weeks ago, I thought I was getting sick again; your interpretation that the renewed sickness was serving for me to stay in the treatment helped. Now I feel OK on that score. But this sadness is different. It is not like depression; it is like moving out of a childhood home or finishing school, or saying goodbye to an old friend. And the exaltation is the new vista, a new beginning with greater strength, a kind of freedom—like feeling that now I am OK, world; it's hard to explain it.

THERAPIST: [The therapist feels the sadness and also the pride.] Powerful feelings.

PATIENT: Yes, and so real, none of those old evasions and hiding feelings, being scared of them. Here I am with full emotions, open and secure. They are powerful, but not scary. I'll never know why people don't express their feelings.

THERAPIST: [The therapist believes the patient thinks he is avoiding her by not sharing his feelings with her.] People?

PATIENT: *(Laughs)* I have only three weeks left; I feel good although I still have lots to learn. And you? I mean how do *you* feel? You worked with me all this time. Do you feel a little touch of loss that I'll no longer be here on Mondays and Thursdays at five P.M.? Or are you glad that I am well and happy? Just a minute, don't answer yet. I don't really want to know. I guess I don't want you to say "I'll miss you," you know. I want you to feel that without your saying it. As if your saying it will reduce it.

THERAPIST: [The therapist thinks he will miss her.] You want to maintain the nature of our relationship without reducing it to just friendship.

PATIENT: Yes, because we are more than friends, different than friends, much deeper, more meaningful. Your saying "I'll miss you" would not do justice to the depth of our relationship. I know you'll wonder about me after I've left. Part of me wants to make friends. But I really wouldn't want that. I am ready to terminate the treatment and not necessarily need to come back. So it isn't just for that reason that I want to keep you as my therapist, but it is too special to be reduced to social contact. Obviously, though, it's time for me to leave therapy, so we'll have to stop in a few weeks.

THERAPIST: No, we don't *have* to, but we're ready to.

PATIENT: You know, you have a way of subtly teaching . . . no, no, no, I don't mean that I should become your student when I'm no longer your patient.

CHAPTER 47

Psychotherapy is like a slow-cooking process that has no microwave substitute

B REAKING THE TIME BARRIER seems to be a goal in many areas of modern life, including psychotherapy. The increasing popularity of short-term techniques is testimony to that quest.

The microwave oven is a prime example of the trend toward brevity—cooking that once took hours now takes minutes. Likewise, over the past few decades the short-term strategies of psychotherapy have radically altered the average time spent in treatment—what once took years can now be provided in months or even weeks.

However tempting the microwave model may be for the clinician, this paradigm is not well applied to actual psychotherapeutic practice. Perhaps our food can be quick-cooked without a loss of quality. But human psychopathology is highly resistant to shortcuts. There are three important barriers to condensing psychotherapeutic practice: the complex nature of the patient's psyche, the naturally unfolding pace of the therapeutic process, and the human constraints of the skilled practitioner. Since the fundamental resistances to and defenses against change come from the unconscious, they are not easily accessible to the patient, never mind the therapist. Because unconscious conflicts take time to reveal themselves to memory, and because neither establishing a joint alliance nor achieving insight occurs instantaneously—no matter how experienced the clinician or how receptive the patient—dynamic psychotherapy is by definition a gradual process of progressions and regressions, of uncovering painful feelings and then warding them off.

Of course, some patients come to treatment with highly circumscribed stresses that can respond to short-term interventions; but these patients may also have lifelong characterological problems that cannot be attended to in brief therapy. Their problems tend to recur under adverse situations, and many individuals may not be well prepared to deal with them without long-term treatment. This is not an indictment of the brief, targeted approaches as much as a recognition of their limitations.

Often patients who receive short-term psychotherapy come back for more, or go to someone else, or seek other treatment. Some of these people become professional patients, searching for help in an assortment of abbreviated approaches. The danger is especially great when short-term psychotherapy is misapplied to those who really need long-term care. Moreover, the durability of improvement from time-limited encounters, however powerful their impact, varies with life circumstances.

The enduring effects of psychotherapy derive from true alteration in the patient's functioning affectively, cognitively, and behaviorally. Clinical experience and experimental research (Weiner 1974; Hoehn-Saric 1978) confirm that all three aspects must be addressed for sustained change to occur: the deepening of affect may produce cathartic effects that are strong but do not last unless they are accompanied by cognitive restructuring; and both of these are insufficient without behavioral change. If the therapist presents to the patient in a direct fashion what he or she understands to be the underlying problem, or addresses in a confrontative way what he or she considers the patient's defenses, the patient may temporarily unfreeze emotionally and give the therapist access to his or her inner world. However, this opening of the doors is usually short-lived; the patient will close them at the first opportunity because they were, in effect, opened without his or her full cooperation.

Another process that takes time is the natural evolution of the therapeutic relationship from its formation to its dénouement. More specifically, it is time-consuming to experience "recollection, repetition, and working through" (Freud 1914b). Anna Freud once said that the shortest distance between two points is not a straight line; obviously, she was referring to the direct approach in psychotherapy. In any event, one must still get to one's destination. Psychology suggests that in order to reach the inner recesses of the mind one has to take a tortuous route. Taking a supposed shortcut will delay the trip; the therapist may either never get to the destination or miss some important spots along the way.

The therapist's human limitations also lengthen the time needed for effective psychotherapy. Understanding the complexity of another person is a strenuous and demanding undertaking, and the therapist must work modestly and patiently in attempts to bring about even minor psychic modification. The establishment, maintenance, and termination of a therapeutic alliance require the skillful balancing of frustration with gratification, professional distance with intimacy, and dependence with independence. Likewise, the techniques of confrontation, clarification, and interpretation have to be carefully adjusted according to how they are received and accepted by the patient; the therapist cannot be rushed.

Returning to the food analogy, the therapist would do well to bear in mind the old adage: "To eat an elephant, take one bite at a time."

CHAPTER 48

Every therapist must be prepared for the element of surprise—which can come only in the psychotherapy experience itself

> The Zen student comes to the Zen Master
> and asks him for a wisdom to guide him.
> The Zen Master writes on a piece of paper:
>   Experience.
> The student is unsatisfied and asks for more.
> The Master writes:
>   Experience experience.   —CEMIL KARASU, 1963

EVEN THE MOST SEASONED CLINICIAN is faced with unanticipated events and outcomes: the conscientious and contented patient who leaves prematurely; the recalcitrant patient who outlasts his or her own threats as well as the therapist's expectations; the highly defended patient who nonetheless dares to open himself or herself to change and get well; or the promising patient who adroitly deigns to remain the same. But even more, what I am referring to here are the immediate, moment-to-moment occurrences that can never be foreseen—the freshness that each patient, each session, and each interchange brings to the therapeutic endeavor. Freud (1913) compared psychoanalysis to a game of chess, a highly structured but spontaneous unfolding that cannot be predicted by its participants; Rollo May, Ernest Angel, and Henri Ellenberger (1958) suggested that "the only thing that will grasp the patient, and in the long run make it possible for him to change, is to experience fully and deeply that [the therapist] is doing precisely this to a real person . . . in this real moment" (p. 83).

My concluding maxim represents wisdom that each clinician must discover alone; it pertains to a phenomenon that underlies and includes

285

other maxims. Indeed, the phenomenon arrives irrespective of our best expertise, most scrupulous planning, or even profoundest portents—and it applies to every patient, every session, and every nuance, as the clinician must continually experience the ongoing therapeutic process anew. Such is the final axiom of psychotherapy, as well as the source of all others.

References

Adler, G. 1986. Psychotherapy of the narcissistic disorder patient. *American Journal of Psychiatry* 143:430–36.

Alexander, F., and T. M. French. 1946. *Psychoanalytic therapy*. New York: Ronald Press.

Appelbaum, S. 1961. The end of the test as a determinant of responses. *Bulletin of the Menninger Clinic* 25:120–218.

———. 1976. The dangerous edge of insight. *Psychotherapy: Theory, Research and Practice* 13:202–6.

Arlow, J. A. 1961. Silence and the theory of technique. *Journal of the American Psychoanalytic Association* 9:44–55.

Balint, M. 1968. *The basic fault*. London: Tavistock.

Bateson, G. 1979. *Mind and nature: A necessary unity*. New York: E. P. Dutton.

Bell, S. 1970. The development of a concept of object as related to infant–mother attachment. *Child Development* 41:291–311.

Brenner, C. 1976. *Psychoanalytic technique and psychic conflict*. New York: International Universities Press.

Brewer, E. 1953. *Dictionary of phrase and fable*. New York: Harper.

Buber, M. 1957. Elements of the interhuman. *Psychiatry* 20:105–13.

Burling, T., E. M. Lentz, and R. N. Wilson. 1956. *Give and take in hospitals: A study of human organization*. New York: G. P. Putnam & Sons.

Calestro, K. 1972. Psychotherapy, faith healing and suggestion. *International Journal of Psychiatry* 10:83–114.

Celsus, A. C. 1935–38. *De medicina*. Cambridge, Mass.: Harvard University Press.

Chessick, R. D. 1974. *The technique and practice of intensive psychotherapy*. New York: Jason Aronson.

————. 1981. What is intensive psychotherapy? *American Journal of Psychotherapy* 35: 489–501.

Culler, J. 1975. *Structuralist poetics*. Ithaca, N.Y.: Cornell University Press.

Davanloo, H. 1978. *Short-term dynamic psychotherapy*. New York: Spectrum.

Davison, G., and G. T. Wilson. 1974. Goals and strategies in behavioral treatment of homosexual pedophilia. *Journal of Abnormal Psychology* 83:196–98.

Dewald, P. 1964. *Psychotherapy: A dynamic approach*. New York: Basic Books.

Ehrenwald, J. 1966. *Psychotherapy, myth and method: An integrative approach*. New York: Grune & Stratton.

Einstein, A. 1969. Autobiographical notes. In *Albert Einstein: Philosopher-Scientist*, edited by P. A. Schilpp, 1–96. London: Cambridge University Press.

Erikson, E. H. 1959. *Identity and the life cycle*. Psychological Issues, Monograph 1. New York: International Universities Press.

————. 1963. *Childhood and society*. New York: W. W. Norton.

Fenichel, O. 1945. *The psychoanalytic theory of neurosis*. New York: W. W. Norton.

Ferenczi, S. [1916–17] 1926. Silence is golden. In *Further contributions to the theory and technique of psycho-analysis*. London: Hogarth Press.

————. [1919] 1926. On the technique of psycho-analysis. In *Further contributions to the theory and technique of psycho-analysis*. London: Hogarth Press.

———— [1920] 1926. The further development of an active theory in psycho-analysis. In *Further contributions to the theory and technique of psycho-analysis*, 198–217. London: Hogarth Press.

Frank, J. 1961. *Persuasion and healing: A comparative study of psychotherapy*. Baltimore: Johns Hopkins University Press.

————. 1974. Common features of psychotherapies and their patients. *Psychotherapy and Psychosomatics* 24:368–71.

————. 1979. What is psychotherapy? In *An introduction to the psychotherapies*, edited by S. Bloch, 1–22. New York: Oxford University Press.

Frank, J. D., and J. B. Frank. 1991. *Persuasion and healing: A comparative study of psychotherapy*. 3d ed. Baltimore: Johns Hopkins University Press.

Freud, A. [1936] 1966. *The ego and mechanisms of defense*. New York: International Universities Press.

Freud, S. [1901] 1953. The psychopathology of everyday life. *Standard edition*, edited and translated by J. Strachey, vol. 6. London: Hogarth Press.

————. [1905] 1953. Three essays on the theory of sexuality. *Standard edition*, edited and translated by J. Strachey, vol. 7, 125–248. London: Hogarth Press.

————. [1909] 1955. Notes upon a case of obsessional neurosis. *Standard edition*, edited and translated by J. Strachey, vol. 10. London: Hogarth Press.

————. [1910] 1955. Five lectures on psycho-analysis. *Standard edition*, edited and translated by J. Strachey, vol. 2. London: Hogarth Press.

————. [1912a] 1958. The dynamics of transference. *Standard edition*, edited and translated by J. Strachey, vol. 12. London: Hogarth Press.

————. [1912b] 1958. Recommendations to physicians practicing psycho-analysis. *Standard edition*, edited and translated by J. Strachey, vol. 12. London: Hogarth Press.

————. [1913] 1958. Further recommendations in the technique of psycho-analysis. On beginning treatment. *Standard edition*, edited and translated by J. Strachey, vol. 12. London: Hogarth Press.

————. [1914a] 1957. On the history of the psychoanalytic movement. *Standard edition*, edited and translated by J. Strachey, vol. 14. London: Hogarth Press.

————. [1914b] 1958. Papers on technique: Remembering, repeating, and working through. *Standard edition*, edited and translated by J. Strachey, vol. 12. London: Hogarth Press.

————. [1915] 1958. Papers on technique: Observations on transference-love. *Standard edition*, edited and translated by J. Strachey, vol. 12. London: Hogarth Press.

————. [1916–17] 1963. Introductory lectures on psycho-analysis, pt. 3. *Standard edition*, edited and translated by J. Strachey, vol. 16. London: Hogarth Press.

————. [1923] 1942. The ego and the id and other works. *Standard edition*, edited and translated by J. Strachey, vol. 19. London: Hogarth Press.

————. [1925] 1959. An autobiographical study, pt. 4. *Standard edition*, edited and translated by J. Strachey, vol. 20, 40–47. London: Hogarth Press.

————. [1937a] 1964. Analysis terminable and interminable. *Standard edition*, edited and translated by J. Strachey, vol. 23. London: Hogarth Press.

————. [1937b] 1964. Constructions in analysis. *Standard edition*, edited and translated by J. Strachey, vol. 23. London: Hogarth Press.

Gabbard, G. O. 1982. The exit line: Heightened transference-countertransference manifestations at the end of the hour. *Journal of the American Psychoanalytic Association* 30:579–98.

Garfield, S. 1974. Values: An issue in psychotherapy. *Journal of Abnormal Psychology* 83:202–3.

Gergen, K. 1981. The meagre voice of empiricist affirmation. *Personality and Social Psychology Bulletin* 7:333–37.

Glover, E. 1955. *The technique of psycho-analysis.* New York: International Universities Press.

Goldberg, C. 1977. *Therapeutic partnership.* New York: Springer.

Greenacre, P. 1954. The role of transference: Practical considerations in relation to psychoanalytic therapy. *Journal of the American Psychoanalytic Association* 2:671–84.

Greenson, R. 1961. On the silence and sounds of the analytic hour. *Journal of the American Psychoanalytic Association* 9:79–90.

————. 1965. The working alliance and the transference neurosis. *Psychoanalytic Quarterly* 34:155–81.

————. 1967. *The technique and practice of psychoanalysis.* Vol. 1. New York: International Universities Press.

REFERENCES

Grice, H. P. 1967. Logic and conversation. Paper read in the William James Lectures at Harvard. Cambridge, Mass.: Harvard University.

Grünbaum, A. 1979. Epistemological liabilities of the clinical appraisal of psychoanalytic theory. *Psychoanalysis and Contemporary Thought* 2:481–526.

Guntrip, H. 1968. *Schizoid phenomena, object relations and the self.* New York: International Universities Press.

Hadley, S. W., and H. H. Strupp. 1976. Contemporary views of negative effects of psychotherapy: An integrated account. *Archives of General Psychiatry* 33:1291–1302.

Harper, R. A. 1959. *Psychoanalysis and psychotherapy: 36 systems.* Englewood Cliffs, N.J.: Prentice-Hall.

Havens, L. 1986. *Making contact.* Cambridge, Mass.: Harvard University Press.

———. 1989. *A safe place.* Cambridge, Mass.: Harvard University Press.

Hoehn-Saric, R. 1978. Emotional arousal, attitude change, and psychotherapy. In *Effective ingredients of successful psychotherapy,* edited by J. Frank et al., 73–106. New York: Brunner/Mazel.

Hogan, D. B. 1979. *The regulation of psychotherapies.* Vol. 1. Cambridge, Mass.: Ballinger.

Horowitz, M., and C. Marmar. 1985. The therapeutic alliance with difficult patients. In *Psychiatry update: American Psychiatric Association annual review,* edited by R. E. Hales and A. J. Frances, vol. 4, 573–85. Washington, D.C.: APPI.

Kiev, A. 1966. Prescientific psychiatry. In *American handbook of psychiatry,* edited by S. Arieti, vol. 3. New York: Basic Books.

Kohut, H. 1971. *The analysis of the self.* New York: International Universities Press.

———. 1977. *The restoration of the self.* New York: International Universities Press.

Kris, E. 1947. The nature of psychoanalytic propositions and their validation. In *Freedom and experience,* edited by S. Hook and M. R. Konwitz. Ithaca, N.Y.: Cornell University Press.

———. 1950. On preconscious mental processes. *Psychoanalytic Quarterly* 19:540–60.

———. 1956. On some vicissitudes of insight in psycho-analysis. *International Journal of Psychoanalysis* 37:445–55.

Kuhn, T. S. 1962. *The structure of scientific revolutions.* Chicago: University of Chicago Press.

Lacan, J. 1977. *Ecrits: A selection.* New York: W. W. Norton.

Langs, R. 1973. *The technique of psychoanalytic therapy.* Vol. 1. New York: Jason Aronson.

———. 1982. Countertransference and the process of cure. In *Curative factors in dynamic psychotherapy,* edited by S. Slipp, 127–52. New York: McGraw-Hill.

Leighton, A., R. Prince, and R. May. 1968. The therapeutic process in cross-cultural perspective: A symposium. *American Journal of Psychiatry* 124:1171–83.

Lesse, S., ed. 1974. *Masked depression.* New York: Jason Aronson.

Levenson, E. 1983. *The ambiguity of change.* New York: Basic Books.

References

Lewin, B. D. 1955. Dream psychology and the analytic situation. *Psychoanalytic Quarterly* 24:169–99.

Lewin, K. 1958. Group decisions and social change. In *Readings in social psychology*, 3d ed., edited by E. E. Maccoby, T. M. Newcomb, and E. L. Hartley. New York: Henry Holt.

Luborsky, L. 1984. *Principles of psychoanalytic psychotherapy.* New York: Basic Books.

Ludwig, A. M. 1966. The formal characteristics of therapeutic insight. *American Journal of Psychotherapy* 20:305–18.

Mahler, M., and M. Furer. 1960. Observations on research regarding the "symbiotic syndrome" of infantile psychosis. *Psychoanalytic Quarterly* 29:317–27.

Mahler, M., F. Pine, and A. Bergman. 1975. *The psychological birth of the human infant.* New York: Basic Books.

Mann, J. 1973. *Time-limited psychotherapy.* Cambridge, Mass.: Harvard University Press.

Maslow, A. H. 1970. Neurosis as a failure of human growth. In *Psychopathology today: Experimentation, theory and research*, edited by W. S. Sahakian, 122–30. Itasca, Ill.: F. E. Peacock.

Masterson, J. F. 1976. *Psychotherapy of the borderline adult.* New York: Basic Books.

May, R., E. Angel, and H. Ellenberger. 1958. *Existence: A new dimension in psychiatry and psychology.* New York: Basic Books.

Naftulin, D., F. Donnelly, and G. Wolkon. 1975. Four therapeutic approaches to the same patient. *American Journal of Psychotherapy* 29:66–71.

Neki, J. S. 1973. Guru-chela relationship: The possibility of a therapeutic paradigm. *American Journal of Orthopsychiatry* 43:755–66.

O'Kill, B. 1986. *Exit lines.* Essex, England: Longman.

Parsons, T. 1951. *The social system.* New York: Free Press.

Pine, F. 1990. *Drive, ego, object, and self.* New York: Basic Books.

Raimy, V., ed. 1950. *Training in clinical psychology.* New York: Prentice-Hall.

Random House collegiate dictionary. 1975. Rev. ed. New York: Random House.

Redlich, F., and R. Mollica. 1976. Overview: Ethical issues in contemporary psychiatry. *American Journal of Psychiatry* 133:125–26.

Reider, N. 1954. The demonology of modern psychiatry. *American Journal of Psychiatry* 3:255–65.

Reik, T. 1949. *Listening with the third ear.* New York: Farrar, Straus.

Ricoeur, P. 1977. The question of proof in Freud's psychoanalytic writings. *Journal of the American Psychoanalytic Association* 25:835–971.

Rogers, C. R. 1957. The necessary and sufficient conditions of therapeutic personality change. *Journal of Consulting Psychology* 21:95–103.

———. 1965. *Client-centered therapy.* Boston: Houghton-Mifflin.

Rogers, C. R., and C. B. Truax. 1967. The therapeutic conditions antecedent to change: A theoretical view. In *The therapeutic relationship and its impact*, edited by C. R. Rogers. Madison: University of Wisconsin Press.

Rosen, V. 1967. Disorders of communication in psychoanalysis. *Journal of the American Psychoanalytic Association* 15:467–90.

REFERENCES

Sandler, J. 1976. Countertransference and role responsiveness. *International Review of Psychoanalysis* 3:43–47.

Schafer, R. 1983. *The analytic attitude.* New York: Basic Books.

Schnabel, A. 1958. Newspaper interview. *Chicago Daily News,* June 11.

Schonbar, R. A. 1965. Interpretation and insight in psychotherapy. *Psychotherapy: Theory, Research and Practice* 2:78–83.

Sifneos, P. E. 1973. The prevalence of "alexithymic" characteristics in psychosomatic patients. *Psychotherapy and Psychosomatics* 22:255–62.

———. 1984. *Short-term anxiety-provoking psychotherapy.* In *Psychiatry Update,* edited by L. Grinspoon, vol. 3. Washington, D.C.: American Psychiatric Press.

Smith, M. L., G. V. Glass, and T. I. Miller. 1980. *The benefits of psychotherapy.* Baltimore: Johns Hopkins University Press.

Spence, D. 1982. *Narrative truth and historical truth.* New York: W. W. Norton.

———. 1990. Theories of the mind: Science or literature? *Poetics Today* 11: 329–47.

Stein, M. 1981. The unobjectionable part of the transference. *Journal of the American Psychoanalytic Association* 29:869–92.

Strachey, J. 1934. The nature of the therapeutic action of psychoanalysis. *International Journal of Psychoanalysis* 15:127–59.

Strean, H. 1980. The unanalyzed "positive transference" and the need for reanalysis. *The Psychoanalytic Review* 66:493–506.

———. 1985. *Resolving resistances in psychotherapy.* New York: Wiley.

Strupp, H. H. 1974. Some observations on the fallacy of value-free psychotherapy and the empty organism: Comments on a case study. *Journal of Abnormal Psychology* 83:199–201.

Strupp, H. H., and J. Binder. 1984. *Psychotherapy in a new key.* New York: Basic Books.

Sullivan, H. S. 1954. *The psychiatric interview.* New York: W. W. Norton.

Sundland, D. M. 1977. Theoretical orientations of psychotherapies. In *Effective psychotherapy: A handbook of research,* edited by A. S. Gurman and A. M. Razin, 189–219. New York: Pergamon Press.

Szasz, T. 1978. *The myth of psychotherapy.* New York: Anchor.

Tarachow, S. 1963. *An introduction to psychotherapy.* New York: International Universities Press.

Torrey, E. F. 1974. *The death of psychiatry.* Radnor, Pa.: Chilton.

Viderman, S. 1979. The analytic space: Meaning and problems. *Psychoanalytic Quarterly* 48:257–91.

Webster's ninth new collegiate dictionary. 1989. Springfield, Mass.: Merriam-Webster.

Weiner, M. F. 1974. Genetic versus interpersonal insight. *International Journal of Group Psychotherapy* 24:231–37.

Weiss, J. 1990. Unconscious mental functioning. *Scientific American,* March, 103–9.

Winnicott, D. W. 1965. *The maturational processes and the facilitating environment.* New York: International Universities Press.

Wittgenstein, L. 1951. *Tractatus logico-philosophicus.* New York: Humanities Press.

References

Wittkower, E. D., and H. Warnes. 1974. Cultural aspects of psychotherapy. *American Journal of Psychiatry* 28:566–73.

Wolitsky, D. L., and P. L. Wachtel. 1973. Personality and perception. In *Handbook of general psychology*, edited by B. Wolman. Englewood Cliffs, N.J.: Prentice-Hall.

Zeligs, M. A. 1961. The psychology of silence. *Journal of the American Psychoanalytic Association* 9:7–43.

Zetzel, E. 1956. Current concepts of transference. *International Journal of Psychoanalysis* 37:369–76.

Index

Acceptance, 135, 159–60
Adler, Gerald, 6, 7
Adolescence, 159
Aggression, 7, 40, 85–86, 89, 200, 246; and communicative intimacy, 104; and cues, 258; and guilt, 144; and transference, 124, 166, 184, 185
Alienation, 226–32; and demoralization, 12; and literal interpretation, 248; and therapeutic setting, 44
Ambitendency, 121
Ambivalence, 183–84, 211
Angel, Ernest, 285
Anger, 37, 67, 165, 262; and Oedipus complex, 244; at therapist, legitimate, 174, 187; and transference, 184, 185. See also Aggression
Anorexia, 227–32. See also Eating disorders
Anxiety, 12, 19, 195; "age" of, 44; and arousal, 56; and minimum dosage, 220; and primal scream method, 58; separation, and transference, 174–75; and silence, 90, 93, 94, 95; and therapeutic setting, 44, 59, 60
Appelbaum, Stanley, 197, 269, 276
Arlow, Jacob, 91
Attention, free-floating: and clinical listening, 67–70; in Freud, 41, 65, 69, 135
Attitude change, 58–59
Authenticity, 80
Autonomy, 120

Aversion therapy, 57
Avoidance, 258, 262

Balint, Michael, 37
Bateson, Gregory, xvi
Bell, Silvia, 23
Bergman, Anni, 22–23, 25; and individuation, 120, 121–22; mild negativism in, 186; "mother after separation" in, 248
Binder, Jeffrey L., 194
Bioenergetics, 57
Bion, Wilfred, 26
Bipolar mood disorder, 12
Birth, psychological, 22–23
"Blank screen" orientation, 39
Bowlby, John, 26
Brenner, Charles, 158, 183, 248
Buber, Martin, 70
Bulimia, 227–32. See also Eating disorders
Burling, Temple, 14

Calestro, Kenneth, 14, 44, 45
Capriciousness, 183–84
Catharsis, 57, 283
Celsus, Aulus Cornelius, 57

295